WOMAN AS MYTH AND METAPHOR
in Latin American Literature

WOMAN AS MYTH AND METAPHOR
in Latin American Literature

Edited with an Introduction
by Carmelo Virgillo
and Naomi Lindstrom

University of Missouri Press
Columbia, 1985

Library of Congress Cataloging in Publication Data
    Main entry under title:

    Woman as myth and metaphor in Latin American literature.

    Bibliography: p. 184
    Includes index.
    1. Latin American literature—History and criticism
—Addresses, essays, lectures.   2. Women in literature—
Addresses, essays, lectures.   3. Myth in literature—
Addresses, essays, lectures.   4. Metaphor—Addresses,
essays, lectures.   I. Virgillo, Carmelo, 1934–
II. Lindstrom, Naomi, 1950–
PQ7081.A1W65   1985   860'.9'98   85–1019
ISBN 0–8262–0460–0

∞™ This paper meets the minimum requirements of
the American National Standard for Permanence of Paper
for Printed Library Materials, Z39.48, 1984.

Drawings by Liz Fett

To our special
friends and colleagues

Acknowledgments

We wish to acknowledge the generous assistance of Arizona State University at all stages of our project. We offer special thanks to Dean Guido Weigend of the College of Liberal Arts and Professor Peter Horwath, Chair of the Department of Foreign Languages, for their kind support and encouragement. We are indebted and grateful to Margaret Jamison and Eleanor Akins, who provided a great deal of assistance in the preparation of the manuscript.

Two of the following essays, those by Richard J. Callan and Ann Marie R. Rambo, were first published in the journal *Hispania*; an earlier version of Carmelo Virgillo's essay appeared in *Women Writers from Latin America: Yesterday and Today,* edited by Yvette E. Miller and Charles M. Tatum (Pittsburgh, Pa.: *Latin American Literary Review,* 1975); and a version of David W. Foster's essay is contained in his *Alternate Voices in the Contemporary Latin American Narrative* (Columbia: University of Missouri Press, 1985).

C. V., Tempe, Arizona
N. L., Austin, Texas
June 1985

Contents

FOLK-POPULAR CULTURE

Introduction

Carmelo Virgillo and Naomi Lindstrom

The essays that make up this collection represent varying explorations of a single topic: the mythic representation of woman in Latin American literature. By this we mean the non-mimetic portrayal of the female, as manifested in larger-than-life figures charged with diverse meanings. To assure plurality of critical perspective, we have sought the collaboration of international scholars who have established themselves in structural and semiological studies, archetypal criticism, analysis of ideological and philosophical content, the placing of literary work within its social context, and discourse analysis. In sum, while the general focus of the book is on myth in literature, it is by no means a survey restricted to mythic criticism in the traditional sense—Jungian and archetypal models. Indeed, we propose to demonstrate that the systematic study of literary myth may proceed by many critical routes, a contention which will be developed further in these introductory remarks.

One may well ask how we arrived at the formulation of *myth and metaphor* to convey the type of representations of woman that interest us here. As the essays themselves make evident, both these terms may be construed in a number of ways by the literary analyst. Yet, myth and metaphor, however diversely defined, are both designations that stand in conceptual opposition to the notion of a literal transcription of reality. To be sure, the mythmaker generates images larger than life and capable of taking a powerful hold on the human imagination; similarly, the innovative user of metaphor relies on analogical, symbolic patterns to achieve this same scope.

Inquiries into mythic figures of woman, when conducted by critics whose main concern is sexual stereotyping, have, however, tended to explore only one aspect of this phenomenon: the harm that such presentations may cause. To mention some of the more memorable investigations, Simone de Beauvoir's groundbreaking study *Le Deuxième Sexe* (1949; English, *The Second Sex*, 1953) devotes considerable space to an appraisal of the myth of woman in literature. The five authors whose texts receive attention all fail to satisfy Beauvoir's criteria for just and

1

adequate representation of women. Her principal grievance is that female characters lack the features of autonomy and free will that are routinely assigned to their male counterparts. According to this analysis, readers of such myth-laden texts come to perceive real-life women as less than fully existent persons. In short, claims Beauvoir, the female literary persona is generally incapable of choice and the exercise of the will. These same notions recur in Kate Millett's popular *Sexual Politics* (1970) and continue to figure in much sex-role analysis of literature.

One would not wish to denigrate Beauvoir's analysis, for she is attentive to the specifics of the texts under study and pursues her central thesis with logical rigor. Yet, it is difficult not to perceive in her work definite signs of limitation or partiality, since only those myths thought to be harmful claim her attention. On the other hand, she suggests strongly that nonmythic female figures are less likely to distort readers' perceptions of women.

Before entering into any consideration of the essays contained in the present volume, we shall offer a brief review of modern, pace-setting research on literary myth and metaphor. We will begin with general works on the subject and then move to those that have a direct bearing on the female persona. In this schematic view, we include not only Latin American literature and criticism but international developments as well, not just critics admiring of nonmimetic images of woman but also those who warn against the distorting power of such images.

Contributors to this renovative effort include, of course, all those scholars who, in examining myth, remain attentive to specifically literary features of the text. Certain authors and works stand out especially for their influence. Northrop Frye's *Anatomy of Criticism* (1957), for instance, must be considered as very significant because of its movement away from the idea that literature contained myths that the critic must isolate and extract for study. For Frye, literature was itself a manifestation of myth, but a highly specialized one requiring a particularly literary treatment. Another key work very prominent for its synthesis of mythic criticism and social commentary is Leslie Fiedler's *Love and Death in the American Novel* (1960; rev. ed. 1966). Fiedler's procedure is to identify mythic patterns in American literature, then use these myths to diagnose collective disturbances in United States society. Such works aroused a good deal of controversy and alerted critics to the expanded possibilities of mythic discussion.

More directly germane to the present volume is the highly original work of Roland Barthes. His concern for everyday manifestations of myth is present in much of his writing, but especially in short pieces known as *mythologies* (collected in French as *Mythologies,* 1957; in English, as *Mythologies,* 1972, and *The Eiffel Tower and Other Mythologies,* 1979) and in his 1966 study of fashionable magazine writing, *Système de la mode.* It is difficult to sum up Barthes's impact on critical procedure, but one can indicate why he stands apart from traditional investigators of myth. Readers of Barthes are encouraged to look at very banal material (such as advertising copy) for the traces of myth encoded within it. Language, as the generator and chief vehicle of myth, receives the closest scrutiny.

These characteristics of Barthes's investigation were of exceptional interest to literary analysts. Clearly, not all literary work manifests the more heroic types of myth, such as the descent to the underworld. A great number of literary texts, nonetheless, can be shown to exhibit more subtle and implicit forms of myth—those that require the most careful decoding. The Barthian emphasis on language also proved stimulating to the literary critics who had found it difficult to concentrate on myth without casting aside the materiality of the text—that is, without the concrete linguistic realization. Barthes had no need to cease discussing myth while closely observing the style of the text; for him, the two aspects were inseparable.

Among the newest literary developments in women's studies are hypotheses about women's writing being propounded by French theorists. Although definitions of a postulated possible "women's discourse" vary, the participants in this debate all share a utopian ideal of a radically innovative writing that would prove subversive of and disruptive to the mainstream tradition of literary discourse in the West. While conventionally acceptable writing is seen as dominated by values that are masculine, rationalistic, logocentric, and linear, the alternative represented by feminine writing would break out of these conceptual molds and avoid the processes of repression that maintain the metaphysics and ideology of the existing society. Julia Kristeva, one of the most important exponents of this possibility, sees the originators of this possible literature as neither necessarily women nor feminized men, but rather cultural radicals who are "feminine" writers by virtue of rejecting the masculine-dominated mind-set of their literary and intellectual tradition. This androgynous ideal differs from that posited by, most notably, Hélène Cixous, whose vision of feminine writing involves not only a breaking free of repressive constraints on discourse but also the inscription into the literary text of experience that is specifically of women. While this debate has not yet made much impact in the United States, its repercussions and those of Lacanian-based French feminisms have made considerable inroads in Britain, resulting in English-language analyses.

Latin American criticism, in its recent period of flourishing, has not failed to make its own mark in the field of literary myth. Eduardo Romano's *Análisis de Don Segundo Sombra* (1968), for instance, is an original investigation into the mythic workings of Ricardo Güiraldes's famous Argentine novel of 1926. Also very influential has been *Imaginación y violencia en América*. This celebrated 1970 book by the Chilean Ariel Dorfman argues forcefully for the positive effects of certain literarily expressed myths. The most attractive characteristic of Dorfman's study—the most immediately perceptible one—is its specific focus on Latin American culture. By asserting his belief that Latin Americans are able to generate and work with their own cultural models, the author helps to combat the notion that myth-oriented critics are otherworldly individuals detached from the realities of their own region. While Dorfman has no doubt borrowed elements from previous non–Latin American studies, particularly Barthes's, he uses his knowledge of Latin American indigenous myth and the current-day elaborations of that body of myth.

Dorfman also impresses readers with his confidence in the validity of mythic writings as potential agents for changing the awareness of social and cultural conditions. Again, one finds here a break with the traditional image of archetypal critics as scholars without relevance to their particular society. To wit, in Dorfman's view, myths of strong, charismatic leadership and inspired rebellion can spur the process of social change forward. Here is, then, a conception of literary myth that differs from the conventional understanding of the term. In fact, contrary to the commonly held notions that literary myth constitutes an abstract reflection of the universal human condition, myths appear in Dorfman's book as almost a pragmatic form of communication.

While the social-mythic analysis just discussed represents one new possibility, other types of investigation have also appeared. Noteworthy among these is "Pruebas y hazañas de Adán Buenosayres," a lengthy semiological study of Leopoldo Marechal's novel *Adán Buenosayres* (Argentina, 1948). The uniqueness of this study, published in volume two of *Nueva novela latinoamericana* (edited by Jorge Lafforgue, 1972), lies most immediately in the manner in which it was composed. In effect, authorship for this analysis is claimed by a team of critics, known as Centro de Investigaciones Adanbuenosayres, who chose to work collectively in order to achieve greater detail and objectivity. The result is another original contribution to the critical appraisal of myth-based writings. The study constitutes in fact an application of linguistic and structural models that unearths and sorts out the abstract patterns of interrelationships at the core of an otherwise perplexing story of spiritual quest.

If the Centro's efforts bespeak the determination of contemporary Latin American literary criticism to reexamine myth-oriented literature and do it justice, no less dedicated has been another group, by now possibly defunct, the Centro de Estudios Latinoamericanos. In *Hacia una crítica literaria latinoamericana* (Argentina, 1976), the group's eleven members (all of whom signed their individual contributions) set out to find what was specifically and uniquely Latin American in the continent's body of literature and what might develop a "properly" autochthonous critical response to it. The point of departure for the *équipe*—their common concern—is the conviction that even though the collective writings of a given area represent a structurally organic phenomenon, they are nonetheless related intertextually to a common literary and sociocultural context. As such, claims Graciela Ricci, one of the most articulate formulators of the group's position, if critics are to successfully evaluate the signifying power and performance of the Latin American text (particularly its ability to emit social messages), they cannot overlook the mythic and symbolic levels of interpretation. In short, myth is the very core of the Spanish- and Portuguese-American literary artifact, and criticism must attend to this central feature.

One additional example of broad application of critical procedure to myth is provided by Walnice Nogueira Galvão. In her well-received *Mitológica Rosiana* (1976), the Brazilian critic does more than look at indigenous myth in the fiction of João Guimarães Rosa: she sets his work within a larger context. The writer, after all, has utilized a great amount of information to effect such contextualization. This seems to lead Galvão to see mythic criticism not as being only about myth, but rather as the starting point for investigating diverse aspects of social and cultural organization. For instance, a study of "A hora e a vez de Augusto Matraga," a story from the 1954 *Sagarana*, becomes an extensive and rather meditative examination of the patterns of signification associated with stigmata.

The emphasis on myth may seem to some observers to go against the current drive to recognize woman's reasoning and enterprising talents, hitherto obscured by the demands of her traditional role. Feminist writers who espouse a rational view of woman are likely to react with some horror to the myth surrounding women's mothering, nurturing, and empathetic capacities. Millett, for one, interprets this legendary material as a pretext for excluding women from the domains of power and decision making; the mythification of motherhood represents to her a strategy of subjugation.

At the same time, there has been a revalidation by feminists of those female myths wherein woman shows such attributes as strength, resourcefulness, and understanding. To wit, there is a frequent assertion that women, in developing new models of behavior, learn not only from their masculine predecessors in business and the professions, but also from a female persona of myth historically either downplayed or shrouded in undesirable mystery. Mary Daly's *Gyn/Ecology: The Metaphysics of Radical Feminism* (1978) exemplifies the positive reevaluation of such figures as the wise-woman, the healer, the spellbinder, and the sorceress. Daly's point is that myth can be a force tending either toward the diminution or the augmentation of woman's status and strength in society, depending upon the way in which the mythic material is elaborated and interpreted.

The feminists' willingness to utilize some manifestations of myth is beginning to make an impact in many areas—not just in the feminist treatise per se. In literature and the other arts, goddess and wise-woman images have taken on a new currency. Writers including Adrienne Rich, Robin Morgan, and Jill Johnston make such figures essential to any reading of their works. With her collection of poems *The Dream of a Common Language* (1977) and her essayistic *On Lies, Secrets and Silence* (1979), Rich emerges as the most explicitly articulate of the rediscoverers of the female myth. In this respect, one should also note the surge of interest in the writings of France's Anaïs Nin (see, for example, *Celebrations with Anaïs Nin,* edited by Valerie Harms, 1973). What seems to be drawing many admirers to Nin is the heavy archetypal, mythic, and oneiric representations of female experience permeating her works.

Having taken a general look at writing that reflects recent trends in feminine myth and metaphor in literature, we now introduce the essays in this collection. We see these pieces as, in some cases, direct continuations of the above-summarized tendencies in research. More specifically, we consider our essays to be the first concerted effort, on the part of an international team of Latin Americanists, to survey the various ways in which the female of the Spanish and Portuguese New World has been mythified in the literature of her given country, in accordance with nativist (Indo/Afro-American) attitudes and universal cultural patterns. The collaborating critics all share the belief that while the ethnic sources and traits of myth may be mere stereotypes, they may also constitute a great stimulus to the imagination. Literary myths of strong and complex women may incite readers to recognize the real-world woman's ability to act independently and to decide who she will be.

Among the strong myths examined in this anthology are woman as a messianic figure; as a noble warrior; as a protean, eternally adaptable urban survivor; as a source of magic wisdom; as an intelligent force pitted against the disorder and violence of the natural world. In many of these cases, woman fills a role with a number of earmarks that could also be considered masculine, such as determination and leadership. Other myths studied here place woman in a more traditionally feminine role, stressing qualities of nurturing, gentleness, and peacefulness. Still, these more conventional mythic depictions are not necessarily the agents of sex-role stereotyping. The virgin mother, for example, may be elaborated in such a way as to emphasize this figure's personal competence rather than the traits of submissiveness and passivity. Our critics have had to use their analytical procedures not only to identify a particular manifestation of myth, but also to evaluate its efficacy in drawing attention to the favorable attributes and potentialities of woman.

Conversely, literary interpreters have also been required to single out and assess the deconstruction of conventions that have historically created feminine myth. Therefore, some of the essays in our book take into account the presence of a new type of female character, one who is too complex and paradoxical to fit any particular form of reductive myth. Such studies address the issue known as *demythification*—a procedure that occurs both in creative works and in critical analyses. It arises from a conviction that unjust distribution of power and wealth is made acceptable partly through the diffusion of myths that support the prevailing order. A clear example is mythic elements constructed by founders and leaders of nations; by extension, one may count in this category ideologists and creative writers associated with the power elite. We mention these myths not only because they are easy to recognize but also because their denunciation has been a major task of those writers who critically question the organization of Latin American society. One such instance is the "parricida" movement in Argentina. Identified and designed by Emir Rodríguez Monegal in his *El juicio de los parricidas* (1956), the movement challenges the values of both conservative and liberal Argentine writers, as exemplified by traditionalists such as Leopoldo Lugones (literary organizer of the 1910 Argentine Centennial) and would-be progressives like Manuel Gálvez. Among the many myths allegedly propagated by these establishment-identified authors are those of woman as a creature of uncontrollable desires, woman as useless ornament of consumer society, and woman as plaything.

In considering with our contributors the writings to be studied, we were particularly eager to move beyond literary works that are conventionally considered most suitable for mythic analysis. In the Latin American field, mythic study tends to focus upon certain nineteenth-century and early twentieth-century works. These texts have in common a highly symbolic figuration, often in female form, of New World realities. Their pragmatic function was typically to increase readers' awareness of specifically American phenomena that a European-style education might otherwise obscure. The forces of barbarism and civilization, the massive power of rivers and jungles, the questing spirit required to surmount the continent's obstacles: all these abstractions received a narrative incarnation in characters of undeniably symbolic stamp. In their search for emblematic representations that would be universal enough to speak to a range of readers, the New World writers often went beyond the simply allegorical to develop archetypal figures. During the early twentieth century, the notions of mythic, telluric forces as a constant in human existence enjoyed a vogue in Latin America, as elsewhere.

As a consequence of such developments, there exists a whole body of writings stretching from Esteban Echeverría's *El matadero* (c. 1838, Argentina) through the great "novels of the earth" of Rómulo Gallegos (Venezuela), Jorge Isaacs and José Eustasio Rivera (Colombia), and Ricardo Güiraldes (Argentina), and from these through such relatively recent myth-oriented writers as Miguel Angel Asturias, the Guatemalan Nobel Prize winner.

Of these overtly telluric and symbolic-archetypal works, only Rivera's *La vorágine* (1924) is treated here. The reason is our desire to establish that a great number of writings can be seen as containing elements of myth so long as the definition of myth in literature is sufficiently flexible and responsive to the peculiarities of the given text under scrutiny. In this context, we are not arguing that all literature is myth, but instead that a close examination of literary works will divulge in many of them mythic processes. We have secured for this collection the analysis of *La vorágine* ("The Archetype of Psychic Renewal in *La vorágine*"), the work of noted Jungian and archetypal critic Richard J. Callan, to show the best type of this longstanding approach. Structured around a questing hero and the dark forces that impede his search, Rivera's work is the very exemplar of the mythic-telluric novel; thus, it virtually invites a classical-style Jungian analysis. This is essentially the treatment it receives from Callan. While directly in the mainstream of archetypal criticism, the study, however, is not so canonical as to hinder its following the peculiar features of Rivera's one-of-a-kind text.

In other cases, we looked especially for analyses of writings that have not been the subject of extensive myth-based studies, our chief purpose being to demonstrate that mythic commentary can be many things and can adapt itself to the features of very disparate works.

Following such guidelines, we have thought it appropriate to include innovative essays like David W. Foster's "Narrative Persona in Eva Perón's *La razón de mi vida.*" To appreciate the singularity of this analysis, one must remember that, although the study of folk poetry and narrative has enjoyed a longstanding acceptance in academic circles, the examination of artifacts of mass culture is still beginning to establish itself as a subarea of literary and cultural studies. In this respect, Foster makes a welcome contribution to a neglected field by looking at a work most known for its power of mass persuasion. Clearly, Eva Perón's autobiography is little more than a pro-Peronist statement, or so it has heretofore been regarded. In Foster's study, however, the main focus of attention is Eva's creation of a literary personality for herself. From such representation emerges the dualistic image of the fascinating *grande dame* and the antipodal figure of the protective and nurturing mother. An additional novel feature of this essay is the utilization of discourse analysis and other current-day models for the study of narrative.

Qualities such as immediacy, accessibility, artistic remove, and alienating effects have long been commented in relation to literature. Their consideration has, nonetheless, only recently benefitted from the further development of the analysis of literary language. Even more recent and somewhat rare has been the discussion of the element of distance in dramatic works. Sandra M. Cypess takes up this task in "Visual and Verbal Distances: Women in the Mexican Theatre." Her essay looks at texts by women dramatists—among them, Elena Garro, Luisa Josefina Hernández, Marcela del Río, Maruxa Vilalta, and Pilar Campesino—to determine the rules of discourse which govern the speech of women in comparison to that of male protagonists. The analysis takes into account primarily whether the feminine persona speaks according to contemporary society's accepted images or whether new patterns are being established. Although the main concern of Cypess's investigation is the deictics of the speech act, along with the rhetorical procedures and stylistic devices employed by the individual playwrights, her essay manifests a second emphasis—the function of the *rhetor* or persuader. Cypess's contention is that the dramatic medium can more easily permit a woman writer to function in this role of spokesperson in a way that does not violate societal expectations regarding her appropriate behavior or even her own past conditioning toward passivity. In her study, Cypess further maintains that the dramatist, by creating personae who incorporate her ideas, is able to convey the impression that she is not speaking in her own voice, when in effect she is the *rhetor* just the same.

Brazil's *literatura de cordel,* as one of the most flourishing folk literatures available today for critical assessment, has often been the topic of descriptive and anthropological studies. Candace Slater ("Ambivalent Representations of Woman within the Brazilian *Literatura de Cordel"*), on the other hand, accords it the close scrutiny of particular texts—an essentially literary approach. Following this procedure, her essay sets forth a typology of mythified female characters mirrored against male figures. The study goes on to examine in some detail the significance of these feminine images as bearers of cultural values.

Since the appearance of Northrop Frye's *Anatomy of Criticism,* there has been a continued attempt to apply the insights of this archetypal-structural work to particular literary texts in many literatures. Fred P. Ellison's "Soledade Persephone: A Cyclical Myth in *A bagaceira"* avails itself of elements drawn from Frye to reexamine a work often lightly dismissed as regional. As such, Ellison's essay enjoys the double distinction of representing the very recent application of Frye-type analysis on Luso-Brazilian texts and the new effort to revindicate the literary artistry of writings, such as José Américo de Almeida's 1928 novel, usually relegated to the category of regional realism.

Using as her point of departure Simone de Beauvoir's classic, *Le Deuxième Sexe,* Naomi Lindstrom ("Arlt's Exposition of the Myth of Woman") probes the dual phenomenon of feminine myth-making and demythification in *Los siete locos* (1929) and *Los lanzallamas* (1931) by Argentine novelist Roberto Arlt. Lindstrom's application of structuralist models and discourse analysis to her investigation clearly demonstrates the potential of such critical procedures when interpreting works of considerable complexity and transcendence. In effect, this essay, while examining how Arlt makes society's mythification of woman an integral element in his fictional creation, dispels any impression that Arlt himself may be guilty of sex-role stereotyping. On the contrary, claims Lindstrom, if one pays attention to the distortions and falsifications of the unstable Arltian characters, it is possible to determine that the novelist, far from falsely mythifying female figures like Hipólita—the focal point of Lindstrom's scrutiny—invokes the mythification process only to denounce and deconstruct such processes.

Gabriela Mistral presents a case that is of special concern because she has been seen as mythifying woman in a way that is at best outdated and at worst socially unhealthy. Mistral's recurrent theme of motherhood as woman's fulfillment has understandably disturbed modern sensibilities. Carmelo Virgillo's essay argues that the use of the themes of woman and motherhood in a poem by Mistral can most profitably be understood if separated from the real-world issue of woman's "biological destiny." Rather than constituting any type of poetic comment upon this social issue, the poem uses the notions of womanhood and mothering as elements in a metaphorical code of much more global sweep. The mechanisms of the cosmos are the overall theme to be explored, while womanly and maternal fulfillment function as parts of a metaphorical structure designed to examine more abstract issues that do not lend themselves to mimetic treatment.

Equally pertinent to the pluralistic scope of the present volume is Matías Montes Huidobro's reevaluation of female divinity in an environment, the Caribbean literary scene, permeated by cross-cultural currents. His study, which takes into account the ritual/cultural expressions related to the *hieros gamos* ("Recovering the Lost Erotic Priestess of Caribbean Tradition"), represents a novel treatment of a theme that has recently attracted the attention of a number of critics: the antinomies of black/white, tribal/Westernized, indigenous/colonial, and other such phenomena. Yet Huidobro, setting aside the often tendentious championing of the tribal elements of culture with a corresponding disparagement of European tradition, focuses on the complexities of both sides of the duality, as well as on their coming together. Because of this, the examination of the divine woman may be viewed in Huidobro's essay not merely as one more attempt to graft the mythic/mystic figure of the Virgin from Spanish tradition onto the American cultural scene but as a way of organizing one's overall view of the world and woman.

Although the other essays in this volume all make original contributions of their own and should be accorded equal attention, space does not permit, and we prefer to leave the last word to our readers. Let it suffice to add in conclusion, that while in the past mythic criticism may have suffered from narrowness, such a flaw is not inherent in the idea of studying myth. In our opinion, the fallacy rests instead with the defective mode of investigation. Few will dispute that myth is difficult to examine within a literary text; resourcefulness and imagination are of the utmost importance in this critical undertaking. With these qualities, the myth-oriented interpreter can be as literary, as sophisticated, and as socially conscious as any other type of investigator. We believe that the essays assembled here will validate two basic premises of this anthology: one, that myth in general and feminine mythic representations in particular are central to much of the literature produced in Spanish and Portuguese speaking America in the last two centuries; and two, that the critical procedures being developed in response to such myth-based writing exhibit the diversity and ingenuity so essential to the appreciation of sophisticated and elusive works.

ARCHETYPAL CRITICISM

1 The Archetype of Psychic Renewal in *La vorágine*

Richard J. Callan

Before ever losing his heart to a woman he had gambled it away to violence, Cova confesses in the flamboyant opening of *La vorágine*.[1] Still, he yearned for the divine gift of ideal love and sought it—after his fashion. In a gesture of chivalry he ran off from Bogotá to the vast plains of Casanare with a girl he seduced, Alicia; then, thinking it over on his first night out there, he realized that her presence was beginning to irk him. He had foolishly attributed to her that which he had never found in any woman. The ideal, he tells himself with fleeting perspicacity, is not to be sought after; one carries it within. His words attempt to express an immemorial experience: "Every man carries within him the eternal image of woman," writes Carl Jung, and to this image he gives the name *anima*, because it *animates* or inspires a man.[2] It is of the utmost importance where the emotions are concerned, Jung explains, because it "intensifies, exaggerates, falsifies and mythologizes all emotional relations with . . . other people."[3] The anima is a personification of a man's suppressed femininity, and it is generally projected onto the woman he loves.

Evidently, Alicia has only fitfully carried the projection of Cova's anima, for it appears at times to dissolve back into the unconscious. A dream of Cova's in which Alicia turns into a tree illustrates this tendency. Cova sees her, naked and disheveled, running away from him through a thicket and into a dark wood; then, coming to a tree, he makes an incision in the bark and begins to drain the sap as if to gather rubber from it. But the tree speaks to him: "¿Por qué me desangras. . . . Yo soy tu Alicia

1. José Eustasio Rivera, *La vorágine* (Buenos Aires: Losada, 1967), p. 11. Subsequent page references in the text will be to this edition. Luis Alberto Sánchez faults the opening pages for their verbiage, but inasmuch as the novel is written in the first person, it can be said in Rivera's defense that the tone immediately characterizes the intemperate disposition of the protagonist. *Escritores representativos de América*, 1ª serie (Madrid: Gredos, 1963), pp. 3, 149.

2. *The Development of Personality*, in *Collected Works* (New York: Pantheon, 1954), 17:198.

3. *Archetypes of the Collective Unconscious*, in *Collected Works* (Princeton, N.J.: Princeton University Press, 1968), vol. 9, pt. 1, p. 70.

. . ." (Why do you bleed me. . . . I am your Alicia . . .) (p. 35).
Among the many symbols of the total unconscious, the most
common is the primordial image of the Great Mother, who represents the balm for every distress, the all-enveloping protection that the state of unfeeling offers. A tree can symbolize the
Great Mother (for example, the olive tree, symbol of Athena);
woods and forests, likewise, signify the unconscious, as well as
anything dark and mysterious. Cova's dream, therefore, shows
his anima (Alicia) slipping back into the unconscious and
becoming indistinguishable from the Great Mother. Cova
appears to be at an early stage of psychic development at which
full emancipation from the Great Mother has not been achieved;
Jung tells us that the anima "invariably appears, at first,
mingled with the mother-image." This is further indicated by
Cova's propensity to Don Juanism, a form of the mother-com-
plex whereby a man, seeking his mother in every woman, is
unable to relate satisfactorily with any woman.[4]

Each progressive level of consciousness is reached through
self-renewal, that is, through a symbolic death or sacrifice leading to rebirth or transformation. Cova seems stalled on the
threshold of the process known as the crystallization of the
anima from the mother archetype. He must disengage his
anima from the Great Mother by what Jungians call the dragon
fight.[5] From the very first page of *La vorágine*, Cova is confused
and highly irascible; often he behaves with infantile preten-
tiousness and freely displays his emotional instability as well as
his need for psychic renewal. Even he is aware of it: a new life is
due to begin for him, he feels; he yearns to "renovar" (renew)
himself.[6] Furthermore, he seems to intuit the nature of his

4. *Archetypes*, pp. 81–82, 85. Jung goes on to say: "What in its negative aspects
is Don Juanism can appear positively as bold and resolute manliness; opposition
to all stupidity, narrow-mindedness, injustice and laziness; willingness to make
sacrifices for what is regarded as right, sometimes bordering on heroism"
(p. 87). These positive factors also apply to Cova in his better moments, and they
are particularly descriptive of his creator, Rivera, who partly projected himself in
his character, according to his biographer, Eduardo Neale-Silva (*Horizonte
humano: vida de José Eustasio Rivera* [Madison: University of Wisconsin Press,
1960], pp. 286–87, 302).

5. Erich Neumann, *The Origins and History of Consciousness*, trans. R. F. C.
Hull (New York: Pantheon, 1954), p. 198.

6. "Debía iniciar una nueva vida, distinta de la anterior" (I had to start a new
life, distinct from the former) (p. 16); "iba . . . anheloso de renovar mi vida y de
rescatarme de la perversión" (I was eager to renew my life and to save myself
from perversion) (p. 24).

dilemma and its remedy. Speaking to Don Rafo, the fatherly guide with whom the young couple travels into Casanare, Cova confides that he is by nature chivalrous to the point that he would sacrifice himself for a lady even if she were not his. Then, referring to the ideal he has set himself, he says he knows that the chimera he pursues is human, and that through it one can attain personal triumph, well-being, and love (p. 24). Goals such as these are, in fact, among those which the anima inspires a man to reach. Only through her can he shake off his natural inertia and accomplish anything, for she is the source of creativity: "Creativity in all its forms is always the product of a meeting between the masculine world of ego consciousness and the feminine world of the soul." Besides, the anima has human features, as Cova says; she is a partner in the sense that she is "a 'you' with whom 'I' can commune, and not a mere idol to be worshipped," in contrast with the awesome Great Mother.[7] The stage is set in the novel for sacrifice and renewal with the object of liberating the helpful feminine image from the unconscious.

In Casanare, Cova and Alicia are soon separated: first in spirit, because although he forces himself to be gallant with her, and thinks he is, she cannot be deceived, and his behavior alienates her. Later they are separated in fact when, during his prolonged absence, she disappears. She has joined the party of Barrera and left for the jungle. Barrera is a sinister entrepreneur, who is recruiting workers with false promises for the odious rubber plantations of Amazonas. All those who follow him become his prisoners. Mortified and enraged by this news, Cova reacts hysterically and plunges into the jungle after them, intent on killing them both, for he is sure that Barrera is his rival.[8] As soon as she withdrew from him, Cova had found himself falling in love with Alicia and even idealizing her (p. 42). In other words, insofar as she was a woman of flesh and blood with a distinct personality of her own, she did not correspond to the lady of his yearnings; but when she became aloof and out of

7. Neumann, *Origins*, p. 335.
8. Actually, his first impetus slackens quickly and he is beset by vacillations for several days, until he and his companions finally set their horses free and board the canoe, which like "a floating coffin" (p. 98) will take them downstream into the jungle.

reach, he could project his ideal upon her, and she became the carrier of his anima.

The departure of Alicia with Barrera and his group has been foreshadowed by another of Cova's dreams. Before ever meeting Barrera, but hating him nevertheless, Cova dreams of Alicia going toward a sinister and lugubrious place to meet Barrera; Cova follows her with a shotgun in hand, but when he tries to shoot his rival, the gun turns into a snake (p. 34). A snake is symbolically ambiguous, combining connotations of both death and life, partly due to its habit of renewing itself by shedding its skin; it is therefore a symbol of rebirth, and the dream hints at this coming event as well.

It would almost seem that Alicia's flight was brought about by some telepathic coercion on Cova's part. By attributing to Alicia an interest in Barrera she never felt, Cova unwittingly forces her into going with Barrera, for as it turns out she did not leave of her own accord, but because Cova's fatuous conduct left her no alternative. At all events, she takes on the form of his anima now, leading him through the jungle and inciting him to surmount difficulties, which he does with unexpected tenacity. She inspires him in the sense that the passion of finding her and Barrera presses him on; in the course of time he learns that she is guilty of no offense against him. The last two thirds of the book (Cova's journal) are a record of his wildly contradictory emotions, his fevers and hallucinations, the portion of wisdom he receives from an older man, and the successful outcome of his quest: overtaking Barrera, he kills him in hand-to-hand combat and rejoins Alicia, who is carrying Cova's first-born.

In outline, Cova's adventure (the descent into the jungle, the slaying of Barrera, and the freeing of Alicia) follows the general pattern of the dragon fight of myth and fairy tale. Like Theseus, Cova makes his way through a labyrinth, slaughters a monster, and runs off with the princess who is the monster's prisoner. The dragon fight is a traditional test of masculinity. According to Jungian psychology, hero motifs of this nature are archetypes of transformation and renewal that exist in the collective unconscious: "The dragon fight is correlated psychologically with different phases in the ontogenetic development of consciousness. The conditions of the fight, its aim and also the period in which it takes place, vary. It occurs . . . wherever in fact a rebirth or a reorientation of consciousness is indicated. For the captive is the 'new' element whose liberation makes further development possible."[9] The labyrinth represents the total unconscious, or Great Mother; the latter is comprised of a helpful aspect and a terrible aspect, which are symbolized respectively by the maiden and the monster. The aim is to separate the helpful from the terrible, the anima-maiden from the monster-Great Mother, to take possession of her and assimilate her creativity into one's personality. Turning back to the novel, the jungle (or vortex, as the title has it) is a fitting symbol for the dark Great Mother; Barrera is a Minotaur-monster in Cova's mind and corresponds to the Terrible Mother, and Alicia is obviously the captive anima to be liberated.

After Alicia has disappeared and Cova is swept into the process of psychic transformation, we find a number of images from the collective unconscious breaking into his journal. Having just heard of her disappearance, he entertains a vindictive fantasy while galloping toward the rancho where he had left Alicia: he pictures the decapitated body of Barrera tied to his horse's tail, and as it drags through the brush, its members scatter behind him until it is reduced to atoms and disappears in the dust (p. 93). Beheading and dismemberment are universally connected with fertility offerings to the earth (the Great Mother), and they express the dread that masculine consciousness has of being swallowed up by the unconscious feminine.[10]

Minutes later, Cova's friend Franco, whose wife has also left with Barrera's party, sets fire to the deserted rancho. As he watches, Cova sees the flames writhe and curl themselves into the pattern of a snake biting its tail (p. 93). The circular serpent that bites its own tail, Uroboros, is the archetypal image of original felicity and corresponds to the earliest psychic state, preconsciousness.[11]

Early in his jungle trip Cova witnesses an Indian bacchanal; his companions take part in it, whereas he, by nature intem-

9. Neumann, *Origins*, pp. 204–5. "Time and again," Neumann continues, "the failure of the dragon fight . . . proves to be the central problem for neurotics during the first half of life, and the cause of their inability to establish relations with a partner."

10. Ibid., pp. 54, 58.

11. Ibid., p. 10.

perate, is ironically the only one to remain sober and chaste (pp. 108–9). Orgiastic festivals are characteristic of the adolescent stage in the evolution of consciousness; the ego is still dominated by the Great Mother, and its tendency to dissolve back into the unconscious is felt to be pleasurable (later, in the hero stage, it is dreaded). But in initiations such as the dragon fight, to resist the lure of the Great Mother is one of the tests of strength designed to beget higher consciousness.[12] The fact that Cova deliberately retains his composure despite external provocation and internal despair, going so far as to invoke chastity for vigor and tranquility, suggests a conquest, at least a temporary one, over the unconscious and a strengthening of ego stability; it is of course one of the necessary steps in the transformation process.

One evening Cova sees a mysterious footprint inexplicably isolated in the sand. It is the mark of a water nymph. That night he listens to the Indian legend of Mapiripana, the Lorelei of the Orinoco and Amazon headwaters. Seated on a tortoise shell drawn by river dolphins, she rides over the waters when the moon is full, singing. By her lascivious charms, she lures men away from reality into an underworld of monstrous spirits where the men are tortured and left to die. Mapiripana is a manifestation of the negative anima, which, in legends all over the world, expresses the well-founded fear of uncontrollable instinctual forces. "¿Quién puede librar al hombre de sus propios remordimientos?" (Who can free man from his own remorse?), Mapiripana admonishes her victims when they beg to be released from their torments (p. 121).

Essential to any initiation drama is that the candidate submit to "death" in one form or another. In the course of Cova's sojourn in the jungle, he suffers several attacks of fever accompanied by delirium, which reduce him to extreme physical and mental weakness and make him fear for his sanity. Any one such experience, to be sure, would suffice to symbolize death followed by rebirth, but we have something more explicit here. Cova takes us along as he struggles through his hallucinations; he hears the sands of the river banks lament their immobility and the waters complain of being engulfed by the ocean (p. 122).

12. Ibid., pp. 277, 310.

Next, he feels stricken with catalepsy, and while icy cold creeps up from his toes, he sees a shadow at his side swinging its scythe over his head. In horror he awaits the blow from Death, and when it comes, his cranium shatters with the sound of tinkling crystal. Franco examines his glassy eyes while Cova shouts inaudibly: "¡Estoy vivo, estoy vivo! Pon el oído sobre mi pecho" (I am alive, I am alive! Put your ear on my breast). But Franco calls the others, and without so much as a tear he says, "Abrid la sepultura, que está muerto. *Era lo mejor que podía sucederle"* (Open a grave, because he is dead. *It was the best thing that could have happened to him*) (p. 123, emphasis added). And Cova listens to the blows of the pickax falling in the sand before he dies. It is particularly significant that the voice of his unconscious should tell him that to die is the best thing for him, because psychologically this is exactly what he needs most.

The sands want mobility and beg him to scatter them to the winds, which he does; the waters in turn want to be still and ask to be held quietly in his hands. This double contradiction reflects an inner polarity in Cova, without which there can be no flow of psychic energy (libido). According to Jung, a living tension between the conscious and the unconscious maintains our psychic balance and regulates the movement of the libido. Inasmuch as the essence of sacrifice and rebirth is the transformation or renewal of psychic energy, and the need for renewed energy can be felt as madness, it is natural that these three concepts—polarity, sacrificial death, and insanity—be linked together as they are here. Mythologically expressed, the Great Mother pursues her son with madness until he offers sacrifice to her. When something of value is given up in sacrifice, energy regresses to the unconscious, provoking a one-sided accumulation. The normal reversion of the psychic process results in a fresh charge of energy for consciousness. It is understandable that until the new release of libido is received, a temporary imbalance occurs, which explains Cova's periods of mental disturbance and insanity. In the first part of the novel, when he feels the need for renewal he often acts without restraint; once he begins the process of renewal, marked by an initial regression, his derangement becomes more acute and frequent, which is normal. In this connection, regression, or energy passing into the unconscious, activates its contents. This accounts for the eruption of archetypal images from Cova's unconscious: dismemberment, circular snake, siren, beneficial death, and others yet to come. Under favorable conditions these images act as transformers of energy, as does the anima for the hero.[13]

Fifty pages later he has reason to fear once again for his mental equilibrium. Now the trees persecute him and send him screaming from his companions, who must hurry after and disentangle him from the underbrush. Later in a quiet mood, he ponders the mystery of death as a prelude to the life he sees all around him. Lianas, insects, and other creeping parasites destroy the great trees of the virgin forest, but alongside the fallen giants sprout the seedlings; pollen flies in the pestilential miasmas; everywhere, death and procreation are bound together as the earth performs her uninterrupted renovations.

During the night a strange stillness takes possession of the jungle: the faint rustle of unknown activities, a phantasmal light followed by foreboding silence. "Es la muerte, que pasa dando la vida" (It is death that passes giving life) (p. 176). Here again, Cova's words, reminding him of the paradoxical law that there can be no life without death, are remarkably appropriate to the psychic state he is traversing. His perception of this law shows that whatever disorders he is suffering, his psyche seems to be basically healthy and in harmony with nature.

As for Cova's feeling of being persecuted by the trees, this is a frequent occurrence for him and for others. Over and over, the jungle is personalized, sometimes in long impassioned apostrophes. She *(la selva) (the jungle)* is spouse, mother, virgin, enemy; she is inhuman, sadistic, and prophetic (pp. 95, 111, 175, 176). Each of these epithets describes typically the Great Mother archetype, which also contains diverse and contradictory symbols.

The intensity with which Cova reacts to the jungle indicates that it has a profound emotional meaning for him, and so it must have had for the author, Rivera. Neale-Silva, his biographer, reports that Rivera was always strongly attracted to nature and to the jungle in particular. During a trip up the Orinoco, he experienced only the jungle's pernicious aspects at first. The shattering of his idyllic concept of the jungle was for him a bitter disappointment. Nevertheless, he was drawn to solitary expedi-

---

13. Jolande Jacobi, *The Psychology of C. G. Jung*, 6th ed. (New Haven: Yale University Press, 1962), pp. 53–57.

tions along its rivers and inland. While it continued to repel him for its brutalizing influence, he also caught the fascination and wonder it held for others.[14] Again, these conflicting emotions are those that the Great Mother generates. Ever ambivalent, she can appear to be attractive and hostile at the same time; she is both positive and negative, good and terrible, and always disturbing.

Rivera's personal response to the jungle suggests that for him it was charged with mana (extraordinary and bewitching power such as archetypes have). As a mana figure, it could be a symbol of transformation: that is, the jungle is capable of transforming psychic energy, a process which is the essence of the rebirth mystery.

Meanwhile, Cova's feelings toward Alicia are in constant flux. Still convinced until close to the end of his quest that she has betrayed him, he draws considerable satisfaction from the thought of her probable sufferings. His declared hatred for her is fed by his wounded vanity in the face of his companions; but when he compares her with other women, he recognizes that she stands above them for her dignity and virtue. At times he reviews her defects to convince himself that her loss was a good riddance, which does not prevent him, when longing for feminine companionship, from realizing that the vague figure in his romantic dreams often turns out to be Alicia. However, he quickly suppresses such thoughts by evoking some crude fantasy about her. Sometimes he lingers over lewd reveries concerning her relations with the gross jungle workers, or he pictures her having become a degenerate slut, given over to her vice (pp. 101, 105, 117, 226). Such erotic daydreaming is a manifestation of the primitive, immature aspect of the anima; for Cova to indulge in it suggests that he has not yet established a feeling relationship with the opposite sex and that he is therefore still emotionally infantile, a fact that is frequently confirmed by other behavior.

The last half of the novel is dominated by the noble figure of Don Clemente. A jungle counterpart of Don Rafo, Cova's fatherly guide in Casanare, Don Clemente is a wise and kindly

14. *Horizonte humano,* pp. 230–31, 244, 251–52. In 1918 Rivera met Franco Zapata, who, with his common-law wife Alicia, had just returned from five years in the tropical jungles. Rivera heard his friend's tales and came under their spell. Franco Zapata was to be a partial prototype of Cova (pp. 146–50).

old man with an uncommon knowledge of the forest; he is in most respects the opposite of Cova. Another personification of the unconscious that often appears at the same time as the anima is the archetype of the wise old man. It symbolizes the self, or the nucleus of the psyche. Knowledge, wisdom, and insight are some of its characteristics, along with a willingness to give advice. At crucial moments, when these qualities are at a premium, it tends to intervene in the guise of an old man. Don Clemente, with his benevolence and other fatherly attributes, is such a figure. He enters the novel immediately after Cova and his crew have lost their canoe and face a bleak future. They stumble onto Don Clemente, who comes to the rescue by guiding them to the nearest settlement, planning their next move, and helping them to execute it. Furthermore, his familiarity with the ins and outs of jungle life is in keeping with the archetype of the wise old man, since the latter is an image of the psychic depths, or nature.[15] It is only natural that to Cova, Don Clemente should personify this archetype.

True to his name, Don Clemente is the first and only one to speak to Cova of pardon: "¡Pero perdone a la pobre Alicia! ¡Hágalo por mí!" (But forgive poor Alicia! Do it for me!) (p. 216). Cova makes no comment, but later, after learning that he has misjudged Alicia, that she has been faithful and is held prisoner by Barrera, he is abashed and admits that his anger is sometimes stupid: "¡Esa varona es buena y yo la perdí! ¡Yo la salvaré! . . . habrás de vernos reconciliados" (That strong woman is good and I lost her! I will save her! . . . you will see us reconciled) (pp. 237, 243). Having fought Barrera and seen his body reduced to the bone by a school of caribes in a matter of minutes, Cova forces Alicia to look upon the skeleton; the sight brings on premature birth pangs. Thus a seven-month baby is born as the immediate result of Cova's reunion with Alicia—in fact, due to the coming together of the hero and the princess. In Rivera's version of the myth, the fruitful consequence of liberating the creative feminine element from the unconscious is clearly and immediately set forth.

The ending of the novel is somewhat fortuitous, as if Rivera were in a hurry to finish: in order to protect his son from a

15. C. G. Jung, *Modern Man in Search of a Soul,* trans. W. S. Dell and Cary F. Baynes (New York: Harcourt, Brace and Co., 1933), p. 215.

plague, Cova and his companions retire a short distance from the camp where they were awaiting Don Clemente, leaving behind directions where he will find them. But he, known to be the best guide of the region, searches five months and never finds them. The jungle has swallowed them up.[16] Here is a man who succeeded in tracking down the bones of his son, buried somewhere in the vast forests of Colombia, Peru, Venezuela, and Brazil, but he can find no trace of five adults and a baby, two large dogs, a litter, and other baggage within a half-hour walk from the camp in a given direction! It may be that this ending demonstrates the jungle's triumph over man, but the argument is not entirely convincing as long as the story of Don Clemente's triumph over the jungle is inserted in the novel.

If Rivera identified with Cova to any extent, as his biographer suggests, his obliteration of Cova from the face of the earth for no inherent reason has an ominous portent for himself. "Experience shows that the unknown approach of death casts an *adumbratio* (an anticipatory shadow) over the life and dreams of the victim," writes Jung.[17] In fact, Rivera died suddenly of a cerebral affliction four years later at the age of forty.[18]

On the other hand, it seems reasonable to suppose that, insofar as Cova's adventure outlined the dragon fight, *La vorágine* was an unconscious exercise in psychic renewal for Rivera personally, just as *Faust* was for Goethe. Since the standard version of the dragon fight ends with the hero being united with the princess, Rivera may have instinctively felt that his version of it should end there, too.

Whatever technical shortcomings *La vorágine* may hold, the fact remains that it continues to be studied and read for its own sake because it is intensely alive. I submit that a primary basis for its continued hold on the reader is that the archetypal pattern it presents elicits a corresponding archetypal response in him and affords him an occasion to partake, unknowingly but nonetheless satisfactorily, in a rebirth drama—an experience analogous to but not to be confused with Aristotelian catharsis.

16. "¡Los devoró la selva!" (The jungle devoured them!) (p. 250). Note the devouring character of the Terrible Mother–jungle.

17. *Man and His Symbols* (New York, 1968), p. 63.

18. Neale-Silva, p. 449. The swallowing up of Cova by the monster he had just overcome in the person of Barrera could indicate that the dragon fight was unsuccessful; see note 9.

It is not likely that Rivera had this purpose in mind when he wrote the novel, nor is it important that he should. Creativity is a function of the anima and therefore issues from the unconscious: "Whenever the creative force predominates, human life is ruled and moulded by the unconscious as against the active will." Jung also tells us that with artists, the collective unconscious predominates over the personal, and that the man need only be its instrument: "The artist is not a person endowed with free will who seeks his own ends, but one who allows art to realize its purpose through him."[19]

19. Jung, *Modern Man*, pp. 169, 170.

2 Soledade-Persephone: A Cyclical Myth in *A Bagaceira*

Fred P. Ellison

Combining both traditionalist and modernist tendencies of the 1920s, José Américo de Almeida's *A Bagaceira (Trash)*[1] is not only a minor classic but also an important forerunner of the Brazilian novel in the 1930s and 1940s, especially of the regionalist and sociologically oriented "novel of the Northeast" that has attracted international attention. It is also an example of the so-called "drought literature" of the Northeast, since one of its thematic features is the drought cycle, involving the unusually severe occurrences in the years 1877, 1898, and 1915 in the arid backlands or *sertão*.[2] During the second of these droughts, a girl in her teens, Soledade, flees with her father and her foster brother to the *brejo*, or moist uplands, that lie between the coast and the desert backlands of the state of Paraíba. There Soledade and the other *sertanejos* from the interior come under the influence of the *bagaceira*, which is literally the place for dumping *bagasse* or cane pulp: by extension and with pejorative connotations, as the author states in the glossary to his work, the *bagaceira* symbolizes "the moral atmosphere of the sugar plantations" (p. 139). *A Bagaceira* has long been interpreted as a social drama reflecting the clash between two very different ways of life: the herdsmen and ranchers in the arid *sertão* and the sugar cane planters, whose system was based on large landholdings and a labor force just emerging from slavery. It is also a tragic love story that could be called neo-romantic and, because of its language, even lyric and poetic.[3]

1. First published in 1928 at João Pessoa by Imp. Oficial. All references, including those to M. Cavalcanti Proença's introductory study (pp. xxvii–lxxxvi), are to the 13th ed. (Rio de Janeiro: José Olympio Editora, 1974) and are included parenthetically.

2. The distinguished critic Alceu Amoroso Lima mentions "drought literature" in reviewing Rachel de Queiroz's *O Quinze* (1930) in his *Estudos*, 5th series (Rio de Janeiro: Civilização Brasileira, 1933), pp. 93–96; see also Jacinto do Prado Coelho, *Dicionário de Literatura*, 2 vols. (Rio de Janeiro: Cia. Brasileira de Publicações, 1967), 2:734–36, s.v. "Nordeste do Brasil."

3. Juarez da Gama Batista, in *A Sinfonia Pastoral do Nordeste* (João Pessoa: Univ. Fed. da Paraíba, 1967), examines certain myths in Almeida's second novel, *O Boquierão* (1935); on p. 62 he calls attention to the "impressionist and neo-romantic" aspect of *A Bagaceira*.

Soledade, whose role is so prominent that the novel might well have been named for her, will inevitably strike readers as an ambiguous figure. The author-narrator's tendency to associate her, perhaps unconsciously, with the sexual promiscuity and moral decay of the *bagaceira* poses one problem because, in spite of this attitude, the text reveals Soledade to be in many ways an admirable young woman. And, paradoxically for the patriarchal society of the Northeast, she demonstrates that she is more than the equal of the male characters who have tried to dominate her: her foster brother, Pirunga, the *senhor de engenho* or plantation master, Dagoberto, and his son, Lúcio, all of whom are attracted to her, and her father, who is anxious to protect the family honor. The complexities of Soledade's relationships with the other characters have lately occupied the attention of such perceptive critics as M. Cavalcanti Proença and Silviano Santiago. The former sees her as an Eve-like figure (p. lxx), the latter, as a kind of Mother Nature.[4] Neither, however, has chosen to pursue this line of interpretation. I hope to show in this essay that Soledade is more than a general nature goddess, indeed that she can be linked specifically to one of the best-known figures of Greek mythology, Persephone (called Proserpina by the Romans), queen of the Lower World. I shall further argue that some of the uncertainties and contradictions that hinder our reading of *A Bagaceira* can be resolved if we "stand back," as Northrop Frye once suggested,[5] from too close a reading of the story, and adopt—as simply one more productive level of analysis and with no pretense of exclusiveness—a mythic or archetypal approach.

Let me acknowledge my indebtedness to Frye's monumental *Anatomy of Criticism* for both a theory and a method of examining myth. While reflecting his deep interest in the anthropology of Frazer and others and in the psychiatry of Freud and Jung, Northrop Frye's view of myth and ritual is limited to belles lettres. He observes the multiplicity of myth, whether in dream world or real world, along with its recurrent aspect in ritual, but he finds it inappropriate for literary critics or theorists to specu-

4. Silviano Santiago, *Uma Literatura nos Trópicos* (São Paulo: Ed. Perspectiva, 1978), p. 122, and ch. 5, "*A Bagaceira*: Fábula Moralizante," pp. 101–22.

5. *Anatomy of Criticism* (1957; reprint, New York: Atheneum, 1966), p. 140. See especially his third essay, "Archetypal Criticism: Theory of Myths," pp. 128–239.

late about its origins—for example, to speculate that it might be a
function of the so-called collective unconscious, as Jung has
hypothesized.[6] Frye has recognized the validity of several
related but divergent definitions of the word *myth*. I find useful
for my purposes his statement that myths are fictions

> in the sense of anonymous stories about gods; in later ages they
> become legends and folk tales; then they gradually become more
> "realistic," that is, adapted to a popular demand for plausibility,
> though they retain the same structural outlines.[7]

I am also interested in the fourth and final essay of *Anatomy of
Criticism*, where according to Frye's theory of genres, literature
may undergo the following fourfold division: epos, drama,
lyric, and prose. The latter is further subdivided into novel,
romance, confession, and anatomy. I hope to show that the category of romance will, if applied to *A Bagaceira*, allow a fresh
vision of the work, particularly in relation to the myth of Persephone.

If one recalls that Demeter, the daughter of Cronus and Rhea
and the sister of Zeus, is the primordial earth mother, and that
Demeter's daughter, Persephone, whose myth we shall examine
later in more detail, is a duplicate of her mother, it is not difficult
to see the links between the Greek myths and those of the narrative we are studying. There are abundant passages in which
Soledade has the characteristics of Demeter-Persephone. For
example, she is significantly associated with nature in its powers
of fecundation and growth, with plants, trees, foliage, flowers,
water, earth, blood, and other signs of fertility. In the following
meeting between Soledade and Lúcio (concerning which the
narrator withholds certain indispensable details until almost the
end of the narrative), the young woman is clearly a fertility goddess:

> Soledade seemed to have been impregnated with all the fra-
> grances of nature. The powerful exhalations clung to her still wet
> skin, as if nature's own blossoms had been spilled over her, as if

---

6. Ibid., pp. 108–9.
7. "Myth as Information," in *Northrop Frye on Culture and Literature: A Collection of Review Essays*, ed. Robert D. Denham (Chicago: University of Chicago
Press, 1978; rpt., Phoenix Books, 1980), p. 74.

her own sexual charms were there in bloom. Even her green eyes exuded a fragrance.

This dizzying and seductive atmosphere drugged his senses, and Lúcio seized the girl's hand, tugging at her fingers as if plucking petals from a daisy. (p. 31; tr. 44)[8]

Soledade is sometimes a goddess of agriculture. Once Lúcio discovers the girl "in the most grotesque of feminine attitudes, sitting on her haunches, digging furrows in a bed of coriander" (p. 74; tr. 91). Another time her interest in animal reproduction, in barnyard and corral, strikes the somewhat prudish Lúcio as immodest, and he blames it on the immoral *bagaceira*.

There is no reason to believe that José Américo had any fertility goddess specifically in mind. He does include, however, passing references to figures or motifs from Greco-Roman mythology, including titans (p. 5), centaurs (pp. 61, 121–23), an odyssey (pp. 27, 51), and a sacred wood (p. 32). Though principally decorative, they do confirm José Américo's interest in mythology. Soledade is once likened to Helen of Troy in Lúcio's mind as a "destroyer of cities" (p. 74). In another scene with Lúcio, the narrator sees the girl as Eve (p. 67), in a traditional version of the origins myth. A chapter picturing the nubile Soledade and the sexually immature Lúcio in a jungle bower is entitled "Neither Dryads nor Hamadryads"; no doubt the title enhances rather than eliminates the mythic connotations. When describing the rape of Soledade by the *senhor de engenho*, José Américo employs the same device: "It had nothing to do with nymphs and fauns . . ." (p. 121; tr. 142). The obviously ironic negatives in these two cases may reflect a playful attempt to justify to other *modernistas* his somewhat conservative retention of Greco-Roman motifs, which had been popularized by the nineteenth-century Parnassian poets of Brazil but were anathema to the nationalist wing of writers with whom José Américo was identified.[9]

The specific connection with the myth of Persephone be-

8. The translations from the Portuguese are my own; numerals in parentheses refer respectively to *A Bagaceira*, 13th ed., and, for further interest, to R. L. Scott-Buccleuch's valuable translation of *A Bagaceira*, entitled *Trash* (London: Peter Owen, 1978).

9. José Américo once had some unflattering words for those writers "who, believing their thoughts are on Brazil, are actually thinking about ancient Greece or the man in the moon" ("Como me Tornei Escritor Brasileiro," in

comes visible through an episode involving Soledade, Dagoberto Marçau, and the wildflower *espia caminho* (road
watcher),[10] popularly believed to resemble female genitalia:

> The scowling plantation master had gone by without looking at
> her. Farther on, he had stooped down and seemed to be gather-
> ing flowers along the way, which in fact is what he was doing.
> Waiting till she caught up with him, he gave them to her—a bou-
> quet of purple—and his sensual features broke into a smile. In her
> embarrassment she accepted them without a second look, but
> she then discovered they were the "road watcher," the indiscreet
> little flower that women find disgusting. Washerwomen would
> put down their bundles on the ground and pull it up or furtively
> grind it under foot. (p. 30; tr. 43)

Cavalcanti Proença believes that Dagoberto's "sensual features"
in this passage (literally, "insatiable snout") indicates a goatlike
figure or perhaps a faun, and, because of a suggestion of horns,
the devil (p. lxix). There are more than enough instances of diabolical behavior to make us see him as an underworld archetype. He is cruel, even sadistic, to his plantation workers, and
he is hated by everyone, especially by his son Lúcio—their
enmity is established from the opening chapter. An exception is
Soledade, who eventually chooses Dagoberto to be her lover.
This development is puzzling, for after following a plot in which
three males are vying for her affection, the reader discovers that
soon after she reached the plantation, the fifty-year-old man
had surprised the virgin Soledade while she was bathing under
a waterfall and made her his.

Soledade's rape by the *senhor de engenho*, in a mythic context
that had already been provided by the omnipresent fertility
motifs, immediately calls to mind Persephone's abduction to the
Lower World by Hades, who fell in love with her and made her

Revista de Antropofagia, vol. 1, no. 6 [October 1928], p. 1, [rpt., São Paulo: Ed.
Abril, 1975]). If José Américo included no indigenous myths in *A Bagaceira*,
another Northeasterner, the Bahian Sosígenes Costa, composed a successful
mock epic called *Iararana*, written about 1932, that prominently joins Greco-
Roman and American gods and goddesses (ed. José Paulo Pães [São Paulo: Editora Cultrix, 1979]).
   10. The eminent folklorist Luís da Câmara Cascudo confirms the custom
requiring "women of the people" to stop and destroy the *espia caminho*,
"thought to be immoral" (*Dicionário de Folclore Brasileiro*, 4th ed. [São Paulo, Edi-
ções Melhoramentos, 1979], p. 312).

his queen. Zeus, Persephone's father, was persuaded to let her return to earth for a part of each year during the seasons of spring and summer and to bring with her a divine child as a symbol of her fecundity.[11] Persephone thus symbolizes the cycle of the seasons and is a goddess of both death and resurrection. With her mother, she represents "two phases of the vegetative powers of the soil, the mother standing for the entire power, latent or active, at all seasons, the daughter for the potency in its youthful aspect."[12]

Persephone's "divine child" parallels Soledade's own child, who is born after Soledade and Dagoberto move to Soledade's family ranch in the *sertão* when the news of their "criminal love" becomes known. The child is born after Dagoberto's death at the turn of the century in an accident that Pirunga may have caused. Fleeing the drought of 1915, Soledade returns with her child to the *brejo*. Soledade's supposed death fifteen or sixteen years earlier corresponds to Persephone's descent into the underworld and is explained in the story by the family's acceptance as truth of the report by Pirunga that he, to save his own life, had throttled her. The fact that she did not die can be interpreted, for purposes of the myth, as a ritual death followed by a rebirth. In terms of imagery, at both the beginning and the end of *A Bagaceira* Soledade is identified with death and the underworld when, as a victim of drought, her beauty is eclipsed and she is described as a skeleton.

The mythographer G. S. Kirk has pointed to analogies between the Demeter-Persephone myth and ancient stories of disappearing fertility deities in certain drought-stricken countries of Asia. The Greek canon refers to the return of the deity on a seasonal basis each year; the Asiatic myths more commonly refer to the return after a series of dry years ended by plentiful rains.[13] Kirk's observation is relevant to the arid region of northeastern Brazil. The final chapter of *A Bagaceira*, "Skeletons

---

11. C. G. Jung and K. Karényi, *Essays on a Science of Mythology: The Myth of the Divine Child and the Mysteries of Eleusis* (New York: Pantheon Books, 1949), pp. 172, 198–99.
12. G. Jobes, *Dictionary of Mythology, Folklore and Symbols* (Metuchen, N.J.: Scarecrow Press, 1961), 2:1257.
13. *Myth: Its Meaning and Functions in Ancient and Other Cultures* (1970; rpt., Berkeley: University of California Press, 1973), p. 197.

Revived," describes Soledade's unexpected reappearance with her child; thus, she can be likened to a fertility archetype or disappearing deity returning from "death" after an absence of a period of years.

The stories of Soledade and Persephone are metaphorically equivalent. Northrop Frye, who has investigated the Persephone myth extensively, including its appearance in five of Shakespeare's plays,[14] believes that a critic need not be concerned with whether the author consciously includes a particular myth, as long as the outlines of the operant metaphor can be discerned. He associates myth with the dream mode, in which desire or repugnance shape the creative process; furthermore, the ritual aspect of myth, a recurrence or periodicity of an experience or a dramatic action (for example, morning and night, phases of the moon, seed-time and harvest, and so on), accounts for its cyclical structure.[15]

Drought literature of northeastern Brazil expresses the *sertanejo's* desire to survive destruction and to return to a renewed and burgeoning *sertão*. The wide dissemination of such writing, which includes folk literature as well as the more evolved forms associated with writing, especially the novel, bears witness to the ritualistic nature of the myth in Brazil. In such literature in general, whatever the geographic setting, analogies to Soledade can be found among scores of fertility deities, along with the corresponding underworld archetypes representing death, disaster, and the scourge of drought.

The mythical dimension of Soledade is more easily understood if we read *A Bagaceira* not as a novel but as a "romance," to use a term still current in English to refer to an idealized form of fiction about heroic deeds; the Portuguese word is *novela*. José Américo's book is usually considered to be a novel, with emphasis upon its allegedly objective presentation of social reality. Northrop Frye makes a clear distinction between these two generic terms:

> The romancer does not attempt to create "real people" so much as stylized figures which expand into psychological archetypes. It is in the romance that we find Jung's libido, anima, and shadow reflected in the hero, heroine, and villain respectively. That is

14. *Anatomy,* p. 183.
15. Ibid., pp. 119–20, 160.

> why the romance often radiates a glow of subjective intensity that the novel lacks, and why a suggestion of allegory is constantly creeping in around its fringes. . . . . The romancer deals with individuality, with characters *in vacuo* idealized by revery, and, however conservative he may be, something nihilistic and untamable is likely to keep breaking out of his pages.[16]

Soledade is certainly more credible as a creature of the author's revery than as an observed social type. Lacking any well-differentiated psychology—the same may be said of the other characters, with the possible exception of Lúcio—Soledade is practically all instinct, and love seems to be her one imperative. There is about her something supernatural, which, as in the following passage, nature seems to be celebrating on the morning she arrives at the plantation with a little band of refugees:

> On that luminous morning, the loveliness of the green forest was alive in an orgy of golden blossoms.
>
> His sensibilities dulled to the splendor of nature, Dagoberto for the first time in his life was disturbed by the flowering gold. The sun seemed to have descended on the tawny jungle. . . .
>
> And once again he closed his unfeeling eyes. Suddenly, he was roused by a faint but startling voice. (p. 8; tr. 17–18)

The solar imagery, which we shall look at presently, points to Soledade; indeed it is a splendid annunciation of her in the early pages of the book. The voice reminds Dagoberto of his long-dead wife; later we are told that not only is she Soledade's first cousin, but she is also practically her double in appearance. Readers of romance are used to this sort of thing and are of course willing to suspend their disbelief. Another instance that taxes our credulity occurs when Soledade's nightgown catches fire from a lamp she is holding:

> Flames enveloped her breast like the spontaneous combustion of her heart. With one violent tug Pirunga stripped the garment from her body, then fled in panic, much more afraid of her and her white body staining the darkness like moonlight, than of any imaginary monster. (p. 102; tr. 121–22)

16. Ibid., pp. 304–5. An early critic, Olívio Montenegro, discussing the characters of *A Bagaceira*, observes, "A angélica pureza de Lúcio, com uma resistência às tentações físicas do amor que por vezes parece negar as qualidades da sua natureza viril; a dedicação canina de Pirunga por Valentim, e o seu crime imprevisto contra Soledade, por mais verdade local que encerrem não excluem uma impressão de fantástico e irreal" (cited by Gonzaga Rodrigues, Nathanael Alves, et al., eds., *José Américo, O Escritor e o Homem Público* [João Pessoa: União, 1977], p. 157).

Nowhere is there any suggestion of bodily injury to Soledade. Are we not in the presence of an almost supernatural figure moving beyond the limitations imposed on ordinary characters, whose actions must be governed by rules of plausibility? Instances abound of the girl's remarkable freedom that allows her to elude almost at will the vigilance of the men of her family, who would enforce the protection of the so-called honor code, a traditional system designed to guarantee a girl's virginity until her father should decide the time of her marriage.[17] The reader, furthermore, is baffled by her ability to return to her father's ranch as the wife (probably common-law wife) of her clan's enemy, Dagoberto, and to continue after his death to reside there for many years rearing their child, even though she had once been given up for dead. There is beyond a doubt an air of "subjective intensity" (to use Frye's term) and unreality about *A Bagaceira* that José Américo himself wanted to rationalize. For example, in the preface he states, "If there is any excess of senti- ment, it is the tragedy of reality itself. Passion is romantic only when it is false." He opposes naturalism as "just the idle gossip of ragpickers—to see clearly is not to see all but to see what is hidden from others." He also declares: "The semi-barbaric soul is a soul only by virtue of its violent instincts. To interpret it with artificial restraint would be to deprive it of its soul" (p. 2; tr.11). Though he never makes clear who are the "semi-barbaric," he may have meant all the archetypal characters of this strange "romance."

As a character identified with the displaced myth of Per- sephone, Soledade is a literary signifier of unusual semantic range. If she is an earth goddess, she is also a sun myth. The text itself calls attention to the elements of her name, *sol* and *edade* (the Portuguese word is *idade*), or "sun" and "age" (the latter in its sound pattern if not in its spelling) (p. 134). The Jungian scholar Erich Neumann, in *The Great Mother,* finds no contradic- tion between earth goddess and sky or sun goddess: moon, stars, and sun are all mythologically the offspring of the "Noc- turnal Mother" and thus associated with the feminine—the patriarchal view of the sun's dominance and of its birth each

17. For a sociologist's view of the clash between the societies of the *sertão* and of the sugar-cane area, and with a glimpse of the role of women under the "honor code," see Roger Bastide, *Brasil, Terra de Contrastes,* trans. Maria Isaura Pereira de Queiroz (São Paulo: Difusão Européia do Livro, 1959), pp. 78–80.

morning reflects a later stage of mythological thinking.[18]
M. Cavalcanti Proença has examined the widespread solar imagery in *A Bagaceira* and has called the sun "the symbol of Soledade's erotic personality," adding: "Soledade is igneous, and
her heat is given off to the men around her" (p. xxxv).

Through such symbolism, and especially through the book's
pervasive fertility imagery, Soledade comes to be associated
with the miracle of growth and renewal that follows the rains in
the *sertão*. Not surprisingly, then, her return to the backlands
with her lover Dagoberto, whose unborn child she carries, coincides with the "reconciliation of heaven with the stricken
earth":

> A miraculous odor filled the sertão. As far as the eye could see,
> imperishable nature was displaying her pristine loveliness, as if
> she had died only for the pleasure of being reborn more beautiful.
> . . . Each tree had on a new dress for the feast of the resurrection.
> (p. 116; tr. 137)

Although the chapter is entitled "Feast of the Resurrection,"
there is no direct reference to Catholic liturgy. With the exception of an occasional religious reference (for example, Soledade's baptismal name is Maria Soledade [p. 36] and a
washerwoman gossips that Soledade is as pretty "as a church
statue" [p. 65; tr. 82]), there is a strange absence of traditional
religious themes anywhere in the narrative, as Mário de
Andrade points out.[19]

Perhaps the most difficult problem of interpretation concerns
Soledade's relationship to the *bagaceira*. The word has, as we
have seen, a widely recognized connotation of sexual promiscuity among the society living and working on the sugar plantation, from the *senhor de engenho's* household to the females of the
lower social orders symbolized by the *senzala*, formerly the slave
quarters. This fundamental process, under way since the sixteenth century, is studied exhaustively in Gilberto Freyre's
famous study, *Casa Grande e Senzala* (1933), which has been
translated into English as *The Masters and the Slaves*.[20] Sole-

18. *The Great Mother: An Analysis of the Archetype*, trans. Ralph Manheim, Bol-
lingen ser. 47 (New York: Pantheon Books, 1955), pp. 212, 233.
19. *Aspectos da Literatura Brasileira, Obras Completas* (São Paulo: Martins, n.d.),
10:9.
20. Freyre, from the neighboring state of Pernambuco, and José Américo,

dade's father, Valentim, fears that the moral pollution of the *bagaceira* threatens his daughter. Lúcio deprecates the "plantation mentality, the legacy of slavery, the stigma of the slave quarters, the corruption of custom" (p. 55; tr. 71). Merely hinted at are the sexual relations between black women and the men of the big house: Lúcio "imagined famous plebeian love affairs. Nor did his abject heart omit humble persons of color. Solomon, the patron saint of the slave quarters: *Nigra sum, sed formosa*" (p. 28; tr. 40). The impressionable youth, evoking Lafcadio Hearn and Baudelaire on the subject of black women, was once on the point of shouting, "Long live the color-blind lovers who embraced Africa and gave Brazil a new race!" (p. 29; tr. 41).

For the narrator, love is a brutal passion that may even be "putrescent" (p. 40; tr. 55). In their flower-canopied huts, women "would give birth once, even twice a year" in "disastrous procreations . . . fecundity frustrated by general misery and wretchedness" (p. 80; tr. 97). Such are the women of the *bagaceira*, and the narrator associates Soledade with them when she is made the topic of their gossip or when she becomes the object of "lascivious looks" (p. 18; tr. 30) from the ragged, half-naked field workers. Her own normal flirtatiousness is, again indirectly, described as bordering on the sensual, especially in scenes of seduction involving her and the reluctant, guilt-ridden Lúcio—each time he sees Soledade he thinks of his own mother, for whose death in childbirth he feels responsible. Lúcio is warned by his black mammy: "A woman is like a fruit: when she drops, she rots" (p. 105; tr. 125). Lúcio has a literary bent and composes aphorisms: "Love is the traveling salesman that propagates the race" (p. 105; tr. 125). As a mature man and the prosperous heir to his father's plantation, Lúcio could enjoy a pun on his own name: if the first syllable, *lu*, "light," represents the fire of his youthful passion, the second, *cio*, "rut," stands for "an excessive romanticism" of the sort that "transformed women into angels or devils no one can love" (p. 124; tr. 157). In the earlier-mentioned preface to *A Bagaceira*, the author anticipates

---

who died on 10 March 1980 at the age of ninety-three, as friends had many interests in common. On the question of Freyre's possible influence on Almeida, see Joaquim Inojosa, *O Movimento Modernista em Pernambuco*, 3 vols. (Rio de Janeiro: Gráfica Tupy Ed., 1968–1969), 1:202–5.

his character's views: "Here love is an inconsequential, lyrical concession to climate and race" (p. 3; tr. 12).

The creation of Soledade as a fertility deity is, no doubt unconsciously, the result of José Américo's naturalistic concept of love between the sexes, which makes idealization unthinkable. That the sort of love represented by Soledade is equated with carnality is illustrated in the chapter "Love Is the Law of Nature," where, in an aphrodisiac setting with Lúcio, Soledade displays the by-now-familiar traits of a nature goddess. Here too are notable examples of the water imagery associated not only with the theme of fertility but also with the content of romance as a specific narrative genre.[21] There is also blood imagery that is consistent with the Persephone archetype (pp. 67–68; tr. 84–85).[22] Soledade's forwardness makes Lúcio wonder once more: "Can her modesty have been contaminated by the bagaceira?" (p. 71; tr. 88). Later, when he discovers that his father has "put one over on him" by winning the love of Soledade, he vilifies her as a prostitute. Actually, the narrator censors himself and merely writes "pu—" or "prosti—."

Here, as in other places in the story, the narrator fails to take the reader fully into his confidence. The text suppresses information to which the reader might have felt entitled. Such withholding, on the other hand, may have some justification as an artistic device to build dramatic tension. The Brazilian critic Silviano Santiago has studied closely the implicit narrator's suppressions in *A Bagaceira*; these may take the form of actual ellipsis points or gross omissions of information in situations where the reader might have expected to be enlightened.[23] Many of the suppressions have to do with sexual discourse:

> The narrative spoke constantly of the "romantic" encounters between Lúcio and Soledade, of the continuing suspicions of Pirunga (who, watching over the young pair of lovers, was like the figure of the narrator himself, who was also keeping watch on them for fear they would commit some act that would have to be suppressed); the narrative *kept still* about all the sexual encounters between Dagoberto and Soledade.[24]

21. Frye, *Anatomy,* p. 160.
22. Neumann, *Great Mother,* p. 286.
23. *Uma Literatura nos Trópicos,* pp. 109–11.
24. Ibid., pp. 110–11.

Little wonder then that the reader may feel perplexed about the progress of Soledade's *amours*. The most striking of the omniscient narrator's suppressions is of course the rape scene, which is revealed toward the end as a flashback to a point early in the story, shortly after the drought victims arrived at the plantation. From the first the text was a series of innuendos and allegations of Soledade's probable immorality in the atmosphere of the *bagaceira*—the case presented by the narrator, though in the third person, is reminiscent of that made by the first-person narrator, Bento, against Capitu in Machado de Assis's *Dom Casmurro* (1900). When Valentim at last learns of his daughter's supposed death at the hands of Pirunga, he is sorry, but he adds: "Fortunately, she is dead, dead and gone. . . . She could not go on living like that! . . . What's done is done. . . . It was the bagaceira!" (p. 129; tr. 152). Valentim's rationalization of his daughter's "death" is given a broader context in lawyer Lúcio's court speech defending Valentim against a charge of murdering Dagoberto's overseer, whom he wrongly suspected of being Soledade's lover. Lúcio accuses society: "Who is more guilty, the defendant who killed a man or society that through its own neglect allowed thousands of people to die? Rather than a criminal, he is the victim of an entire people's lack of solidarity" (p. 130; tr. 152). The lawyer refers to the fact that the Brazilian government had not taken steps to correct the effects of the periodic drought.

But in the entire book there is never a word in defense of the young woman who is an innocent victim of rape, then falls in love with her ravisher, elopes with him to the *sertão*, lives with him, attempts to avenge his death, and later bears his child. Nor is Soledade ever shown to be corrupt in the environment of the *bagaceira*, as scandalmongers would have it. The narrator offers no evidence of any violation of the moral law. The most serious charge against her would be that she conceals her relationship with Dagoberto from her father and thus is indirectly responsible for the murder of Dagoberto's go-between by Valentim. M. Cavalcanti Proença has spoken of Soledade's loneliness— indeed "solitude" or "loneliness" are standard lexical meanings of her name:

> The loneliness of one who, in every respect a lady, moves dazzlingly through the 300 pages of a novel, without finding any-

one who understands her. When the book is finished, the question remains: to what extent have sex, pique at Lúcio for his timidity, powerlessness in the face of force, or love itself, contributed to her surrender to Dagoberto? Whom did she really love? The son or the father? Both? Neither? (p. lxvii)

Why, on the surface at least, does the narrator leave the reader in doubt about the worth of Soledade as a person? Why does he disparage or suppress her possible motives for an idealized love? Perhaps one reason is that she represents a subversion of the traditional patriarchal values concerning the role of women, whether in the *brejo* or in the backlands. Not only does she elude the vigilance of her father and her foster-brother, Pirunga, but she ultimately escapes their authority by finding her own freedom and by surviving her ritual death. She towers over Dagoberto, who as plantation master is the highest symbol of authority. When she and he leave the *brejo* for the *sertão*, "she is the one in charge," in Pirunga's words (p. 115; tr. 135). During a dangerous hunt for Soledade's pet jaguar, she and Pirunga lead the way, with Dagoberto in the rear. From first to last she rejects the submission expected of her in the patriarchal Northeast.

Soledade-Persephone is a powerful character based on a powerful archetype. Perhaps this explains M. Cavalcanti Proença's acute observation: "As may happen in works of art, the achievement went beyond the proposal: contrary to her creator's plans, the heroine became a remarkable figure of a woman, winning not only the hearts of all the men but the first place in the book itself, which became the 'novel of Soledade'" (p. xxix). The male domination implicit in Dagoberto's initial possession of Soledade gives way to an ever stronger affirmation of the power of the archetypal feminine, quite unlike the instances of the Demeter-Persephone archetype investigated by Susan Gubar in her article "Mother, Maiden and the Marriage of Death: Women Writers and an Ancient Myth":

> The marriage of death becomes a symbol of daemonic male power which simultaneously effects the destruction of the girl and the desecration of nature . . . . The grievous separation of mother and maiden implies that in a patriarchal society women are divided from each other and from themselves. The renewal promised by the birth of a divine child can never cancel out the pain and sorrow of its conception since it means the continuance

of the myth, which is no less a tragic cycle than the rhythm of the seasons.[25]

On the contrary, Soledade's "eternal return" is in accordance with the rhythm of fertile and infertile years in the backlands and proclaims the central theme of the romance: on a mythic level, the victory over natural disaster and death; on a social plane, the promise of greater unity between the desert *sertão* and the fertile uplands and coastal plantation areas—that is, "the two Northeasts," as they are sometimes called. The archetypal Soledade completely overshadows the rationalist, progressive-minded Lúcio, who is ridiculed in the text as a "little god" despite his success in improving the material existence of his workers. Soledade's child—Lúcio's half brother—is, like Lúcio, the offspring of a *brejo* father and a *sertão* mother. But, unlike the failed Lúcio, the boy symbolizes a new generation and the hope of unifying the two radically different areas of this venerable and long-suffering part of Brazil.[26]

The Persephone myth provides fresh insight into the some-times ambiguously presented love story of Soledade and her suitors; it also helps to explain the durability of the narrative, its unflagging appeal to Brazilian readers after more than fifty years. Despite the patriarchal prejudices of the narrator, the unconscious resonance of this ancient and widespread arche-type in the minds of readers contributes to an appreciation of Soledade as a fertility figure and at the same time as a disappear-ing goddess who is a fitting symbol of the cycle of death and resurrection represented by drought. Finally, at the level of the "unsaid" and as a prime example of what was no doubt creative (unconscious) dreaming on the part of the author, the Per-sephone myth brings a sense of ritual solemnity to the romance that has thus far gone unnoticed.

25. *Women's Studies* 6 (1979):305.

26. This is a major theme in José Américo de Almeida's *A Parahyba e Seus Prob-lemas* (João Pessoa: Imp. Oficial, 1924), an ambitious study of his native state and the source of much of the documentation for socio-economic problems taken up in *A Bagaceira*. The same message of cultural assimilation and unity was enunci-ated with artistic emphasis in Euclides da Cunha's classic *Os Sertões* (1902). See Gilberto Freyre, "Euclides da Cunha and the Sertão," reprinted from *Vida, Forma e Côr* (1962), in *The Gilberto Freyre Reader,* trans. Barbara Shelby (New York: Alfred A. Knopf, 1974), pp. 200–203; see also my own "O Drama Edipal do Romance *A Bagaceira,*" in *Aufsätze zur Portugiesischen Kulturgeschichte* 14 (1967/1977):146–51.

DISCOURSE ANALYSIS

3 Visual and Verbal Distances in the Mexican Theater: The Plays of Elena Garro

Sandra Messinger Cypess

The concepts developed by Michel Foucault regarding the use of discourse bring to our attention the fact that implicit in a system of discourse are rules and restrictions, privileges and exclusions.[1] The rules that govern the production of discourse and the procedures that control, select, organize, and redistribute it are expressions of a culture handed down from generation to generation. In Latin American culture, women have generally been considered silent figures, submissive to the patriarchal powers that govern their society, whether they be the fathers of the family or of the Church. Women's real distance from the centers of power can be translated linguistically as a restriction in the production of discourse in literary texts. It is pertinent in this regard to remember Foucault's contention that the fact of writing itself is a systematic conversion of the power relationship between the controller and the controlled; that is, the one who has the power also controls the written word (the discourse).

In applying this concept to the literary tradition, it is apparent to many readers, as Virginia Woolf reminds us in *A Room of One's Own*, that although women may have been visually present as images in literature, they have been verbally absent from the literary tradition as producers of discourse. In regard to the Mexican theatrical tradition, from the time of Sor Juana Inés de la Cruz in the seventeenth century to the modern period there has been a general absence of women dramatists, according to the records of the literary-critical tradition.[2] The socio-economic changes of the twentieth century have enabled women to assume more active roles in society, including that of authorship. Now that there are increasing numbers of Mexican women dramatists, it is important to focus on the nature of their produc-

1. See *The Archaeology of Knowledge*, trans. A. M. Sheridan Smith (New York: Pantheon, 1972), p. 216. The appendix entitled "The Discourse on Language" is especially useful.
2. See my article "¿Quién ha oído hablar de ellas? Un repaso de las dramaturgas mexicanas," *Texto Crítico* (México), no. 10 (1978), pp. 55–64.

tion of discourse and how their texts contribute to the cultural mythology of the image of women. I will begin my study of visual and verbal distances in the Mexican theater by analyzing the plays of Elena Garro (1920–).

When Carlos Solórzano referred to Elena Garro in his *Teatro latinamericano en el siglo XX,* he called her "mujer de excepcional talento y de extraordinaria receptividad" (woman of exceptional talent and extraordinary sensitivity).[3] In commenting on her three one-act plays first produced in 1956, Solórzano concluded that *Un hogar sólido (A Solid Home), Andarse por las ramas (Beat Around the Bush),* and *Los pilares de doña Blanca (The Fonts of Doña Blanca)* brought to the Mexican theater "una nueva frescura que se apoya en el lenguaje popular y en breves fábulas que son como juegos en las que se advierte una profunda y rara dimensión poética" (a new freshness based on popular language and short, gamelike fables that reveal a profound, unusual poetic dimension) (p. 181). Despite such early praise and Garro's subsequent production of six additional one-act and two three-act plays, her dramatic work has received little critical attention. While initial readings saw in her work a dichotomy between reality and fantasy and a tendency toward the evasion of reality, more recently the social aspect of her drama has been recognized, in particular her exploration of woman in society.[4] A reading of her plays from a semiotic perspective brings forth the variety of women as well as the underlying exploration of the processes that shape signification.

My analysis of Garro's production of discourse is based on a semiotic perspective, or the study of signs and sign systems and the function of these systems within a cultural, performative context, a method utilized in a growing number of studies of the drama.[5] By applying semiotic methodology we may study the

3. México: Editorial Promaca, 1964, p. 181. Further page references to this work will be cited parenthetically in the text.
4. See Frank Dauster, "El teatro de Elena Garro: evasión e ilusión," *Revista Iberoamericana,* no. 57 (1964), pp. 84–89; reprinted in *Ensayos sobre teatro hispanoamericano* (México: SepSetentas, 1975), pp. 66–77 (page numbers will refer to this edition of the article). Gabriela Mora, "*Los perros* y *La mudanza* de Elena Garro; designio social y virtualidad feminista," *Latin American Theatre Review,* 8, 2 (1975), pp. 5–14.
5. See Raúl H. Castagnino, *Semiótica, ideología y teatro hispanoamericano contemporáneo* (Buenos Aires: Editorial Nova, 1974); Susan Wittig, "Toward a Semiotic Theory of Drama," *Educational Theatre Journal* 26 (1974):441–54; and Anne Ubersfeld, *Lire le théâtre* (Paris: Editions Sociales, 1978).

production of meaning on stage, taking into consideration not only the linguistic system but also the spatial relations (the proxemics) and the kinesic or gestural codes. A reading that analyzes only the semantic or referential level of the dialogic interchanges without considering the other dramatic codes may derive an interpretation that appears to support a stereotyped image of woman on Garro's stage. I would suggest, however, that by decoding the dialogic interchanges and the reciprocal actions of the dramatic moment, it becomes apparent that Garro's texts explore the relationship between expression and content, or between signifier and signified. The texts, therefore, question the very nature of the linguistic system that has generated our concept of society, including the stereotyped image of woman. The key plays in this system are *Andarse por las ramas (Beat Around the Bush)* and *El encanto, tendajón mixto (Enchantment: Five and Dime)*.

As a title, *Andarse por las ramas* has a popular metaphoric connotation: it is a cliché that signifies talking around a subject without getting to the point, to beat around the bush in the English equivalent. A colloquial expression, it implies that one is speaking indirectly. The denotative level of the phrase, literally in Spanish "to go along the branches of a tree," is almost always ignored. One may assume from the title, then, that the play will deal with the theme of indirect speech, in the sense of pretexts. However, it would be a superficial reading of the play to conclude that it is merely "la ilustración de otro refrán" (the literal rendering of another proverb) in the same manner as Buenaventura's *En la diestra de Dios Padre*.[6] In fact, not only is the polysemous nature of the phrase presented, but also an illustration of the general signifier-signified to generate a sign function.

Since semiotic theory is important to my reading of the text, I shall repeat the following passage of Umberto Eco in regard to the concept of sign as an introduction to my own discussion:

> A semiotic relationship exists when, given any material continuum, it is segmented, subdivided into pertinent units by means of an abstract system of oppositions. The units which this

6. Solórzano, *Teatro*, p. 182. Willis Knapp Jones also calls the play a work based on the proverb and sees it as "a disconnected presentation of people who somehow achieve integration," in *Behind Spanish American Footlights* (Austin: University of Texas, 1966), p. 490. My interpretation of the play contradicts his reading.

system makes pertinent constitute, according to Hjelmslev, the *expression plane,* which is correlated (by a code) to units of a *content plane,* in which another system of oppositions has made pertinent certain (semantic) units through which a given culture "thinks" and communicates the undifferentiated continuum which is the world. The sign, therefore, is the correlation, the function which unites two "functives," expression and content. But the "functives" can enter into different correlations; correlations are mobile, and a given object can stand for many other objects, which is how one can explain the ambiguity, the semantic richness of the various types of language and the creation, the modification, the overlapping of different codes.[7]

As we shall see, the expression plane of "andarse por las ramas" enters into mobile correlations and stands for both the metaphoric and literal content functives. Two different codes are created that allude to different signifying processess, to different systems of behavior and approaches to "reality."

That Don Fernando, who is said to represent reason, uses the signifying process that is metaphorical, while Titina, who is related to lunar-*lunático* (lunatic), uses the literal signifying process, is an ironic inversion of the rational, patriarchal universe. That is, the father figure, Don Fernando, speaks indirectly, evading the literal level. His wife Titina, whom Don Fernando considers to be irrational, in the here and now of the drama keeps to the direct content functive of the sign. While their disagreement in this case is based on a connotative-denotative difference, in other situations their disagreements will derive from a different interpretation of signifieds; that is, the content with which they fill the linguistic signifier will be conflicting, with Titina providing an imaginative, open, more magical reading. Ultimately, we may conclude that Titina's procedures resist permanence and closure, while Don Fernando relies on the authority and tradition of convention to determine meaning.

Let us return to the specific elements of the text. The proxemic code places Don Fernando at the head of the table, just as he is the head of the family. His exalted position of power is verified on the linguistic level when his wife Titina addresses him using formal Spanish linguistic forms. "¿Ha pensado usted, don Fer-

7. Umberto Eco, "Looking for a Logic of Culture," in *The Tell-Tale Sign: A Survey of Semiotics,* ed. Thomas Sebeok (Lisse/Netherlands: Peter de Riddle Press, 1975), p. 15.

nando de las Siete y cinco, en donde se mete los lunes?" (Have you ever wondered, Don Fernando of the Five-o-seven, where Monday goes?).[8] In this utterance, Titina not only uses the *usted* form, but also gives him a full title: "Don Fernando de las Siete y cinco." The name *Fernando* has historical significance as an allusion to the king of Spain at the time of the Conquest, Fernando de Aragón. As Dauster points out, the chronological reference 7:05 refers to the fact that Fernando always expects to eat at that time. While seven may be considered a magical number, the specifics of 7:05 may imply that any sense of magic inherent within him has been destroyed by his immersion in the artificial world of conventional chronology. On the other hand, the semantic level of Titina's previous statement alludes to her imaginative conception of time.

In contrast to Titina's deference to her husband, Don Fernando addresses his wife with the informal familiar *tú*, often in the imperative mood. Contrast her formal "Perdone, don Fernando. ¿Quiere usted que traiga . . .?" (Excuse me, Don Fernando. Shall I bring you . . .?) (p. 84) with his curt "¡Justina, Justina! te estoy hablando. ¡Responde!" (Justina, Justina! I'm talking to you! Answer!) (p. 85).

On the kinesic level, the family's joint action concerns the evening meal, in particular the drinking of a bowl of soup. This act represents Don Fernando's whole mechanistic, rational outlook on life. As he eats, he continually looks at his watch, for soup must be served at a particular time, and each day a specific but different soup must be served. In contrast to his mechanical movements he says that the time is 7:07, a doubling of seven that might imply a magical moment, but Don Fernando is not privileged to see the magic. For him, 7:07 marks an arbitrary convention to which he gives egotistical meaning. It is past the time for him to eat a specific food. The ritual of soup, like other rituals of his life, are self-reflective, ego-centered acts.

For Titina, on the contrary, a bowl of soup reflects the creativity of the universe, the natural world rather than the mechanistic system: "En los platos de sopa a veces caen estrellas, hay eclipses, naufragios" (Sometimes stars drop into the soup, there are eclipses, shipwrecks) (p. 85). In this situation

---

8. Garro, "Andarse por las ramas," in her *Un hogar sólido y otras piezes en un acto* (Xalapa: Universidad Veracruzana, 1958), pp. 82–83. Further references to this play will be cited parenthetically in the text.

Titina shows her flexibility and creativity. Their different responses to the sign *soup* are repeated with other sign functions.

Lunes (Monday), for example, as a signifier is acknowledged by Don Fernando as an arbitrary choice to express its content: "Los lunes son una medida cualquiera de tiempo, una convención. Se les llama lunes como se les podría llamar pompónico" (Mondays are just a way of marking off time, a convention. They could just as well be called pomponic) (p. 84). Here Don Fernando offers us another way of saying that the signifier-signified relationship is arbitrary, a social convention that functions to convey meaning. Titina refuses to accept his association: "Pompónico no sería nunca lunes. Pompónico sería algo con borlas" (Pomponic would never be Mondays. Pomponic would be something with tassels on it) (p. 84). This response does not negate the arbitrary nature of the signifier-signified relationship; rather it shows a nascent rebellious spirit that attempts to reject old social codes and instill new ones.

Further examples of Titina's rebellious spirit are presented by her kinesics. When Don Fernando commands her to speak, her response is not verbal, but rather kinesic. According to the stage directions, she goes to the back of the stage, and on the back wall draws a house whose door she opens and through which she disappears. Above the wall, the branches of a tree appear, and Titina returns to stage presence seated on top of the branches of a tree. While she is accomplishing this act of distancing, motivated by Don Fernando's command, he talks to the empty chair where she had been sitting at the table. As the following dialogue takes place, Titina is literally "por las ramas," while Don Fernando employs the term metaphorically.

Don F.: —Siempre haces lo mismo. Te me vas, te escapas. No quieres oír la verdad ¿Me estás oyendo?

Titina: (desde el árbol) Lo oigo, Don Fernando.

Don F.: (a la silla vacía) La locura presidiendo mi casa. La fantasía a la cabecera de mi mesa. La mentira impidiendo que sirvan los jitomates asados de los lunes. Y tú sin oírme. Las mujeres viven en otra dimensión. La dimensión lunar. ¿Me oíste? Luuunaar.

Polito: Titina te oye y también te oigo yo.

Don F.: Se escapa y lo peor de todo es que a ti también te enseña a irte por las ramas.

> Titina: (desde el árbol) Yo no creo que sea malo irse por las ramas.
> Don F.: (a la silla vacía) Irse por las ramas es huir de la verdad.
> Titina: Las ramas son verdad. Polito, dile a tu papá que las ramas son verdad. (p. 86)

> Don F.: You always do just that. You get away from me, you escape. You don't want to hear the truth. Do you hear me?
> Titina: (from up in the tree) I hear you, Don Fernando.
> Don F.: (to the empty chair) Madness rules in my house. Fantasy at the head of the table. Lies, keeping Monday's stewed tomatoes from getting on the table. And you, not hearing a word I say. Women live in another dimension. The lunar dimension. You hear me? Luuunaar.
> Polito: Titina hears you, and I hear you, too.
> Don F.: She gets away and the worst of it is, she's teaching you to beat around the bush, too.
> Titina: (from up in the branches) I don't see anything wrong with beating around the bush.
> Don F.: To beat around the bush is to run away from the truth.
> Titina: The bush is truth. Polito, tell your papa that the bush is truth.

Before analyzing the dialogue and the spatiotemporal aspects of this scene, let us consider first the utterance that caused the action. Don Fernando had addressed a command to Titina, "¡Responde!" (Answer!). He expected her to respond verbally to his command to speak. Second, her movement away from him to a house of her own creation are gestures that signify her rejection of the world view represented by Don Fernando. That she cannot verbally address him and explain her rejection reflects her cultural position as the silent Mexican woman. Yet she has been able to communicate her intent to rebel, if not to Don Fernando, certainly to the reader/audience (henceforth referred to as R/A). Furthermore, it is also important to note that the receivers of Titina's utterances—Don Fernando on one hand, Polito their son with the R/A on the other—see two different sign systems in function.

Don Fernando addresses an empty chair as if Titina were sitting there. He calls her previous ideas about soup irrational and labels her behavior with the metaphor "irse por las ramas" (beat around the bush), which to him means "huir de la verdad" (run away from the truth).

Yet despite his kinesic and proxemic behavior, Titina is indeed spatially located on the branches of the tree and not in the chair. Don Fernando appears to be unaware of this, despite being convinced that he has his feet on the ground, that he is rational and knows the truth. The R/A sees that Titina is on the branches, so that her statement "Las ramas son verdad" (The bush is truth) appears true. Also, in contrast to Don Fernando's statement, "Aquí se trata de tener los pies honestamente en el suelo" (The thing is to keep your feet honestly on the ground) (p. 87), Titina responds with a reference to the natural configuration of the tree: "Las ramas tienen los pies en el suelo" (The bush has its feet on the ground). In order to understand the implications of this dialogue we should go beyond the denotative level. Titina uses "ramas" (bush) and "árbol" (tree) to signify truth and reality, while for Don Fernando "ramas" contradicts "pies en el suelo" (feet on the ground) and is associated with "huir de la verdad" (run away from the truth). We notice in this syntax that he refers to "la verdad" (the truth), whereas Titina says, "las ramas son verdad" (the bush is truth). The use of the definitive article by Don Fernando implies there is one truth, which is the equivalent of saying that there is one expression-content correlation. Don Fernando represents the naive view that the sign is a set signifier-signified relationship, while Titina acknowledges the multiplicity of correlations.

Perhaps it would be helpful here to refer to the cultural meanings that have been associated in the past with the sign function *tree*. One of the possible meanings attributable to the tree has been noted by Mircea Eliade, who has found that it has been used to symbolize absolute reality, reality that goes above and beyond the limits of everyday reality.[9]

On the basis of this symbology, Titina's association with the tree could suggest her connection with absolute reality, as was already alluded to in her reading of the soup.[10] Moreover, as befits the polysemous nature of signs in this text, a correlation in two directions seems possible: Titina-branches-tree—earth and

9. In Juan Cirlot, compiler, *Dictionary of Symbols* (New York: Philosophical Library, 1962), p. 328.
10. Gloria Feman Orenstein, *The Theater of the Marvelous* (New York: New York University Press, 1975), discusses Garro's presentation of absolute reality in relation to three other plays, *El encanto, tendajón mixto, Los pilares de doña Blanca,* and *La señora en su balcon.*

Titina—tree branches–absolute reality. Like the tree, Titina is connected both to the earth and to the upper spheres. Furthermore, as with Titina's reading of the soup, her relationship to the earth is not egocentric, as is Don Fernando's. She is not dependent upon her individual contact to be related to it, but is part of a continuum of being: Titina—branches—tree—earth—reality. Although Don Fernando literally has his feet on the ground, and Titina literally does not, his insistence that he knows the reality and the truth is undermined by the visual impact of Titina in the branches of the tree while he addresses an empty chair. That Titina's perspective is supported by the dramatic context is verified in the proxemic code of the play. From the R/A's view, Titina is on a higher level than Don Fernando physically and by extension, epistemically; that is, her system of knowledge is verified in contrast to Don Fernando's. Don Fernando remains in the narrow limits of the house while Titina can see over the walls; her vision is expanded, as we suggested by her association with the tree. Semiotically, Don Fernando can be read as a sign of the patriarchal social system rejected by Titina because of its restraints and restrictions.

It is interesting that Don Fernando does acknowledge a difference between himself and Titina on the basis of a generic category. As quoted above, he complains that "Las mujeres viven en otra dimensión. La dimensión lunar" (Women live in another dimension. The lunar dimension). This idea is based on a stereotyped perception that Cirlot alludes to: "When patriarchy superseded matriarchy, a feminine character came to be attributed to the moon and a masculine to the sun."[11] As patriarch, Don Fernando reasserts the moon-woman association and includes, too, the idea that the moon is a nonrational dimension, for he doubts Titina's rationality.[12] Here it may appear that Garro is agreeing with the traditional concept that the moon is representative both of the feminine and of lunacy. However, only Don Fernando makes this association, since he interprets signs in a narrow sense. For him, Titina is a nonrational being, a lunatic. If, on the other hand, the moon is also considered a representative of multiplicity, as Titina is in regard to her reading of signs, then the symbol is not negative. In

11. *Dictionary of Symbols*, p. 204.
12. Before she leaves his house Don Fernando asks Titina, "Por última vez. ¿eres capaz de ser racional?" (p. 86).

matriarchal terms, it is a fertile, unifying sign: "The moon not only measures and determines terrestrial phases but also unifies them through its activity; unifies, that is, the waters and the rains, the fecundity of women and of animals, and the fertility of vegetations."[13] To live in a lunar dimension, therefore, need not be negative or a sign of insanity; it can instead point to the greater, extended reality already mentioned in connection with the sign *tree*, a reality that in literary terms is related to the surrealists' concept of absolute reality.

Gloria Orenstein has related Garro's plays to the surrealist aesthetic.[14] While she does not analyze *Andarse por las ramas*, this play certainly supports Orenstein's observation. The play's vision of reality goes beyond the phenomenological and suggests instead an association with Breton's concept: "Je crois à la résolution future de ces deux états en apparence si contradictoires qui sont le rêve et la réalité en une sorte de réalité absolue, de surréalité" (I believe in the future merging of these two states, in appearance so contradictory, of dreaming and reality, into a sort of absolute reality, a surreality).[15] If we recall Titina's reading of the soup, her ability to draw a house and enter it, and her poetic language in general, all this would relate to Breton's "dream sequences"; those are the experiences she would add to Don Fernando's view of reality to create absolute reality.

Although Titina appears to realize with Breton that "L'imagination est peut-être sur le point de reprendre ses droits" (Imagination may well be on the verge of reclaiming its rights), her husband has rejected her and her perspective.[16] Their son Polito supports her, as one meaning of his name (*polo*, in English *pole*) implies. As a child Polito has not yet entered into the narrow world of signs represented by Don Fernando. But when he repeats the imaginary ideas of his mother, his father becomes upset: "¡Van a reprobar a este niño en la escuela!" (They're going to flunk that kid out of school!) (p. 87). The school, an institution of society, correlates with Don Fernando's ideas of reality and will reject Polito, just as Don Fernando refuses to accept Titina's views.

13. Cirlot, *Dictionary of Symbols*, p. 204.
14. See note 10 above.
15. "Manifeste du surréalisme (1924)," *Manifestes du Surréalisme* (Paris: Jean-Jacques Pauvert, 1972), p. 48.
16. Ibid., p. 21.

While Polito is at one extreme from Don Fernando in his ability to read beyond the trivial aspects of everyday reality, Lagartito, the young man who meets with Titina in the second half of the play, ultimately performs in the same limited way as Don Fernando. At first, he briefly tries to respond to her imaginative universe. His responses, however, exist only on the linguistic level, for when he attempts to bring her back home, he thinks only of her home with Don Fernando: "Voy a llevarte a tu casa" (I'm taking you home) (p. 90), he informs her very officiously, a directive that Titina interprets as a return to the narrow meaning of reality. Her response is once again to scale the heights of the tree.

It is important to note that each directive expressed in terms that would limit her activities receives a nonverbal, active response from Titina. She leaves the man who has addressed her and returns to the back of the stage to draw her own house, which she reenters, only to reappear on the branches of the tree (pp. 90–91). The repetition of this act reinforces its sign function not as lunacy, an irrational content, but as a deliberate action reflecting her rejection of the narrow world of both Don Fernando and Lagartito. At first, Lagartito, like Don Fernando, does not see that Titina has ascended the tree, and he continues to address the space she had occupied. Her physical distance from him and her superior stance again indicate that her perspective is affirmed in contrast to the inferior position of Lagartito.

An interesting variation occurs in the dialogue between the two progresses. Unlike Don Fernando, who is lost in his rational world, Lagartito attempts to follow Titina in her imaginative universe, as signalled by his utterance "Titina, ¡yo quiero ser lunes!" (Titina, I want to be Mondays!) (p. 92). Here he acknowledges the multiplicity of signifieds for a signifier. When Lagartito repeats Titina's verbal phrases, it is an indication that he enters into the same system as she. Unlike Don Fernando de las 7:05, he is able to see her on the tree.

> ¡Titina! ¡Mírame Lagartito! (Lagartito se vuelve, la mira entre las ramas y se acerca.)
> Lagartito—Dame la mano, Titina (Titina le alarga el brazo. Lagartito le toma la mano.) (p. 95)

Titina: Look at me, Lagartito! (Largartito turns, looks at her in the tree, and comes over)
Lagartito: Give me your hand, Titina (Titina reaches out. Lagartito takes her hand).

Although Lagartito visually acknowledges Titina's presence on the tree, touches her, and verbally communicates with her, he cannot sustain this relationship. He is unable to continue in her world of extended reality. When a coquettish woman passes him in the street and stares at him, the special relationship between him and Titina is broken. He relinquishes his contact with Titina and her world and follows the woman in the street, who is the ordinary signifier of woman, a reified essence of woman for Titina: "Tus pies, Lagartito, están hechos para recorrer aceras, oficinas y señoras. Tus pies y tus ojos" (Your feet, Lagartito, are made to take you down sidewalks, through offices and ladies. Your feet and your eyes) (p. 96). In that phrase, *señoras* is on the same level as the objects, sidewalks and offices.

Titina realizes Lagartito's inability to reach her heights in the reference to his *pies (feet)*, a signifier used previously in association with Don Fernando and his rational world. His failure is based on his feet and his eyes, on his physicality and limited imagination. The importance of the relationship between eyes and the ability to see expanded reality will be repeated with greater elaboration in *El encanto, tendajón mixto (Enchantment: Five and Dime)*.

That Lagartito ends up as limited as Don Fernando is visually apparent at the play's end. The two men are proxemically related when they both pass Titina, who is still in the branches of the tree. She is described as being "acomodada como un pájaro" (snug as a perching bird) (p. 96), yet their references to her position are negative. Each man's verbal comments are examples of indirect speech references to Titina's position. Fernando sings, "Uy, uy, uy, qué iguana tan fea / que se sube al árbol" (Uy, uy, uy, what an ugly lizard / up that tree), and Lagartito adds, "No te andes por las ramas uy, uy, uy, uy" (Don't beat around the bush, uy, uy, uy, uy) (p. 96). It would not be an exaggeration to say that metaphorically they both "andan por las ramas" (beat around the bush) in reference to Titina's existence in the tree, a signifier whose signified they are capable of interpreting only along normalized lines. If we, too, interpret Titina's position in the tree in their terms, then "el dicho popular se ha convertido en triste realidad" (the old proverb turned into a sad reality).[17] But one should question if it is really a "triste realidad" (sad reality) for Titina to be distanced from the patriarchal system of Don Fernando and Lagartito. Their use of the saying represents a patterned regularity in which the multiplicity of possible and arbitrary relationships between a signifier and signified has been narrowed by their social system to admit only one acceptable sign function. Their code stresses conformity while Titina's stresses innovation, a symbolic inversion within the communicative system. If we move to the proxemic code, we see that Titina, who as a woman has been shown verbally and kinesically to be in an inferior social position to her husband (recall the linguistic forms of address and her position at table), on stage has enjoyed a superior position. While she is silent, her sign function communicates an ascendant role, another inversion of the communicative system.

In regard to the social function of symbolic inversion within the communicative system, Barbara Babcock-Abrahams sees such deviations as a "way of 'playfully' calling to attention the classificatory systems that regulate the social world they 'manipulate' . . . and thereby question or dispute or at least comment upon the existing order of things."[18] Titina functions, then, in a way that playfully calls attention to the classificatory systems regulating the social world that would require her to live alongside Don Fernando. That she breaks away from him physically and linguistically, and existentially as well, can be considered the beginnings of a revolution, or at the very least an affirmation of an expanded vision of reality. It is not an exaggeration to suggest that Titina's actions are an attack against the patriarchy, for as Nelly Furman reminds in an article on textual feminism, "To refuse the authority of a signified means rejecting the status of defined object in favor of the dynamics of becoming and privileging the freedom of process rather than the performance of product."[19]

Although the dominant positive image is Titina, the female

17. Dauster, "El teatro de Elena Garro," p. 72.
18. Quoted in Wittig, "Toward a Semiotic Theory," p. 447.
19. "Textual Feminism," in *Women and Language in Literature and Society,* ed. Sally McConnell-Ginet, Ruth Borker, and Nelly Furman (New York: Praeger, 1980), p. 49.

protagonist, Garro affirms the supremacy not of one gender over another, but of a sign system that favors multiplicity over uniformity, freedom of expression over conformity. It is a perception of the world that includes "lo racional" (the rational) as well as "la dimensión lunar" (the lunar dimension). Garro repeats this integrative vision in *El encanto, tendajón mixto*.[20] Once again, the woman protagonist asserts this perception of multiplicity: (Mujer) "No importa que el hombre pierda el camino en los caminos de la mujer que son muchos y más variados que cualquier camino real" ([Woman]: It doesn't matter if man loses his way in the ways of woman, there are so many, and each so different, more than any real/royal way) (p. 142).

This statement reiterates the message of *Andarse por las ramas*. Unlike Titina, who is always a visible entity but not always verbally communicative, the unnamed woman of *El encanto* appears first as a disembodied auditory image, a pure signifier, to three men lost on *el camino real*. The signifier *real* in that phrase has two possible signifieds: either as a reference to *royal* road or as *real* road (reality). For the men, their social system (referred to in the royal connotation) is their reality. The real road here will be shown to be as unidimensional and limited as Don Fernando's rational world. But unlike Titina, who was not able to integrate either of the two men into her extended reality, in *El encanto* the woman is able to achieve greater success, for one of the three men responds to her enchanted or extended view.

The play begins with a narrator who introduces the story of the three muleteers lost in the shadows. The youngest, Anselmo, appears ready to travel beyond the limits of ordinary reality. As he asserts, "Todo está al alcance de los ojos, sólo que no lo sabemos mirar" (Everything is in sight, it's just we don't know how to look at it) (p. 132). His statement explains, too, why Don Fernando did not see Titina, but Anselmo not only sees the woman, he unites with her. Anselmo knows how to see and understand signs.

Anselmo's words are magically responded to not by his companions, but by the voice of a woman, "Hasta mis ojos están al alcance de los tuyos" (Even my eyes are in sight of yours) (p. 132). Notice that the woman repeats the image of eyes.

20. *El encanto, tendajón mixto*, in *Un hogar sólido y otras piezas en un acto*, pp. 129–49. Further references to this play will refer to this edition and will be cited parenthetically in the text.

Whereas the tree was used in *Andarse* as a symbol for extended reality, here Garro uses eyes as a sign to refer to the process of seeing as a spiritual act, as an act of understanding.[21] The eyes (the understanding) of the woman are within the reach of Anselmo. Her vision of extended reality comes to be shared by Anselmo because he is willing to respond fully to her, in contrast to Lagartito, who is inconstant in his relation with Titina.

In this play Garro also refutes Don Fernando's limited vision of woman as a solitary member of "la dimensión lunar." Here the woman says, "El hombre nace encantado y de la mujer depende que así siga o que luego nada más que las piedras mire" (Man is born enchanted and it's up to woman whether he keeps it or just goes around looking at rocks) (p. 138). As a child, man is like Polito, still enchanted or in the realm of the imagination. He leaves that state only when he ignores woman to concentrate on *piedras* of the ground of the rational world.[22] Anselmo is still part of the "dimensión lunar" while his companions have left it. It is not simply because Juventino and Ramiro are older and therefore further from the state of enchantment; in addition, unlike Anselmo, they consider themselves to possess *razón*. As Juventino remarks to Anselmo, commenting on the young man's interest in the woman: "¡Te dejas llevar muy pronto! Por causa tuya nos tenemos que ir; todavía no gozas razón" (You really get carried away! Now it's your fault we have to leave. You still haven't got the use of your reason) (p. 139). Juventino and Ramiro can be equated with Don Fernando in that they side with reason, while Anselmo is still not identified with this narrow view.

For Anselmo, woman is linguistically and epistemologically equal to the world: "¡hallarla a ella es hallar al mundo!" (finding her is finding the world!) (p. 140). She is real to him, whereas for the others she is an apparition, a she-devil. They see with the eyes of ordinary reality and cling fiercely to their *camino real*, which for them is more secure than the path offered by the woman. In response to their narrow vision, the woman expresses her interpretation of their reality:

> Un viejo como tú es un hombre muerto. Así naciste. Nunca

21. See Cirlot, *Dictionary of Symbols*, p. 95.

22. The correlation *piedra/camino real* is suggested by the narrator's description: "Los caminos eran entonces más largos, eran de piedra y los nombraban camino real" (p. 129).

supiste encontrar el filo del agua, ni caminar los sueños, ni visitar a las aguas debajo de las aguas, ni entrar en el canto de los pájaros, ni dormir en la frescura de la plata, ni vivir en el calor del oro. No sembraste las corrientes de los ríos con las banderas de las fiestas, no bebiste en la copa del rey de copas. Tú no naciste. Tú moriste desde niño y sólo acarreas piedras por los caminos llenos de piedras y te niegas a la hermosura. ¡Tu cielo será de piedra por desconocer a la mujer y no habrá ojos que de allí te saquen! (pp. 147–148)

An old man like you is a dead man. You were born that way. You never learned how to find the edge of the storm, or stroll across dreams, or visit the water beneath the water, or go inside the birds' song, or sleep on the cool of silver, or live in the warmth of gold. You never sowed the river currents with festival banners; you never drank from the goblet of the playing-card King of Goblets. You were never born. You died ever since you were a child and all you do is lug rocks down the rocky roads and turn away from beauty. You'll go to a rocky heaven because you never knew woman and no eyes can break you loose from there!

The above speech contains many provocative images that cannot be fully examined in the scope of this essay. We should notice, however, certain aspects of the linguistic level. First, the woman uses the familiar form in addressing the man; she does not consider herself to be subservient. Also, her use of the preterite verbs expresses the finality of her reading of his death-in-life existence. Each phrase is a negative to describe the two men's denial of the imaginative, enchanted reality to which their lack of understanding, their lack of knowledge of woman, has led them. They are like stones, unresponsive to the larger reality that can be achieved only through integration with woman.

Anselmo, on the contrary, sees *la hermosura (beauty)* and woman as the key to extend reality:

Mujer—Dime, Anselmo Duque ¿tú me ves como soy?
Anselmo—¿Yo? Yo te veo como eres: resplandeciente como el oro, blandita como la plata, hija de las lagunas, rodeada de pájaros, patrona de los hombres, baraja reluciente, voz de guitarra, copa de vino buscada desde el primer día que fui Anselmo Duque, y hallada este tres de mayo . . . . (p. 140)

(Woman): Tell me, Anselmo, do you see me as I am?
(Anselmo): Me? I see you as you are: shining like gold, smooth as silver, daughter of the still pools, birds all around you, patroness

of men, a glistening stack of cards, voice like a guitar, a glass of wine I've sought since the first day I was Anselmo Duque, and found this Third of May.

A comparison of Anselmo's speech with the woman's shows that many of the same images are repeated.[23] Moreover, on the level of sign functions, Anselmo attributes the beautiful, bright, and musical signifieds to the signifier *woman*.

In order to signify that he desires to continue his relation with her and accept her vision of reality, he must accept the cup of wine she offers him, a cup that shines like a star. His act of drinking from her cup as a method of initiation onto her *camino (way)* has clear sexual implications. At the same time, the signs associated with the act also repeat the content of multiplicity we found in *Andarse*. The cup is related to a star, which is also how Titina was described by Lagartito: "Y tú la estrella cuyos cinco picos son más blancos que la estrella más blanca . . ." (And you the star whose five points are whiter than the whitest star) (p. 95). The sign *star* nearly always alludes to multiplicity. Once Anselmo drinks "la copa de las estrellas" (the wineglass of the stars) (p. 142), which signals his integration with the woman, with multiplicity, the action on stage is as surprising as Titina's drawing of the house. At the first sip from the cup, Anselmo, the woman, and the store called "El encanto" disappear from the scene. Anselmo's union with the woman has removed him from the *camino real* of his friends onto another level of reality.

When they disappear both acoustically and visually, the stage returns to darkness, but where there had been three men on the *camino real*, now there are two. Ordinary reality has been reduced, but extended reality has been enriched. Anselmo has disassociated himself from his two companions, from reason and convention, and entered "El encanto," or rather reentered the state of enchantment into which he had been born. Like Titina, Anselmo has refused the authority of the signifieds of the two men in favor of a dynamic, imaginative universe in which authority and tradition are rejected. It is important to note that although *Andarse por las ramas* takes as its point of departure the clichéd linguistic phrase to explore the possibility that every sign function or cultural entity can enter into a multiple set of

23. For a discussion of the imagery in relation to the alchemical symbols used by the surrealists, see Orenstein, *The Theater of the Marvelous*, pp. 110–13.

correlations, *El encanto, tendajón mixto* performs the same function using archetypal topoi. The signifiers that are exposed range from Eve and the Holy Grail to the surrealist's *amour fou*.

It is possible to read Anselmo's journey as a variation of the Grail quest. According to the traditional version, the youngest of the knights sets forth in search of the holy cup. The quest is a long and lonely journey that will prove successful only to the man who is innocent and pure of heart, that is, without knowledge of woman. Garro inverts this tradition, this sign function, by having the youngest initiate the journey to a new reality not in a state of sexual innocence, but rather by means of his union with woman, as signaled by his drinking from her cup. Here the cup unites man and woman.

One might see that kinesic act as symbolic of traditional motif of man losing himself in a woman because of erotic love, a popular surrealist theme, as we know from Breton's *L'Amour fou*. While Juventino and Ramiro read the event in the traditional way, in the text Anselmo does not consider himself lost; rather, he interprets his union with the woman to be enriching: "ella me dio los ojos para que mirara lo que ahora miro y los sentidos para que entrara en los placeres que ahora encuentro" (She gave me the eyes to see what I'm seeing now and the senses to know what I'm knowing now) (pp. 148–149).

Juventino and Ramiro try to lure Anselmo away from the woman in order to return with them to *el camino real* by reminding him of his mother. They attempt to fight the power of the woman with the power of another woman, the mother figure. One might interpret this as an inversion of the battle between the old kind and the new, in which the cycle of life is regenerated by the victory of the new king. Here Garro has replaced the male signifiers with women.

Finally, another traditional female archetype is referred to on the kinesic and linguistic levels. The woman appears to recreate the actions of Eve as she urges Anselmo to drink the cup of wine: "Bébala, Anselmo" (Drink it, Anselmo), she urges, as Eve urged Adam to eat of the fruit of the tree of knowledge. In this play, however, the woman is not betraying man with her directive. In Garro's version she leads man toward knowledge, not out of the Garden, but into an Eden of "otra luz, otros colores, otras lagunas" (another light, other colors, other still pools) (p. 147). The sign of woman has been inverted from Evebetrayer to guide toward enchantment. As in *Andarse,* Garro has inverted each sign function of the traditional system and offered new meanings for the signifiers that suggest new possibilities for the image of woman. Orenstein has observed, "In this play, Garro has created the prototype of the new female surrealist protagonist, according to the Bretonian ideal woman. She is a seer, in revolt against conventional interpretations of reality, a poetess-alchemist who makes the imaginary real for the initiate."[24] While that statement appears all-inclusive, I would add to it. For it is not just the Bretonian ideal woman that Garro creates but an ideal couple, a union of male and female. Titina in her tree has been replaced by the integrated Anselmo-*mujer* of *El encanto.* The victory of an integrated vision of extended reality is a precarious one, of course, which Garro recognizes by leaving on stage the two men still on their *camino real* vowing to do away with "el encanto," but Garro at least has done her part to create positive feminine images.

24. Ibid., p. 113.

4 Narrative Persona in
Eva Perón's *La razón de mi vida*

David William Foster

No vaya a creerse por esto que digo que la tarea de Evita me resulte fácil. Más bien me resulta en cambio siempre difícil y nunca me he sentido del todo contenta con esa actuación. En cambio el papel de Eva Perón me parece fácil. Y no es extraño. ¿Acaso no resulta siempre más fácil representar un papel en el teatro que vivirlo en la realidad? (p. 94)[1]

Do not think by this that "Evita's" work comes easily to me. Rather, it always turns out to be difficult, and I have never felt quite satisfied in that role. On the other hand, the part of Eva Perón seems easy. And it is not strange. For is it not always easier to act a stage part than to live it in person? (p. 63)

The Peronist period (1946–1955) may not have encouraged the production of much in the way of lasting literary merit,[2] but it did produce one document of undeniably paraliterary interest: Eva Duarte Perón's *La razón de mi vida* (1951). This work presents itself as a personal statement by President Juan Perón's wife, herself a charismatic national leader. The paraliterary nature of this book lies neither in the questionable quality of its expressive style nor in the presumedly overt fictionality of the "facts" it purports to set forth and interpret. Rather, in this essay I will examine *Razón* as a paraliterary text for (1) the discourse structures it manipulates to create a narrative persona that gives coherence to the story and (2) its value as an implicit contribution to written popular culture in Argentina. The text is interest-

1. Eva Perón, *La razón de mi vida* (Buenos Aires: Ediciones Peuser, 1951). All quotes are from this edition and will be cited by page number within the text. Translations are taken from Eva Duarte Perón, *Evita by Evita: Eva Duarte Perón Tells Her Own Story* (New York: Proteus Publishing Co., 1978, 1980). No translator is specified.
2. Concerning the literature of Peronism, see Ernesto Goldar, "La literatura peronista," in *El peronismo* (Buenos Aires: Carlos Pérez Editor, 1969), pp. 139–86, and Martin S. Stabb, "Argentine Letters and the Peronato: An Overview," *Journal of Inter-American Studies*, nos. 3–4 (1971):434–55. See also Goldar's *El peronismo en la literatura argentina* (Buenos Aires: Editorial Freeland, 1971), and Andrés Oscar Avellaneda, "El tema del peronismo en la narrativa argentina" (Ph.D. diss., University of Illinois, 1973).

ing both for the figure of Eva Perón that it propagates (its contribution to the myths of Eva Perón inside and outside Argentina)[3] and for what it implies about the Argentine public's criteria for written literature.[4] (I am using *literature* in the broad sense of written texts, without reference to the pretensions at fictionality—a relative rather than absolute distinction—and at identification with the norms of high culture.)[5]

It is necessary to distinguish between Eva Perón as author of *Razón* and Eva Perón as the narrative persona of that text (whether that persona is fictional or accurate in some usefully documentary fashion is an issue for professional historians).[6] It matters little, therefore, whether the "real" Eva Perón authored the text published over her name. Eva Perón the author is as much a product of political fiction as Eva Perón the narrator is the product of narrative fiction. I will not examine the documentary relationship among reality, author, and narrative persona. Rather, I will be concerned with the narrative principles that underlie *Razón*. These include strategies for elaborating and maintaining the image of a coherent narrative persona, and the textual markers—rhetorical procedures, stylistic devices, structural features—that enhance that image by imposing on the reader a particular way of reading and understanding the text. Concomitantly, such an analysis will address the issue of how

3. The many images of Eva Perón are examined in the anthropological study by J. M. Taylor, *Eva Perón: The Myths of a Woman* (Chicago: University of Chicago Press, 1979). There has been a rash of recent book publications on Eva Perón. The majority of them border on yellow journalism and are not pertinent to this study. Several Argentine studies available on Eva Perón are listed in Taylor's bibliography. One publication, typical of the revisionist interpretations of Eva Perón by the Argentine left in the midseventies, is not listed by Taylor: *Eva Perón* (Cuadernos de Crisis, no. 7; Buenos Aires: Editorial del Noroeste, 1974). The first popular-culture analysis of Eva is provided by William Katra, "Eva Perón: Populist Queen of Hearts," *Latin American Digest* 14, 2 (1980):6–7, 19–20. Katra quotes from *Razón* extensively.

4. There are only fragmentary studies on the Argentine reading public. One of the most authoritative is Adolfo Prieto, *Sociología del público argentino* (Buenos Aires: Ediciones Leviatán, 1956). See my analysis of Prieto's work in "Adolfo Prieto: Profile of a Parricidal Literary Critic," *Latin American Research Review* 13, 3 (1978):125–45.

5. For issues related to this position, see Barbara Herrnstein Smith, *On the Margins of Discourse: The Relation of Literature to Language* (Chicago: University of Chicago Press, 1978).

6. For a discussion of the interpenetration of "literary" and "historical" versions of "real" events and persons, see Hayden V. White, *Tropics of Discourse: Essays in Cultural Criticism* (Baltimore: Johns Hopkins University Press, 1978).

Razón is an example of Argentine popular culture, not so much from the point of view of the sociopolitical goals that publication of the text may have had, but from that of the reader codes that it implies.[7]

*   *   *

The distinction between Eva Perón, author, and Eva Perón, narrator, is especially necessary in attempting to answer one of the fundamental questions raised concerning a text: How does it justify itself? How does it defend its claim to our attention?[8] Clearly, *La razón de mi vida* was published as part of the propaganda program of the Peronist government. Evita's death within seven months of the publication made the book particularly useful. In its frantic attempts to shore up its crumbling power, the Peronist government strove to mythify and beatify Eva. As a political tract, *Razón* was but one element in a continuing political struggle, used specifically as required reading in Argentine public schools.[9] In this sense, the text does not need to expound or to imply intrinsic justifications: it circulated widely not because of the inherent eloquence of its rhetorical strategies but because it was imposed on one group of readers and insinuated itself on another by virtue of its participation in a range of myth-making activities surrounding the figure of Eva Perón. Beyond the reasonable assumption that millions of students read it because it was an obligatory textbook, there is no reliable index

7. I have been able to find no useful study of *Razón* in the extensive literature on Peronism. There has been a lot of attention in recent years to "reader codes" for both literary and nonliterary texts. One major statement is in Roland Barthes, *S/Z*, trans. Richard Miller (New York: Hill and Wang, 1974), and the issues are summarized by Jonathan Culler, *Structuralist Poetics: Structuralism, Linguistics, and the Study of Literature* (Ithaca, N.Y.: Cornell University Press, 1975). A somewhat different approach is provided by Wolfgang Iser, who is concerned with how the meaning of the text, rather than being inherent, is realized by the act of reading: *The Implied Reader: Patterns of Communication in Prose Fiction from Bunyan to Beckett* (Baltimore: Johns Hopkins University Press, 1974).

8. The principles of discourse contracts are discussed by Mary Louise Pratt in her *Toward a Speech Act Theory of Literary Discourse* (Bloomington: Indiana University Press, 1977), and in Teun A. van Dijk, *Pragmatics of Language and Literature* (New York: American Elsevier, 1976). I have applied some of these principles to the Argentine tango in "Narrative Rights in the Argentine Tango" (unpublished).

9. Goldar, in his section on "Evita" in *El peronismo en la literatura argentina*, mentions a story by David Viñas, "El privilegiado," in which, among other indignities, a schoolteacher is required to read and teach *Razón* (p. 65).

of how many purchasers actually read the book and derived either aesthetic or intellectual satisfaction from doing so.

By contrast, read today without either the political or the emotional coercion that supported its publication thirty years ago, *Razón* may be seen as a discourse text that must justify any claim to our attention. It may be examined to identify the pretensions at privileged communication by Eva Perón the narrator. All discourse texts are forms of privileged communication in the sense that they lay claims to our attention; if we read or listen to them, we are according them the "privilege" of our interest. In return, the text must justify that privilege by complying with criteria of interest, concision, adequate exposition, and the like. Texts rarely address themselves overtly to how they are justified, although the storyteller's trope, "Listen to the marvelous tale I am about to tell, for you have never heard anything like it before," is one example of a text stating its claim on the audience's interest. More customarily, texts employ oblique or subtle references to presentational strategies that are, in addition to elements of stylistic enhancement, procedures for implying how the text presents itself as interesting and unique.

One of the salient features of *Razón* supports the foregoing observations concerning narrative privilege and self-justification. Unlike historical, autobiographical, or documentary texts, *Razón* does not claim to be an interpretation of the real-life events it refers to. The literature on any major political event is filled with analyses by impartial observers, by interested parties, and by prominent participants. Peronism is no exception. However, against the wealth of material propounding this and that interpretation of the movement, *Razón* is characterized not only by its references to specific events but also by its refusal to analyze them or discuss the narrator's own intervention in them. That is to say, unlike a conventional autobiography, *Razón* does not pretend to chronicle the successive events of Eva Perón's life and the details of her participation in the major activities of her husband's government. True, there are references to recognizable occurrences and comments concerning Eva's involvement with them, like her attempts to free Perón after his arrest in October 1945 (chapters 8 and 9). The reader of a conventional biography would eagerly expect to have Eva's version of what happened, what she did, what was said, along with an explanation of the complex emotions she must have felt. Yet, aside from references to the bare facts of what occured, the reader receives only a general statement on the woman's intense efforts on Perón's behalf and her overall sense of elation over her relationship with the Leader.

Indeed, the historical and personal events described by *Razón* can only be followed adequately by a reader already familiar with the "history" underlying the text, either through direct knowledge of occurrences, as was the original audience of the book, or through documentary information provided by the large body of writings about the Peróns, as is the current reader. But, if interpretational (auto)biography or historical documentary is not the goal of *Razón*, what is? How does the narrator justify the privilege of her discourse?

The first of the fifty-nine chapters closes with the following words:

> Yo misma quiero explicarme aquí.
> Para eso he decidido escribir estos apuntes.
> Confieso que no lo hago para contradecir o refutar a nadie.
> ¡Quiero más bien que los hombres y mujeres de mi pueblo sepan cómo siento y cómo pienso...!
> Quiero que sientan conmigo las cosas grendes que mi corazón experimenta.
> Seguramente muchas de las cosas que diré son enseñanzas que yo recibí gratuitamente de Perón y que no tengo tampoco derecho a guardar como un secreto (p. 14).

> I would like to make myself clear about this.
> That is why I have decided to write these notes.
> But I do not do so to contradict anyone or to prove anyone wrong.
> Rather I would wish my fellow citizens, men and women, to know how I feel and think!
> I want them to share in the great things I experience in my heart.
> Surely many of the things I shall say here are teachings I received freely from Perón and which I have not the right to keep secret. (pp. 3–4)

Thus, Eva does not set out to refute or contradict the many scurrilous opinions that had circulated concerning her origins and objectives (although there are, in fact, several direct and indirect allusions to views she feels compelled specifically to repudiate). Rather, she provides an accurate portrait of the feelings, emotions, and sentiments that distinguish her from her mentor (Juan Perón), from her enemies, and, indeed, from the entire Peronist movement. The basis of such a distinction is the "reason" of her intuitive feelings, which are presented as virtually paradigmatic of conventional feminine emotiveness. Read from a present-day feminist perspective, Eva's self-portrait is as unconsciously parodic as it is paradigmatic of the shibboleths concerning masculine mind versus feminine heart.

Razón is not organized in accord with any discernible logic of metahistorical or philosophical discourse, and we have already discussed how it does not follow the outlines of an autobiographical narrative. Presented in vignettes that run four to five pages apiece, the work emphasizes key topics of Eva's participation in the Peronist movement. Thus, the image that emerges of the narrator's appeal to the reader is essentially fragmentary, without either the reasoned exposition one associates with a political essay or the concentrated, systematic symbolism characteristic of self-conscious literature. Nevertheless, a general pattern underlies *Razón* and supports the narrator's claim to our attention by reinforcing a coherent persona for her. This persona sees herself as essentially unique, possessing a sense of mission. Her unique task and the depth of her perception of the goals and values of that mission set Eva Perón, the historical figure, apart from the rest of her countrymen. Her story is, therefore, a privileged version of events. This persona seeks to demonstrate how she embodies a range of "natural"—and presumably more authentic—feelings that refute the worn and corrupt prejudices of traditional culture in Argentina. And this persona promotes a level of intuitive knowledge that makes her narrative valuable as an interpretation that only she can provide.

The most important of these distinctions concerns that of the "natural" versus the "cultural." This distinction reinforces not only the uniqueness of Eva's role, in contrast to the masculine—and military—logic of Perón's leadership, but also her virtuous sincerity, in contrast to the devious mediocrity of her enemies. In such a formulation, the patterns of culture—the myths and rituals by which a society defines what is proper versus what is unacceptable and confers meaning on the former while discarding the latter as nonsense—are seen as arbitrary conventions that stifle the "natural" spontaneity of man. All societies develop codes of cultural behavior (and, in the course of history, borrow from each other). The classic mind defends them as necessary for imposing order on chaotic human drives, while the romantic mind denounces their tyranny because they shackle the natural, creative impulses of mankind.[10]

Razón uses this dichotomy to range the oppression of traditional Argentine culture, with its roots in the French and English elite and its rigorous class distinctions, against the freedom inherent in Justicialism (Peronist political thought). The latter seeks to destroy degrading social categories and to dignify man, who, in the purity of the pursuit of decency without pretensions, is viewed as fundamentally good. Ruling-class prejudices, which dismiss the poor as "animal-like" and lacking in the higher sentiments of civilized man, are refuted in favor of the image of the *descamisado* as a noble innocent whose sentiments are all the more profound because of their ingenuousness:

> Yo he oído muchas veces en boca de "gente bien", como ellos suelen llamarse a sí mismos, cosas como estas:
>
> —No se aflija tanto por sus "descamisados". Esa "clase de gente" no tiene nuestra sensibilidad. No se dan cuenta de lo que les pasa. ¡Y tal vez no convenga del todo que se den cuenta!
>
> Yo no encuentro ningún argumento razonable para refutar esa mentira injusta.
>
> No puedo hacer otra cosa que decirles:
>
> —Es mentira. Mentira que inventaron ustedes los ricos para quedarse tranquilos. ¡Pero es mentira!
>
> Si me preguntasen por qué, yo tendría solamente algo que decirles, muy poco cosa. Sería esto:
>
> —¡Yo he visto llorar a los humildes y no de dolor, que de dolor lloran hasta los animales!
>
> ¡Y por agradecimiento, por agradecimiento sí que no saben llorar los ricos! (p. 163)

---

10. The study of "nature" versus "culture" and the structuring myths of the latter that account for the former have been major contributions of Claude Lévi-Strauss's anthropological theories. One of his principal statements concerns the opposition between the "raw" (nature) and the "cooked" (culture): *Le Cru et le cuit* (Paris: Plan, 1964), translated into English by John and Doreen Weightman as *The Raw and the Cooked* (New York: Harper and Row, 1969). See also the interpretation of William Faulkner's *Go Down, Moses* by Wesley Morris in *Friday's Footprint: Structuralism and the Articulated Text* (Columbus: Ohio State University Press, 1979), pt. 1, "The Pilgrimage of Being."

> I have often heard from the lips of the "upper classes," as they
> are accustomed to call themselves, things like these:
> "Do not worry so much about your *descamisados*. That kind of
> person does not have our sensitivity. They do not understand
> what happens to them. And perhaps it is better on the whole that
> they do not."
> I can find no reasonable argument with which to refute this
> unjust lie.
> I can do nothing but tell them:
> "It's a lie. A lie you, the rich, invented yourselves, so as not to
> be troubled. But it's a lie."
> If they asked me why, I would have only one thing to tell them,
> very little. It would be this:
> "I have seen the humble cry, but not from pain, for even ani-
> mals cry from pain! I have seen them cry out of gratefulness!
> And out of gratefulness, the rich, indeed, do not know how to
> cry. (p. 110)

Although not developed in any systematic fashion, the patterns of binary opposition in *Razón* between corrupt, artificial
culture and innocent, spontaneous nature are extensive. In
addition to intuition versus disingenuous mediocrity (see chapter 14, "¿Intuición?"), *descamisados* versus oligarchy, sincerity
versus cynicism, there are several eulogies of radical spontaneity versus dispassionate methodicalness. Ironically fore-
shadowing how Eva's frenetic activities contributed to breaking
her fragile health, *Razón* speaks over and over again of her mar-
athon campaigns, her late hours (one photograph, showing her
waving from her car as a clock marks 5:40 A.M., has subsequently been widely circulated on the covers of the album and
published text of Webber's musical *Evita*),[11] her chidings by
Perón for her long absences from his side, and so on. *Razón*,
despite the constant reminders that Eva's activities are only an
extension of Perón's political and social programs, runs the risk
of praising her intense spontaneity at the expense of Perón's
rational calculations. The following page, from chapter 44,
"Cómo me pagan el pueblo y Perón," is typical of the encomium
of freewheeling disorder:

> Además yo he sido siempre desordenada en mi manera de
> hacer las cosas; me gusta el "desorden" como si el desorden fuese

11. Andrew Lloyd Webber and Tim Rice, *Evita: The Legend of Evita Perón
(1919–1952)* (New York: Avon, 1979).

mi medio normal de vida. Creo que nací para la Revolución. He vivido siempre en libertad. Como los pájaros, siempre me gustó el aire libre del bosque. Ni siquiera he podido tolerar esa cierta esclavitud que es la vida en la casa paterna, o la vida en el pueblo natal.... Muy temprano en mi vida dejé mi hogar y mi pueblo, y desde entonces siempre he sido libre. He querido vivir por mi cuenta y he vivido por mi cuenta.

Por eso no podré ser jamás funcionario, que es atarse a un sistema, encadenarse a la gran máquina del Estado y cumplir allí todos los días una función determinada.

No. Yo quiero seguir siendo pájaro suelto en el bosque inmenso.

Me gusta la libertad como le gusta al pueblo, y en eso como en ninguna otra cosa me reconozco *pueblo*. (p. 143)

Also, I have always been disorderly in my way of doing things; I like disorder as though it were my normal way of life. I think I was born for the revolution. I have always lived at liberty. Like the birds, I have always liked the fresh air of the woods. I was not even able to tolerate that degree of servitude which is part of life in one's parents' home or the life of one's home town. Very early in life I left my home and my town and since then I have always been free. I have wished to live on my own, and I have lived on my own.

That is why I could never be a functionary, which means being tied to a system, chained to the great machine of State and fulfilling a definite function there every day.

No. I want to continue to be a bird, free in an immense forest.

I enjoy liberty as the people enjoy it, and in that, more than anything else, I recognize that I am completely of the people. (pp. 163–64)

The narrator of *Razón* offers what purports to be a unique conception of political activism, rather than any particular version of events. This eschewal of the hoary model of the "insider's story" in favor of a special mode of self-conception is the basis of the narrator's appeal to the reader and the privileged character of her persona.

*   *   *

One of the rhetorical ploys used by the narrator of *Razón* is to speak of dramatic roles and to oppose artificial theatricality with the authenticity of her spontaneous vitalism. The most significant use of this ploy in *Razón* is in chapter 16, "Eva Perón y

Evita," followed by chapter 17, "Evita." Running a little less
than four pages, chapter 16 sets forth the disjunction between
the wife of the president as defined by the protocol of Argentine
tradition and the wife of the supreme leader of Peronism as
defined by the privileged mission she has been called to fulfill.
This chapter indicates both the rhetoric of *Razón* and the terms in
which the narrator posits the antithesis that justify the uniqueness of her discourse:

> Pude ser una mujer de Presidente como lo fueron otras.
>
> Es un papel sencillo y agradable: trabajo de los días de fiesta,
> trabajo de recibir honores, de "engalanarse" para representar
> según un protocolo que es casi lo mismo que pude hacer antes, y
> creo que más o menos bien, en el teatro o en el cine.
>
> En cuanto a la hostilidad oligárquica no puedo menos que
> sonreírme.
>
> Y me pregunto: ¿por qué hubiese podido rechazarme la oligar-
> quía?
>
> ¿Por mi origen humilde? ¿Por mi actividad artística?
>
> ¿Pero acaso alguna vez esa clase de gente tuvo en cuenta aquí, o
> en cualquier parte del mundo, estas cosas, tratándose de la mujer
> de un Presidente?
>
> Nunca la oligarquía fué hostil con nadie que pudiera serle útil.
> El poder y el dinero no tuvieron nunca malos antecedentes para
> un oligarca genuino.
>
> La verdad es otra: yo, que había aprendido de Perón a elegir
> caminos poco frecuentados, no quise seguir el antiguo modelo de
> esposa de Presidente. . . .
>
> No nací para eso. Por el contrario, siempre hubo en mi alma un
> franco repudio para con "esa clase de teatro".
>
> Pero además, yo no era solamente la esposa del Presidente de
> la República, era también la mujer del conductor de los argen-
> tinos.
>
> A la doble personalidad de Perón debía corresponder una
> doble personalidad en mí: una, la de Eva Perón, mujer del Presi-
> dente, cuyo trabajo es sencillo y agradable, trabajo de los días de
> fiesta, de recibir honores, de funciones de gala; y otra, la de Evita,
> mujer del Líder de un pueblo que ha depositado en él toda su fe,
> toda su esperanza y todo su amor.
>
> Unos pocos días al año, represento el papel de Eva Perón; y en
> ese papel creo que me desempeño cada vez mejor, pues no me
> parece difícil ni desagradable.
>
> La inmensa mayoría de los días soy en cambio Evita, puente
> tendido entre las esperanzas del pueblo y las manos realizadoras

de Perón, primera peronista argentina, y éste sí que me resulta
papel difícil, y en el que nunca estoy totalmente contenta de mí.
(pp. 85-88)

> I might have been a President's wife like the others.
>
> It is a simple and agreeable role: a holiday job, the task of
> receiving honors, of decking oneself out to go through the
> motions prescribed by social dictates. It is all very similar to what
> I was able to do previously, and I think more or less successfully,
> in the theater and in the cinema. . . .
>
> The truth is different. I, who had learned from Perón to choose
> unusual paths, did not wish to follow the old pattern of wife of
> the President. . . .
>
> I was not born for that. On the contrary, there was always in my
> soul an open repugnance for that kind of acting.
>
> But also, I was not only the wife of the President of the
> Republic, I was also the wife of the Leader of the Argentines.
>
> I had to have a double personality to correspond with Perón's
> double personality. One, Eva Perón, wife of the President, whose
> work is simple and agreeable, a holiday job of receiving honors,
> of gala performances; the other "Evita," wife of the Leader of a
> people who have placed all their faith in him, all their hope and
> all their love.
>
> A few days of the year I act the part of Eva Perón; and I think I
> do better each time in that part, for it seems to me to be neither
> difficult nor disagreeable.
>
> The immense majority of days I am, on the other hand,
> "Evita," a link stretched between the hopes of the people and the
> fulfilling hands of Perón, Argentina's first woman Peronista—
> and this indeed is a difficult role for me, and one in which I am
> never quite satisfied with myself. (pp. 57-59)

The oppositions here are clearly set forth. The following chapter then develops further the figure of Evita and her unique role.
There is no particular subtlety either in this disjunctive scheme
or in its textual elaboration. *Razón*, used as a document directed
toward a popular audience, uses the most overt strategies of signification. It also eschews any pretense at the sort of concentrated articulation that provides the "pleasure of the text" for the
reader of high literature. Indeed, the dominant figure of diction
in Eva Perón's book is the disjunctive formula "not A, but
[rather] B," a stylistic device that unambiguously specifies what
is to be valued by explicitly juxtaposing it with what is to be
repudiated. Two examples of this procedure in the chapter I

have quoted will suffice: "Nunca la oligarquía fué hostil . . . [not A] / La verdad es otra . . . [but rather B]." "No nací para eso. [not A] / Por el contrario . . . [but rather B]." No text is free of rhetoric, and the most unpretentious forms of discourse are characterized by commonplace rhetorical formulas that, because of their frequency in our everyday speech, seem natural. Without entering into a thorough analysis of the stylistic features of *Razón*, we may say that its forms of verbal expression fluctuate between the automatic devices of everyday speech and the crowd-arousing bombast that typified the political addresses of both of the Peróns. One such device, which precedes the two examples of disjunctive listing I have quoted, is the series of three rhetorical questions in which Eva wonders why the oligarchy cannot accept her. (There is a disingenuous candor about *Razón*, as Eva zeroes in on all of her traits that so infuriated the opposition; the only notable ones she "overlooks" are her reputed past as a prostitute-courtesan and her rough-hewn accent and grammar.)

A functional irony underlies *Razón*, and I use the phenomenological qualifier to avoid the intentional fallacy of ascribing the irony to the conscious strategies of the author. This irony resides in the overlapping images of the narrator as self-effacing and the narrator as the lone figure on the stage of her own drama. The self-effacement of the narrative persona combines feminine demureness ("We women can't always understand the complexity of things"; "A woman only thinks with her heart"), devotion to Perón ("What I am I owe to Perón"; "What I am doing is only to enhance Perón and his programs"; "To understand me is to understand Perón"), and the desire to go down in history not as an important political figure in her own right but as an effective instrument of the movement she represents. Characteristically, the narrator speaks of herself in this regard in the third person, as though both Eva and Evita were dissociated from the identity of the narrative voice:

> Quisiera que de ella [Evita] se diga, aunque no fuese más que en una pequeña nota, al pie del capítulo maravilloso que la historia ciertamente dedicará a Perón, algo que fuese más o menos esto:
> "Hubo, al lado de Perón, una mujer que se dedicó a llevarle al Presidente las esperanzas del pueblo, que luego Perón convertía en realidades."

Y me sentiría debidamente, sobradamente compensada si la
nota terminase de esta manera:
"De aquella mujer sólo sabemos que el pueblo la llamaba, cari-
ñosamente, *Evita.*" (p. 95)

I would like it to be said of her, even if only in a small footnote to
the marvelous chapter which history will certainly devote to
Perón, something more or less like this:
"There was, at Perón's side, a woman who dedicated herself to
conveying to the President the hopes of the people which later
Perón converted into realities."
And I would feel duly compensated—and more—if the note
ended like this:
"All we know about that woman is that the people called her,
fondly, *Evita.*" (pp. 63–64)

By contrast, there is hardly a sentence of *Razón* that is not predi-
cate to the *yo* of the narrator.

This dissociation is not only between the first person of the
narrator and the portrait of the double personality of Eva-Evita.
It affects also the interplay between the image of the radical
innocent projected by the ploys of self-effacement and the
image of the Great Woman sharing with her readers her "private
knowledge" of Perón, his thoughts, and his goals. In many
cases, these confidences—the letters Perón sent Eva, sentiments
he shared with her, and the emotional turmoils of critical
moments like the October 1945 struggle against Perón's incar-
ceration—are typical of "true confessions" magazines. On many
other occasions, the information shared with the reader summa-
rizes the motives behind the activities of the Peronist couple. In
this case the information is not so much new, being a rehash of
previously published propaganda and political speeches, as it is
emphasized by virtue of the autobiographical context that
frames it. The text may make use of disclaimers to the effect that
it is difficult for Evita to describe what went on in Perón's heart,
but the entire rationale of *Razón* is precisely to provide a privileged explanation, through the persona of the narrator, of
Perón's and Peronism's deepest meanings.

*   *   *

I have attempted to demonstrate that the self-alleged uniqueness of Eva Perón's *La razón de mi vida* rests on the dichotomies
and binary oppositions that underlie its presentation of Eva's

role in her husband's government. This system of oppositions sustains the book's image of Peronism in its struggles against what the narrator calls the futility of the past one hundred years of national history (in 1852 the dictator Juan Manuel de Rosas was defeated at Caseros, and Argentina began the establishment of a European, liberal society that Peronism set out to supersede). The validity of this pattern of oppositions depends, of course, on the assumptions that the reader brings to *Razón*. That is to say, the pattern of oppositions that the narrator establishes from the outset in *Razón* will only be convincing to a reader who accepts the conception of Argentine social history implicit in the book and the explicit references to the events of the 1940s. The reader must accept the distinction between nature and culture, between *descamisados* and oligarchy (liberal faith would hold that, by personal effort, the humblest citizen can become a wealthy Argentine landowner),[12] between mind and sentiment, between tradition and revolution, between, in a word, Eva Perón and her enemies. Only then does *Razón* function as a productive semiotic text, providing an internally reasonable version of certain phenomena and, thereby, justifying the discourse privilege of the feminine narrative persona.

Undoubtedly it is difficult to read *Razón* in this fashion today. Indeed, *Razón* read in the 1980s invites the same sort of bemused, outraged, condescending readings that befall most of the texts of popular culture in the hands of readers who consider themselves of superior sophistication. *Razón* is without question a document of Argentine popular culture, not because it is the product of the mass industry responsible for national television or women's and sports magazines, but because it was written by an author who was addressing herself to a broad-based popular audience and who was in fact a product of the same culture as that audience. It is in this sense that *Razón* must be read within the conventions of popular literature,[13] not so much because it is an inherently puerile text, but because many of its discourse conventions—from the short sentences and paragraphs and the

12. One of the paradigmatic liberal interpretations of Argentine history is Henry Stanley Ferns, *Argentina* (London: Benn, 1969).

13. Concerning the conventions for reading popular literature, see the important theoretical statement by James Mallard, "Prolegomena to a Study of the Popular Mode in Narrative," *Journal of Popular Culture* 6, 1 (1972):1–19. One of the major researchers on Spanish-language popular literature and its scholarly analysis is Andrés Amorós; see his *Subliteraturas* (Barcelona: Ariel, 1974).

abundant exclamation marks to the high-frequency vocabulary and the rhetorical strategies of the confidential narratives all supported by a conventional image of sex roles—are inescapably those of the popular culture that still prevails in much of the West.

The American reader insensitive to the values that dominated Argentina during the Peronist period or the Argentine reader either disdainful of or disillusioned with the myths of the Peróns cannot help but read *La razón de mi vida* as self-serving, as intellectually and emotionally dishonest, and as a superb example of literary kitsch. It is unlikely that even supporters of Peronism, like the novelist Leopoldo Marechal, were able to read Eva Perón's book as innocent poetry. Nevertheless, there is a semiotic coherence underlying *Razón*, supported by the narrative persona who appeals to the reader's interest in well-defined terms. Whether the image of a woman's privileged access to a position of powerful influence is accurate or not is less important than the internal coherence of her narrative. Read on its own terms as either a serious political statement or a "fictional narrative" artfully designed to strike responsive chords in a sympathetic audience, *Razón* deserves its important role as an eloquent example of the literature produced by popular Peronist culture.[14]

14. Significantly, Joseph R. Barager includes a segment from *Razón* in his collection of historical documents relating to Peronism: *Why Perón Came to Power: The Background to Peronism in Argentina* (New York: Alfred A. Knopf, 1968), pp. 203–5.

THE MAKING AND UNMAKING
OF MYTH

5 The Female Persona in the Spanish American Essay: An Overview

Peter G. Earle

In literature as in life, Hispanic American woman has been built into a patriarchal hierarchy, within which she has been assigned a greater organic than spiritual role. For the same reason she is more often adapted to a synthetic cultural view than developed as a dynamic portrait. The most representative essays in nineteenth- and twentieth-century Spanish American literature display a male presence of monumental (heroic or demonic) proportions, in reiterative contrast to a female diffuseness bordering on absence. Man is up front, directing or deforming things; woman is part of the environment—immediate or mystical—or of the author's symbolic system. He is singular; she is plural; he is the sun; she, the satellite. But she is rich in her ambiguous diversity, which is foreseen in the multiple features and gestures of the Aztec goddess Coatlicue, who, like the cosmos itself, is a jumble of contradictions: erotic, domineering, compassionate, cruel, motherly, aggressive, serene, cataclysmic.

Most essays of the past two centuries, like the domino games played in casinos and cantinas throughout the Hispanic world, are a masculine activity. Seldom forgotten but often displaced, woman waits in the shadows until the game is done and it's time to go home or for the poetry to begin.

In the realm of fiction one need only compare the dynamic portraiture of women in nineteenth-century European literature (Tolstoy, Pérez Galdós, Balzac, Flaubert, James) with the swooning Marías, Elviras, and Amalias of the nineteenth-century Spanish American imagination. It isn't a simple matter of cultural machismo; it's that and a number of other things: Catholic Marianism, a belated development of psychological perspicacity among Spanish American writers; the virgin-prostitute ambivalence underscored by Octavio Paz; a general obsession with the frontier image up to and considerably after 1900; and a deeply ingrained feeling of historical original sin common to most Spanish American intellectuals (a feeling that underlies most Spanish American counterutopian thought), a continuing concern, that is, with the root and flower of Latin American underdevelopment.

The most casual reader knows that the female presence is more dynamic in poetry and fiction than in essays. Venus and the Virgin appeal more to the emotions than to the mind. In Latin America that basic difference is particularly evident, for the reasons just enumerated, and often within the work of a single author. For example, José Vasconcelos, who vaguely alludes to the female function in his master plan for racial perfection (progressive eugenic beautification: "los feos no procrearán") in *La raza cósmica*, but who in *Ulises criollo* relives with specific nostalgia the amorous relationships of his adolescence and early adulthood; or José Martí, whose repertory of cultural and political heroes is invariably masculine in his essays on North and South America, but who laments, also with specific nostalgia, the fate of "la niña de Guatemala" in a frequently anthologized poem of *Versos sencillos*; or Ezequiel Martínez Estrada, who is a bleak analyst of Argentina's historical frailties in *Radiografía de la pampa*, but who also creates Marta Riquelme in the short, allegorical novel with that title. Marta is portrayed in a series of contradictory suggestions, ranging from demonic to saintly; she is presented as the dubious emblem of history and society and, at the same time, as a compendium of all that is unfathomable in the female psyche.

Every literary movement retains some of its force long after it has ceased to be a fashion; for example, romanticism in the several symbolist trends that developed in the late nineteenth century, and in the surrealist metamorphoses that took place in the first half of the twentieth. Positively or negatively, the romantic image of women and girls persisted for a long time in Spanish American literature, in ways quite analogous to their compartmentalization in society. In a strange documentary yet poetic novel, *Una sombra donde sueña Camila O'Gorman* (1976), the Argentine poet Enrique Molina adapts a historical episode to poetic experience. In the repressive era of Jual Manuel Rosas, Camila O'Gorman runs away with a priest. Rosas orders their arrest and an intensive search and capture is carried out by the military. At Camila's father's request, she and the priest are condemned to execution by a firing squad. Dispensable as this poor female is (her shame is underlined by her pregnancy), she can still serve a worthwhile liturgical function: just before the execution she is ordered to drink a liter of holy water, so that her child can pass to the other world properly (in this case, umbilically) baptized.

In a recent short essay I mention the crucial effect that North America, through its leaders, its mass media, and its business interests, has had on Latin Americans' ideas about themselves.[1] One receives a graphic impression of this phenomenon from John J. Johnson's book *Latin America in Caricature*. Most of the cartoons reproduced by Johnson elaborate two theses which he sums up as follows:

> First, because of the universal beneficence of its brand of equality and individualism and the superiority of its enterprise and technology, the United States has a civilizing burden in respect to Latin America. Second, Latin Americans are inferior to the point of inspiring little respect or trust and lack the wisdom to know what is best for their own security and economic well-being or to rule themselves effectively.[2]

The three predominant stereotypes under which Johnson classifies his selection of cartoons are children, blacks, and women. The children misbehave, the blacks don't know anything, and the women are passive and vulnerable. Those are the basic traits attributed to the "other" Americans in most of our newspaper cartoons since the 1890s. Although Latin Americans are not inclined to accept that denigration in the light of rational self-analysis, the long barrage of stereotyped imagery has had its subliminal effect. That is, it has tended to complement, though not to confirm, the widespread and deep complex of historical original sin: to be born Latin American is equivalent to coming to bat with the count already at two strikes. Children, blacks, and women (misconduct, ignorance, and vulnerability) are three kinds of victims who in the unending struggle between the haves and have-nots seem to characterize those geographical entities now fashionably gathered under the euphemism "developing countries."

So in the essay the female persona (read *mask*, and psychological tendency) has special importance as image. Image—a

1. Peter G. Earle, "Carta de los Estados Unidos: Notas sobre la interdependencia," in *Los ensayistas*, nos. 10–11 (1981), pp. 185–88. All translations in the text of this chapter are by the author.

2. Austin: University of Texas Press, 1980, p. 114.

mental picture, a sense impression, an evocation, an epiphany or revelation, a symbol—has virtually unlimited potential in the writing and reading of Spanish American literature. I use the term as an embodiment of Jung's concept of the archetype: the conscious and self-conscious person in the foreground; the personal and collective unconscious in the background. The background is where the female presence must be sought in the essay, for the background (historical thought, indelible myths, recurrent archetypes, utopian longing, counterutopian disillusionment, psychological defense mechanisms) is where its cultural significance is to be found. Myth is the refuge or lost home to which the mind repeatedly retreats; it resists change and merges present, past, and future. According to Philip Rahv, "Myth is reassuring in its stability, whereas history is that powerhouse of change which destroys custom and tradition in producing the future. . . . Hence what the craze for myth represents most of all is the fear of history."[3] If, on the one hand, many Latin Americans have interpreted their history as a continuing spectacle of inferiority or—as the cartoons in Johnson's book emphasize—of an inherent inability to deal with circumstances, and have rejected that spectacle in the name of revolutionary action, many others have unintentionally accepted it in the name of tradition. The vulnerable female has been a permanent statue in the museum of tradition, and myth is the vital force that has tried to keep the statue in its (her) place.

The Mexican Revolution could be used as a turning point in the Spanish American essay between two perspectives. Before the revolution woman is usually excluded or, in contemporary sociological usage, "marginalized." After the revolution she is dealt with as an ambiguous presence. Before, religion and a paternalistic notion of decorum relegated her to a passive domestic status. Afterward, as the consciousness of history stimulated a redefinition of New World culture, the traditional mannequin was overturned without being replaced. The cultural female idol, mostly decorative or at best sentimentalized, had become a cultural female question mark.

But, question mark or idol, her function in the essay is still largely instrumental, a function that can be divided into three

3. *The Myth and the Powerhouse* (New York: Farrar, Straus and Giroux, 1965), pp. 6–7.

main categories: cultural, aesthetic, and historical. Seldom has the Spanish American essayist dealt seriously with more than one of these categories—to say nothing of all three. By contrast, the Mexican muralist painters Diego Rivera, José Clemente Orozco, and David Alfaro Siqueiros, together with a younger artist, José Luis Cuevas (a master visionary within the medium of the grotesque), have frequently succeeded in bringing them together. It is curious that an awareness of self and enigmatic circumstance is often more readily and strikingly captured by a gifted painter than by a gifted essayist; curious, that is, when one considers that awareness of self and circumstance is the prime motivation of both.

The triple function (cultural, aesthetic, historical) of the female prevails in those works that tend to lyrical, intimate expression. It is either absent or invisible in most of those that have come to be considered as "classics": for example, Domingo Faustino Sarmiento's *Facundo* (1845), José Enrique Rodó's *Ariel* (1900), or José Carlos Mariátegui's *Siete ensayos de interpretación de la realidad peruana* (1928), each of which has a pronounced historical mystique. *Facundo* is a hymn to materialistic (and positivistic) civilization; public education and the orderly exploitation of natural resources, in the semiutopian, semirealistic view of Sarmiento, would leave no place for the barbarian likes of his provincial antagonist, Juan Facundo Quiroga. With *Ariel* Rodó rejected the materialism of which Sarmiento was the prophet and which, since 1845, had flourished in the Gilded Age of development in the United States. His essay, under the guise of a long-winded commencement address, is a spiritual journey into the abstract and, at the same time, a tentative declaration of Hispanic American cultural independence based on classic values: Greek freedom of inquiry and intellectual elitism; Carlyle's and Emerson's heroism as a weapon against mediocrity; Catholic intuitions (versus Puritan austerity) of an aesthetic culture: genius tends ultimately to the cult and idealization of beauty. Despite its esoteric tone and its limitations as an elitist message for elitist readers, *Ariel* did constitute an important move toward cultural independence; it clarified and emphasized the need for a new awareness of the facts that the Latin American countries were different from other countries, that Latin America should build its future on intellectual and moral values rather than on material values, and that the economic success of the United States should not be taken as a guide for universal progress.

Mariátegui, neither a liberal positivist like Sarmiento nor a liberal elitist like Rodó, sought the socialist solution. In the longest and probably most valuable of his *Seven Essays*, "El proceso de la literatura," he declares, "Traigo a la exégesis literaria todas mis pasiones e ideas políticas, aunque dado el descrédito y degeneración de este vocablo en el lenguaje corriente, debo agregar que la política en mí es filosofía y religión."[4] An explicit disciple of Marx, Mariátegui believes that literature as well as history is "process" and moves toward a communistic, utopian ideal. He theorizes that Peruvian literature, together with other Hispanic American literatures, undergoes three stages of development—colonial, cosmopolitan, and national—in a trajectory that moves from servile imitation to the assimilation of new influences and, ultimately, to intellectual independence "and the well-balanced expression of [a nation's] own personality."[5] Though he persistently used the term *Indoamérica*, he was not a separatist spokesman for the indigenous. He confessed in fact that he had acquired his best education in Europe, an experience that had led him to believe that there could be no salvation for Indo-America without Western science and thought.

Passionate in their philosophical convictions, prophetic in their historical perception, paternalistic in their urge to lead the New World's masses into the mainstream of modern civilization, Sarmiento, Rodó, and Mariátegui didn't consciously include the female, either as a theme or as a motif, in their works. The only exception, in these three essays, is Mariátegui's chapter (16) on the poetry of Magda Portal, in which he recognizes the importance of female poets (Mistral, Ibarbourou, Agustini) in twentieth-century Spanish American literature. Mariátegui throughout the 1920s reiterates his thesis of the decadence of bourgeois art and social values; on the other hand, poetesses, as opposed to "nihilistic, game-playing and skeptical" poets, had brought new vitality and "greater biological energy" to the lyric art. It was and is, of course, a Marxist pre-

---

4. *Siete ensayos de interpretación de la realidad peruana* (Lima: Amauta, 1968), p. 182.
5. Ibid., p. 189.

cept that women's progress is one of the measures of social progress.[6]

Among all Spanish American essayists, Rubén Darío has written the greatest number of *elogios* to the female. In his period of creative activity (1885–1915), Darío had little interest in the feminist cause. For him women were a kind of elixir, magic figures in his sensual landscape wherever he found himself—in Paris, the tropics, Mallorca, Málaga, Buenos Aires, or southern France. His aesthetic experience is displayed in many chronicles and travel pieces from 1893 on, as well as in his poetry. Darío, we shouldn't forget, made more money on his prose than on his poetry and consequently wrote more of the former than of the latter. His best collections of *crónicas*, essays, and criticism are *Los raros* (1893), *España contemporánea* (1901), *Peregrinaciones* (1901), *Tierras solares* (1904), *Opiniones* (1906), *Parisiana* (1909), *El viaje a Nicaragua e Intermezzo tropical* (1909), and *Todo al vuelo* (1912).

Rubén Darío had the autobiographical vigor in prose that he had in poetry; like other poets of great natural power (Whitman, Neruda, Paz) he was the all-consuming subject who mastered a virtual galaxy of objects. Animated, sensual, exhilarating, or ethereal as his women usually were, they were a magic element of the atmosphere; they had greater significance as objects—nineteenth-century art objects—than as subjects—although occasionally there was a portrait, such as that of a beautiful blonde North American captivated in turn by the magic of Gustave Moreau's portrait of Salomé in the Palace of Fine Arts in Paris ("Los anglosajones" in *Peregrinaciones*); her concentration radiates intelligence; she is one of those "rare and sublime statues of feminine flesh inhabited, in exceptional cases, by a sensitive, dreaming soul." In *El viaje a Nicaragua* Darío describes his return to his native country after a fifteen-year absence. In and around Managua the luxurious flowers are so dense that life seems to congeal "in a concentrated block of time," like that experienced by the sleeping beauty in a forest. On a coffee plantation in the nearby hills Darío is impressed by tall indigenous and mestizo maidens whose physiques suggest "fatigantes y agotadores cariños solares." In the streets of Málaga *(Tierras solares)* the women are a moving festival of "marvelous living

6. Ibid., p. 256.

roses." In the gardens of Versailles ("Jardines de Francia," *Parisiana*) he hears the distant song of a woman, "El canto es melodioso, ardiente, profundo." On visiting the Generalife ("Granada," *Tierras solares*) he evokes the image of the sultan of Granada's second wife, Zoraida, and walks along the galleries that "awake one's urge to sigh and to kiss."

Darío didn't lack a historical consciousness. Rather, the female phenomenon was his refuge from everyday space and time, a passive presence in human terms, but one that never failed to excite his sentiments and feelings, a bridge, as it were, that always led to the artistic vision.

As Octavio Paz and Susan Sontag repeatedly remind us, modern thought seeks the Self in the Other. Sontag enumerates: "Europe looks for its image and its own impressions in the exotic settings of other continents; rationality finds a new dimension in sexual ecstasy or loses it in drugs; consciousness measures its own meaning in the unconscious."[7] Or as Wallace Stevens has put it in one of his finest poems:

> Two things of opposite natures seem to depend
> On one another, as man depends
> On a woman, day on night, the imagined
>
> On the real. This is the origin of change.
> Winter and Spring, cold copulars, embrace
> And forth the particulars of rapture come.[8]

This complementary oppositeness is a fundamental feature of Western modernist culture. Norman O. Brown has interpreted it in Freudian terms in *Life against Death*; Julio Cortázar has had intuitions of it in *Rayuela*, as he later explains to Luis Harss in the latter's *Los nuestros:*

> It's the notion of what I call figures. It's the feeling—which many of us undoubtedly have but which I've experienced with particular intensity—that aside from our individual destinies we are part of figures unknown to us. I believe we all create figures. For example, at this moment we may be forming part of a structure that extends, say, two hundred meters from here where there are probably other persons who don't know us just as we don't know

7. See her essay in *Claude Lévi-Strauss: The Anthropologist as Hero*, ed. Eugene Nelson Hayes and Tonya Hayes (Cambridge: M.I.T. Press, 1970), pp. 184–95.

8. "Notes Toward a Supreme Fiction," in *Collected Poems of Wallace Stevens* (New York: Alfred A. Knopf, 1957), p. 392.

them. I continually sense the possibility of connections, of cir-
cuits that may close and make us interdependent, outside all
rational explanation or normal human relationships.[9]

Cortázar's "figures" (structures of the unknown) are the equivalent of what Paz and Sontag have classified as "the Other" (and
otherness), and it is in that mysterious interrogative region that
many contemporary Hispanic American writers have placed the
female persona, a persona that is easily blurred into a presence
or sharpened into a symbol. Before the Mexican Revolution,
which in literature and the arts caused a cultural redefinition
and a renaissance of historical thought throughout Latin America (it coincided with the Argentine university reforms of 1918
and, a few years later, with the workers' APRA movement in
Peru), women were excluded from the essay or, as in the case of
Rubén Darío, aesthetically marginalized; after the revolution
they constituted a new, largely ambiguous presence. In its sim-
pler manifestations, this macho-conceived dualism persists, as
Luis Cardoza y Aragón has remarked in the fourth and last section of his *Guatemala: las líneas de su mano,* noting that in the
twentieth century as well as in the sixteenth, "Woman is treated
in diametrically opposed ways: with medieval gallantry, as in
chivalric tournaments and, at the same time, she is reduced to
submission and ignorance."[10] The gallantry removes her from
the sphere of the immediate; the reduction limits her vision and
cuts short her initiative.

Analogous effects are perpetuated by mass culture, imported
from the country best prepared to transform mass culture into
an industry. In their best-selling *Para leer al Pato Donald* (22 editions from 1972 to 1981), Ariel Dorfman and Armand Mattelart
show with abundant examples that the voluminous imported
world of Walt Disney is an idealless utopia without mothers,
fathers, sons, or daughters (every character in the Disney comic
strips is an uncle or an aunt, a niece or a nephew) and without
any suggestion of male-female love or sexuality. It is a contrived
society, organized to evolve in a world without passions, save
one: the magic realism of everyone's quest for gold. "Disney-
landización es una dinerización" (Disneylandization means

---

9. Luis Harss and Barbara Dohman, *Into the Mainstream: Conversations with
Latin American Writers* (New York: Harper and Row, 1967), p. 227.
10. 1st ed., Mexico City: Fondo de Cultura Económica, 1955, p. 65.

profit motivation). But that moneyfication is consistently unproductive; no one builds, creates, or produces. Rather, remunera-
tion is gained through wile, ingenuity, or simple deception.
Disneyland, Disney World, and Disney literature are purified
images of the First World's material assets (in the concrete, its
content). The catch, of course, is that the potential symbolized in
those assets is not accessible to the impoverished masses of
Aztecland (Mexico), Inca-Blinca (Peru), Inestablestán (Vietnam),
or the elusive Central American republic of San Bananador. The
purified image demands elimination or displacement of erotica
and, consequently, of the female in her "dangerous" contexts of
lover, seductress, untimely mother, or frivolous interrupter of
organized (masculine) enterprise. Hippies, burglars, commu-
nists, and Third World revolutionaries are lumped together in a
universal brotherhood of delinquency and ignorance; their
presence is required as model targets for the expeditionary
forces of Disneylandia. Woman, on the other hand, is not car-
icatured but neutralized. One wonders, not without irony, if the
venerable Disney had foreseen the late twentieth-century con-
vergence of his sterilized North American girl-woman with her
docile, marginalized counterpart in Latin American literature.
Since the essay is a genre in which circumstances (biographical,
historical, social, cultural, or political) are reflected more
directly and *consciously* than in poetry or fiction, it should be
recalled that *Para leer al Pato Donald* was written as a political
attack by the Chilean left (Allende and Unidad Popular had been
in power a little over a year when the book appeared) against
cultural colonialism in Latin America. Donald Duck was the
metaphor for North American middle-class attitudes, a device,
thought Dorfman and Mattelart, for indoctrinating the Latin
American child and, within that indoctrination, of strengthening Latin American barriers against female initiative.

  With *El perfil del hombre y de la cultura en México* (1934) Samuel
Ramos continued on a conscious level what the muralist painters and the first novelists of the Mexican Revolution had begun
on an intuitive level: a cultural reevaluation of Mexican history.
Leopoldo Zea, Edmundo O'Gorman, Octavio Paz, and
Abelardo Villegas would extend and modify Ramos's psychological approach, mainly through a comparison of Mexican history and culture with the history and culture of other parts of the
modern world. Paz, in *El laberinto de la soledad* (1950; revised and

enlarged, 1959), is the essayist who has dealt most thoroughly and conscientiously with the female image in Mexico: that is, with the traditional ambivalence that was born with the sixteenth-century juxtaposition of Guadalupe, the immaculate Mother-Novia, and Malinche, the illegitimate Mother-Concubine. Neither Malinche or the Virgin of Guadalupe, Paz is quick to point out, became the active goddesses that have prevailed in other cultures. They are fundamentally passive.

> Guadalupe es la receptividad pura y los beneficios que produce son del mismo orden: consuela, serena, aquieta, enjuga las lágrimas, calma las pasiones. La Chingada es aún más pasiva. Su pasividad es abyecta: no ofrece resistencia a la violencia. Es un montón inerte de sangre, huesos y polvo. Su mancha es constitucional y reside, según se ha dicho más arriba, en su sexo. Esta pasividad abierta al exterior la lleva a perder su identidad: es la Chingada. Pierde su nombre, no es nadie ya, se confunde con la Nada, es la Nada. Y sin embargo es la atroz encarnación de la condición humana.[11]

> Guadalupe is pure receptiveness, and the blessings are of the same order: she consoles, assuages, pacifies, wipes away tears, cools passions. La Chingada [Malinche and all her symbolic descendants] is still more passive. An abject passivity: she puts up no resistance to violence, she is an inert composite of flesh, blood and dust. Her frailty is inherent and resides, as is stated above, in her sex. This passivity, always exposed, leads to her loss of identity: she is the Chingada. She loses her name, she's nobody, she's lost in the void, she is Nothingness itself. And yet, she is the bizarre incarnation of the feminine condition.

In chapter 5, "Conquista y colonia," Paz refers to the life and works of Sor Juana Inés de la Cruz, who, without becoming in the true sense a woman of science or a philosopher, lived the ideas of her time (seventeenth-century colonial Mexico); she was an intellectual who effectively wielded the intellectual's weapons. One of her weapons was "La respuesta a Sor Filotea," in which she claimed her right to speculative as well as logical thought. According to Paz, knowledge for its own sake was not a basic feature of Hispanic Golden Age thinking, least of all in the atmosphere of ecclesiastic suspicion of the New World colonies.

11. *El laberinto de la soledad* (Mexico City: Fondo de Cultura Económica, 1976), p. 77.

Thus, "Su doble soledad, de mujer y de intelectual, condensa un conflicto también doble: el de su sociedad y el de su feminidad."[12] Her career ended in silence, in a world that was "closed to the future."

"La dialéctica de la soledad" was written as an appendix for the 1959 edition; in it the author recognizes André Breton's influence *(L'Amour fou)* and seems to show also the influence of Denis de Rougemont. I refer to his view that society is constitutively opposed to the free exercise of love, since "La mujer vive presa en la imagen que la sociedad masculina le impone" (Woman lives as captive inside an image created for her by male society),[13] and that any attempt a woman might make to free herself ("Love is choice") is an infraction of society's law. Poetry and love relocate woman in her pristine freedom, in "el tiempo del Mito" (mythic time); Eve in the garden of paradise; love is the urge to begin again. Utopia, as Paz understands it, is a modern longing to return to the "original" mythical age of freedom, even though that longing is expressed in the form of rational planning. In his utopia woman would be free.

In a lighter but still significant vein, Mariano Picón-Salas comments on the devitalization of woman in twentieth-century upper-class society. The symbolic locales are Maracaibo ("a city still more susceptible than Caracas to this wealth without style or roots") and the country club residential area overlooking Caracas. The transitional period is from 1925 to 1945, "when whisky and soda replaced Mediterranean wines," and when ladies once possessed of "a bird's native gift of conversation," graceful manners, and spirituality, became the stultified devotees of card games and highballs. This we are told in *Comprensión de Venezuela* (1950). In parts of his *Regreso de tres mundos* (1959), Picón-Salas reveals a susceptibility to feminine charm comparable to that of Vasconcelos in *Ulises criollo.* Like Vasconcelos he expresses feelings more akin to the romantic seducers of other eras than to modernistic poets of an erotic inclination such as Paz and Neruda, for whom love is, truly and repeatedly, the urge to begin again. Vasconcelos and Picón-Salas, as well-read and widely experienced as they both were, were scarcely women's liberationists; they were old-time liberals at heart. Paz, though

12. Ibid., p. 103.
13. Ibid., p. 178.

not a socialist militant like Pablo Neruda, was until recently a revolutionary in spirit.

I said at the beginning that in the Hispanic American essay man is up front, directing or deforming things, and that woman is part of the environment. He's the sun; she, the satellite: the equivalent—one might say—of the background in a male's portrait of a male, or of an etherealized figure in a male's portrait of a female. But is it always to be that way? What, if anything, can change this auxiliary female status into something closer to equality? Probably nothing that a man could do; so far the only notable change has resulted, as one might logically suppose, from a woman's taking over herself the work of writing. More than a few Spanish American women have excelled since about 1950 in the art of literary criticism (and literary criticism *is* an art, not a linguistic science). Not so many have distinguished themselves as creative essayists. Two radiant exceptions are the poet Gabriela Mistral and Victoria Ocampo, founder and director of *Sur*, which appeared in 1931, Spanish America's finest little magazine or literary journal. Mistral, whose important volume of poems *(Tala)* Ocampo had published in 1938 under the auspices of *Sur*, also wrote a great deal of prose: essays, prologues, prose poems, testimonies. But only very recently did some of this begin to appear in book form, having been held back, inexplicably, by her literary executors.

Ocampo was born of a wealthy family in 1890, the eldest of six girls. She was discreetly indulged and sensitively educated in French, English, and Spanish. Her family background and cosmopolitan upbringing were similar to those of Jorge Luís Borges. Her written work, like his, was often the product of creative reading. On the other hand, *el juego* (literature and thought as a perspective on chance, metaphysical mysteries, or the actions of false gods) did not interest her. She was a humanist first and an intellectual second; her writing was a continual offering. Figuratively as well as literally, women in a man's world are expected to give of themselves. For the same reason, female poets in Hispanic America have traditionally been more prominent than female novelists or essayists; in the early twentieth century Gabriela Mistral, Delmira Agustini, Juana de Ibarbourou, and Alfonsina Storni acquired fame—as poets. Ocampo, who studiously avoided writing verse, insisted on cultivating the essay with the same intensity that characterizes the essays of Montaigne, Emerson, Unamuno, and her close friend Ortega y Gasset. Her compatriot Fryda Schultz de Montovani has set forth Ocampo's case as well as anyone.

> ¿Por qué se ha de criticar como un defecto el que una mujer hable *desde sí* y de lo que la rodea, de sus propias experiencias, en pura prosa conversacional, como quería Gabriela, si las que lo hacen en verso a nadie escandalizan, y de que lo hicieran los hombres, desde Montaigne acá, no sólo a nadie asusta, sino que inspira confianza y establece un diálogo con el lejano y actual lector? Es que la superficial y maliciosa hablilla—a veces masculina, pero a la que ayudan también las del otro género—suele cebarse en la mujer que se atreve a decir sencillamente *yo creo, yo he visto, yo pienso*. . . . Pero tales experiencias forman la materia honrada de que se nutren los libros de esta escritora y por ello nada mejor que el título común en que insiste para definirlos y autodefinirse: testimonios.[14]

> Why is it considered a defect for a woman to speak *of herself,* her surroundings and her own experiences in direct conversational prose—as Gabriela [Mistral] advocated—while those who do the same in verse shock no one? Nobody is disturbed by what men do, since Montaigne's time. Not only is nobody disturbed: confidence is gained through the kind of dialogue that reaches the distant yet present reader. It's because frivolous and malicious criticism—often masculine but sometimes abetted by the other sex—is customarily aimed at the woman who dares say, simply, *I believe, I have seen, I think*. . . . But those are the experiences that have vitalized this woman's books. And there could be no better title than the one she insisted on to define them and to define herself: Testimonies.

And *Testimonios* is the title of ten volumes of her essays. Like Borges, Ocampo read deeply; but she knew people much better than did Georgie (Jorge Luis's mother and Ocampo both called him that), who was always more aloof. And her friendships with Count Keyserling, Ortega y Gasset, Stravinsky, Waldo Frank, Tagore, Gabriela Mistral, and Virginia Woolf were very direct sources of literary inspiration for her. Without ever being a joiner or an organizer, Ocampo was a feminist, a liberal, and a pacifist. In addition to being a clear thinker and a sensitive recreator of the past, *her* past, she was a master portraitist, as one

14. *Victoria Ocampo* (Buenos Aires: Ediciones Culturales Argentinas, 1963), p. 44.

can see in "Fani," an evocation of her Spanish servant who stayed with her forty-two years, and in "Gabriela Mistral y el premio Nobel." In "Mi deuda con Ortega," written on the occasion of Ortega's death, she recalls a promenade on a spring afternoon by El Escorial in the Spanish writer's company. She had mentioned to him her impressions of the scene, in which historical evocations, the conversation, the landscape, and the aroma of spring formed a "symphony" within her. Ortega reproached her for her love of music ("La música te pierde"), believing, as he did, that music removes a necessary barrier between the precise and the imprecise; music was an open invitation to confusion. Now, years later (1955), Ortega had died, and Ocampo thought of how she might have responded to him on that spring afternoon:

> Since I am I and the world that surrounds me, according to *your* philosophy, and since there is no life *in abstractio,* this perishable instant fuses you for always with these towers and these salons, with the blue mountain ridge and above all with an intangible fragrance in the air; a fragrance on which I'll drift one day to meet you.[15]

Ocampo, whose persona was her strength and motivating force, is still the radiant exception, a rare example—together with Gabriela Mistral—of female self-definition in twentieth-century Spanish American literature. It is not encouraging to think that the closest parallel to Victoria Ocampo in the Americas has not been in this century (or in the nineteenth or eighteenth) but in the seventeenth: Sor Juana Inés de la Cruz, who, in the most religiously deadening and unspeculative period of the colonial era, was its liveliest and most speculative writer. Much history has yet to pass or many cultural changes will have to take place before the female image in the Spanish American essay can move from its still traditional status—passive, in the background, symbolic—to an active, autonomous status. Man is still in the foreground; woman is still part of his environment, the object waiting to become subject.

---

15. *Testimonios* (Buenos Aires: *Sur,* 1958), p. 106.

6 The Presence of Woman in the Poetry of Octavio Paz

Ann Marie Remley Rambo

In reading the poetry of Octavio Paz, one is struck by the central place of woman, the sense and presence of her. She seems to be the focal point of both his philosophy of life and his poetry. In this study we shall examine the various forms in which woman appears and attempt to determine the role that each form plays in Paz's poetic expression.

An understanding of Paz's concept of poetry in general is essential to an understanding of the presence of woman in his work. He considers poetry a function and an experience of life along with all other experiences, especially those of a sensual, corporeal nature. Of special interest to us here are Paz's own words on poetry found in Max Aub's *Poesía mexicana, 1950–60*. Paz says of this concept that he has shared with his contemporaries: "La poesía era una actividad vital más que un ejercicio de expresión: no queríamos decir algo personal como personalmente realizarnos en algo que nos trascendiese . . . para nosotros el poema era un acto o sea era un ejercicio espiritual. A todos nos interesaba la poesía como experiencia . . . como algo que tenía que ser vivido" (Poetry was more a vital activity than an exercise in expression: we didn't want to say something personal so much as to realize ourselves personally in something that might transcend us . . . for us a poem was an act, it was a spiritual exercise. Poetry interested us all as an experience . . . as something which had to be lived.)[1] To put it another way, the basis of his poetry is the forms and functions of nature.

The central theme of Paz's philosophy is the tragic longing of man to merge his identity in a union with all life. For him, life and poetry are so closely related that his poetry becomes an active part of his search for an explanation of existence. Solitude, death, sensual pleasures, nature, and love are all important themes.

Paz equates poetry and love as instruments in this search for a metaphysical union: "Veíamos en la poesía una de las formas

1. Quoted from Max Aub, *Poesía mexicana, 1950–60* (México: Aguilar, 1960), pp. 17–18.

altas de la comunión. No es extraño así que amor y poesía nos
pareciesen las dos caras de una misma realidad" (We saw in
poetry one of the high forms of communion. Thus it isn't
strange that love and poetry appeared to us to be two faces of
one single reality).[2] In Paz's collection of essays on poetics, *El
arco y la lira*, he explains how love, like poetic ecstasy, can lead to
a union and why the union is desired: "El amor nos suspende,
nos arranca de nosotros mismos. . . . Y sólo en ese cuerpo que
no es el nuestro y en esa vida ajena podemos ser nosotros mismos. . . . Y ese ser 'otros' no es sino un recobrar nuestra naturaleza o condición original. Experiencia de la unidad e identidad
final del ser" (Love suspends us, it pulls us out of ourselves. . . .
And only in that body which is not ours and in that life of
another can we be ourselves. . . . And that being "other" is
nothing more than recovering our nature or original condition.
An experience of unity and final identity of being).[3]

Love then, as a prime experience, becomes central to Paz's
poetic expression, and woman is the most basic and obvious element in the experience of love: "La mujer . . . es el aliento corpo-
ral más visible del mundo. . . . Ella nos exalta, nos hace salir de
nosotros y, simultáneamente, nos hace volver" (Woman . . . is
the most visible corporeal breath of life in the world. . . . She
exalts us, she makes us emerge from ourselves, and, simul-
taneously, she makes us return [to ourselves]).[4] Paz has also
said of the theme of physical love in his long poem "Piedra de
sol": "El tema central es la recuperación del instante amoroso
como recuperación de la verdadera libertad, 'puerta del ser' que
nos lleva a la comunicación con otro cuerpo, con los demás
hombres, con la naturaleza. . . . Y el puente que nos lleva . . . es
la mujer" (The central theme is the recuperation of the moment
of love as the regaining of true liberty, "the doorway to being"
which leads us to communication with another body, with other
men, with nature. . . . And the bridge which takes us across . . .
is woman).[5] This is the key to his treatment of physical love in
all his poems.

    This idea, which could easily give rise to a loose erotic

2. Ibid., p. 18.
3. Mexico City: Fondo de Cultura Económica, 1956, p. 130.
4. Ibid.
5. Quoted from Emmanuel Carballo, "Octavio Paz," in *México en la cultura*,
no. 493 (24 August 1958), p. 3.

expression, is instead controlled and reformed by Paz into an idea in which woman functions as an instrument and a symbol of transcendence. Throughout Paz's major volume of collected poems, *Libertad bajo palabra*, woman appears in three forms. She is the brief universal image of the girl, the mother, the frustrated woman, or the evil woman. She is then the beloved in a love relationship that expresses both the positive and the negative sides of love. Finally she appears in a transformed natural state in which there is a fusion of her feminine qualities with those of natural objects.

In the first instance she is seen as a brief image contributing to the creation of an atmosphere or to the presentation of a moment of emotion or sensation that is not necessarily essential to the central subject. The four figures of the girl, the mother, the frustrated woman, and the evil woman—her four basic manifestations—represent the complete woman in all her facets.

Paz's vision of the girl represents the universal qualities of feminine youth. She is always seen in a positive light, as an image of freshness or a symbol for an ideal. In "Alameda" she is "doncella de los reflejos . . . / súbita estatua de fuego" (maiden of reflections . . . / sudden statue of fire) (p. 13).[6] In "Primavera y muchacha" he addresses her, "Tú resplandeces al filo del agua y de la luz / Eres la hermosa máscara del día" (You shine at the edge of water, at the edge of light / You are the beautiful mask of day) (p. 97). In "Semillas para un himno" she is "Como el sol la muchacha que se abre paso / como la llama que avanza" (Like the sun [is] the young girl who opens up the way / like the flame that advances) (p. 105). In these examples she is related to nature, the joy of a new day, the visual and refreshing effects of light. The frequency of these optimistic images suggests the poet's almost subconscious vision, as it were, of woman as a part of nature, a vision he cultivates to gain understanding, to achieve tonality, and to infuse his poetry with the presence of woman.

The figure of the mother appears rarely, although the essence of maternity is present in many poems. Paz envisions her as the universal and natural mother. In "Adiós a la casa" Paz has written, "Quisiera decirte adiós, besar tu falda, / niña, mujer, fan-

6. Octavio Paz, *Libertad bajo palabra* (México: Fondo de Cultura Económica, 1960), p. 13. All other poetic quotations will be from this volume unless otherwise stated.

tasma de la orilla, / Madre, quisiera decirte adiós" (I would like to tell you goodbye, to kiss your skirt, / girl, woman, phantom of the shore, / Mother, I would like to tell you goodbye) (p. 139). Here is his universal feminine figure capable of motherliness and of love. She is all feminine things in one. Her supernatural power is related to the image of "la orilla" (the shore), suggesting the shore of life at which the poet stands.

Opposing the vision of the woman who represents the power of love fulfilled is that of the woman who suffers the anxiety of failing to complete her generic role. She is the contrast to the girl, to the mother, and to the beloved. Representing neither idealization nor danger, she can only be pitied as the most pathetic figure of the group. This type of woman is exemplified in the poem "Virgen." After having passed from innocent youth to old age leading a barren life, the woman cries out to be an undefined deity: "llueve sobre mis senos arrugados, / llueve sobre mis senos arrugados, / llueve sobre los huesos y las piedras, / que tu semilla rompa la corteza, / la costra de mi sangre endurecida" (Rain down on my withered breasts, / rain on my withered breasts, / rain on the bones and the rocks, / let your seed break the hard shell, / the scab of my hardened blood). Once again the poet has related woman to the phenomena of nature. "Llueve" suggests rain and the symbolic qualities of water, which refresh and make fecund. An equation is established between "huesos" (bones) and "piedras" (stones) that suggests their similar qualities. Analogous are the ideas of sap flowing beneath the bark of plants and of blood flowing in the human body. The rain sent by this natural god is "semilla" (seed), capable of penetrating or breaking open with new life the bark of plants and the shell that encases listless blood.

Woman as an evil contrary to man appears also, in contradistinction to the idealized visions of the girl and the mother. Often this evil woman is portrayed as an almost surrealistic fantasy figure. She symbolizes the basic dangers in the male's relationship with the female, the potential loss of his individual personality and character, the embodiment of his physical and psychological fears. Paz sees her as potentially poisonous, ensnaring, capable of seizing and strangling his masculine spirituality, intellect, and freedom. In "Piedra del sol" we see this example: "yo vi tu atroz escama, / melusina, brillar verdosa al alba, / dormías enroscada entre las sábanas" (I saw your horrible scales / smooth, gleaming greenly at dawn, / you were sleeping coiled among the sheets). Here there is a fusion of woman and snake in which each shares the qualities of the other. This type of woman is especially characterized by the terms "atroz escama . . . brillar verdosa" (horrible scales . . . gleaming greenly) and "enroscada" (coiled), and by the connotations of treachery and sexuality that the serpent bears in all literature and symbolic expression.

The figures of lovers and physical love form the second stage in Paz's development of the presence of woman. The beloved is the central figure, and it is through her that Paz must seek a spiritual union with all life. When the love relationship is successful, the world and the beloved are transformed. When the relationship is unsuccessful, the world is an empty, lonely existence in which physical love is an act of desperation. In both instances we see the beloved in the light of the poet's state of mind, developed in accord with the atmosphere surrounding her. We encounter a successful relationship in "Estrella interior":

> La cama era un mar pacífico
> Reverdecía el cuarto
> Nacían árboles, nacía el agua
> Había ramos y sonrisas entre las sábanas
> . . . .
> Pájaros imprevistos entre tus pechos
> Plumas relampagueantes en tus ojos
> Como el oro dormido era tu cuerpo
> Como el oro y su réplica ardiente cuando
>   la luz lo toca.

> The bed was a calm sea
> The room grew fresh and green
> Trees sprouted, water appeared
> There were branches and smiles among the sheets
> . . . .
> Sudden birds between your breasts
> Flashing feathers in your eyes
> Your body was like sleeping gold
> Like gold and its burning reply when
>   the light touches it.

Paz metamorphosizes familiar objects into objects of nature and intermingles the two worlds. In this atmosphere, the poet is linked philosophically and physically to woman and hence to all natural life. We find the figure of woman related to the nature symbols of trees and water, which suggest fecundity, profundity, and power of life. The woman is seen indirectly in the manifestations of these things. She is described with more detail in the last four lines of the poem cited above, in which all her reality is linked to birds and to effects of light. She is a visual image in an optimistic setting, and the poet has no need for a tactile reassurance of her presence.

In contrast to this last poem, the negative side of love appears in poems set at night and concerned with the tangible presence of the human body with its assurance of reality. The symbolic night setting obscures visual reality as well as the sensations of crime or guilt. These ideas are manifest in "Al tacto":

> Los lechos son ceniza
> y el amor un crimen compartido
> . . . petrificada soledad del alma
> entre seres y cosas,
> terror de la conciencia
> . . . ¿es el amor, acaso,
> un terror compartido,
> frente a frente los cuerpos
> rodeados por la nada sin tacto?

> Beds are ashes
> and love a shared crime
> . . . petrified solitude of soul
> between beings and things,
> terror of consciousness
> . . . is love, perhaps,
> a shared terror,
> bodies face to face
> surrounded by nothingness without feeling?

These pessimistic poems contain little of the glorified relation of woman to nature and few visual images like those in the previous poem. We read here instead the most purely intellectual preoccupations of the poet, objectified by images such as "los lechos son ceniza" (beds are ashes), "petrificada soledad del alma" (petrified solitude of soul), and "frente a frente los cuerpos rodeados por la nada sin tacto" (bodies face to face surrounded by nothingness without feeling). The poet expresses his doubt that love can lead him to a union with humanity, and in an empty environment he voices his feelings of isolation. He sees love at this moment as a crime of union committed in obscurity for the purpose of experiencing a sensation of life that will counterbalance the terror of the nothingness. In this darkness the tactile presence of woman is the only reality.

In his search for the totality of existence, Paz has logically, as we have seen, made woman the point of departure. With this totality now found and the union with life completed, the poet enters a third phase where he records the effect of this upon him. In the poems of this stage, nature is made the ideal, the basis of femininity, and the figure of woman is transformed and subordinated to this ideal.

Because woman and nature represent both physical solidity and spiritual profundity to the poet, they always appear related through the same three poetic symbols of water, earth, and the tree. Water, as a universal poetic symbol, suggests fecundity, timelessness, continual change, and purity leading to spirituality. Technically, it suggests flow or leap of motion and reflection of light, two predominating elements in Paz's description of woman and nature. The earth represents a solid basis of life, profundity, and substance. Sustained by both water and earth, the tree stands between the two and represents life, based in reality and reaching vertically toward the infinite. As an image, the tree suggests movement and the members of the human form. Since their qualities represent what Paz idealizes in woman, these three symbols with their many variations carry the feminine presence through all the poems.

We see the fusion of the figure of woman with earth and water in the following lines from "Estrella interior":

> Reposa la mujer en la noche
> Como agua fresca con los ojos cerrados
> A la sombra del árbol
> Como una cascada detenida en mitad de su salto
> Como el río de rápida cintura helado de pronto
> . . . .
> Como el agua del estanque en verano reposa
> En su fondo se enlazan álamos y eucaliptos
> Astros o peces brillan entre sus piernas
> La sombra de los pájaros apenas oscurece su sexo
> Sus pechos son dos aldeas dormidas
> Como una piedra blanca reposa la mujer

Como el agua lunar en un cráter extinto
A la orilla del agua a orilla de un cuerpo.

Woman reposes in the night
Like cool water with eyes closed
In the shade of a tree
Like a waterfall stopped in the middle of its leap
Like a river with rapidly moving waist frozen suddenly
· ·
Like water in a pool reposes in the summer
In her depths poplars and eucalyptuses entwine
Stars or fish sparkle between her legs
The shadow of birds scarcely obscures her sex
Her breasts are two sleeping villages
Like a white rock woman reposes
Like lunar water in an extinct crater
At the shore of water at the shore of a body.

In the first few lines we notice the use of similes in series, which establish a rhythmic pattern and form the basis for the transformation. In these lines the woman is constantly compared to water. Suddenly the poet passes from the use of similes to a direct metaphor in which the woman is the water: "En su fondo se enlazan álamos y eucaliptos" (In her depths poplars and eucalyptuses entwine). He then expands the metaphor from the body of water outward to include surrounding land— "Sus pechos son dos aldeas dormidas" (Her breasts are two sleeping villages)—and as a climax exalts the physical substance of woman and of nature: "Como una piedra blanca reposa la mujer" (Like a white rock woman reposes). The focus of the poem returns to the body of water—"Como el agua lunar" (Like lunar water)—and to the image of the woman and a body of water: "A la orilla del agua a orilla de un cuerpo" (At the shore of water at the shore of a body). This last line sustains the equality and the fusion between the two. The use of the term "a la orilla" (at the shore) objectively indicates the shore of the body of water, and subjectively indicates the brink of a new life for the poet, the potential entrance into the life of another.

Further suggestive of this physical and spiritual penetration of woman and of nature by the poet, we see also in "Estrella interior" that Paz places the masculine in opposition to the feminine, surrounding her in nature as a cloud, sky, bird, or water: "voy por tu cuerpo como por el mundo / . . . como la nube por tu pensamiento" (I go through your body as [I go] through the world / . . . as a cloud through your thought); "pájaros imprevistos entre tus pechos" (sudden birds between your breasts); "la rodean mis miradas como agua" (my glances surround her like water). He has the masculine penetrate the feminine as stars, fish, and light rays: "Astros o peces brillan entre sus piernas" (Stars or fish sparkle between her legs). These elements obviously emphasize "lo femenino" in nature and enhance the sensuality the poet attributes to it.

A cinematographic technique is employed here, blending one image into another in a gradual process involving a sense of motion. The fluctuation between simile and metaphor and the periodic repetition of series of images or similes with run-on verses and omission of punctuation all play an integrated central role in creating a sense of motion and in making a smooth, seemingly subconscious transition from woman to nature.

To maintain simplicity and to express clearly the universal concepts with which he is dealing, Paz uses a basic vocabulary of generic terms. Woman is always "mujer," the parts of her body are simple "piernas," "ojos," "brazos," "pelo" (legs, eyes, arms, hair). Natural objects are similarly expressed. A tree is always only "árbol," water "agua," earth "tierra" and stone "piedra."

When Paz omits the use of simile, it results in the complete transformation of woman, as in the poem "En la calzada." Through the use of tree images in an expanded metaphor, the fecundity of woman becomes that of the tree:

> Quisiera detener una joven,
> cogerla por la oreja y plantarla entre un castaño y otro;
> regarla con una lluvia de verano;
> verla ahondar en raíces como manos que enlazan en la noche
>   otras manos;
> crecer y echar hojas y alzar entre sus ramas una copa que canta;
> brazos que sostienen un niño, un tesoro, una
> jarra de agua, la canasta del pan que da
> la vida eterna;
> . . . rozar su piel de musgo, sus pies de savia y luz,
> hablar con ella un lenguaje de árbol de enfrente;
> envolverla con brazos impalpables como el aire que pasa,
> rodearla, no como el mar rodea a una isla, sino como la
>   sepultura;

reposar en su copa como la nube ancla un instante en el cielo sin
olas.

I would like to stop a young woman,
catch her by the ear and plant her between two chestnuts;
spray her with summer rain
see her put down roots like hands that entwine
    in the night with other hands;
grow and send out leaves and raise among her branches a
    crown that sings;
arms that bear a child, a treasure, a
jar of water, the basket of bread that gives
eternal life;
. . . to brush against her mossy skin, her feet of sap
    and light,
to speak with her a language of close-by tree;
enfold her with arms impalpable as the passing
    air,
surround her, not like the sea surrounds an island, but
    like the grave;
to lie back in her crown like a cloud anchors an
    instant in a sky without waves.

We notice the equating of woman to a natural object and the
further elaboration of the attributes of both within a natural
framework: "su piel de musgo, sus pies de savia" (her mossy
skin, her feet of sap). The tree, in the fusion, is given human
capabilities, modified by its own nature: "hablar con ella un
lenguaje de árbol de enfrente" (to speak with her a language of
close-by tree).

The poet himself enters into this lengthy metaphor, transformed also into a natural being in masculine contrast to the
tree: "envolverla con brazos . . . como el aire que pasa" (enfold
her with arms . . . like the passing air); "rodearla, no como el
mar rodea a una isla" (surround her, not like the sea surrounds
an island); "reposar en su copa" (to lie back in her crown). The
poet resorts to structural patterning in the run-on verses and in
the use of series of lines, each of which begins with an infinitive.
This time, punctuation is used to achieve pauses in the rhythm
and intonation and to divide sense groups clearly, creating a
rhythm that is almost rhetorical in sound and yet subconscious
in its flow.

In content the poem has three outstanding points. First we

notice that the poet has chosen a girl as the figure of transformation. The poem is an expression of Paz's future desires, of what he ideally would like to do. The woman represents what he can do in the present and what he has done in the past. The girl is the possibility, the freshness of a future opportunity, an unattained ideal.

Second, the poet himself enters in an intimate, optimistic, and sexually symbolic manner. Through his actions the ideal is to be attained. The girl and the tree are to be instruments for the fulfillment of the poet's physical, psychological, and spiritual desires. That which is ideal and that which is sexual are blended in the poet's expression: "regarla con una lluvia de verano" (to spray her with summer rain); "verla ahondar . . . crecer y echar hojas y alzar entre sus ramas una copa que cante; / brazos que sostienen un niño" (see her put down . . . grow and send out leaves and raise among her branches a crown that sings; / arms that bear a child).

Finally, the manifestation of this ideal is "un niño, un tesoro, una / jarra de agua, la canasta del pan que de la vida eterna" (a child, a treasure, a / jar of water, the basket of bread that gives eternal life). The presence of the child binds the ideal to human reality and represents the fruit of a fulfilled love. The term "tesoro" (treasure) labels the ideal as it exists in the poet's mind, but in the images of bread and water this ideal is expressed in terms not of a resultant fruit to be kept and cared for but of a life-giving substance to be consumed. This "niño" (child), fruit of the poet's desire, is the basic bread and water that renew and sustain his life, the substance of his communion with mankind. Too, the "niño" is the product of woman and of nature, which the poet has cultivated to give a form to his desires and his love, a form through which he attains his ideal.

It is clear, then, that much of Paz's philosophy in life and in poetry centers on woman. She and her relationship to man through love represent the means by which man can communicate with all life. A definite relationship can be seen between the philosophical importance of the three forms of feminine presence and the technique and imagery of their expression in the poems: (1) Starting with the universal but real woman, the poet develops her in some detail into several general types. She is always related to nature, and she is always portrayed in brief, objective images. (2) The beloved is the instrument through which the poet seeks to reach an ideal state. Her function is to transport and elevate him to a higher expression. She appears in pessimistic and optimistic settings, representing the dual viewpoints of physical love. When she is successful, the world is transformed for the poet into a new reality of natural beauty, and she in turn is transformed by this. (3) Feminine objects in nature represent the sublimation of woman as seen through the eyes of the poet, in harmony with all life. She is a woman fused with nature through a technique that blends series of visual images and similes into sustained metaphors of universal symbolic importance: water, trees, and earth. The most interesting and successful stage is this last, which uses the other two as its background and basis. It is here, where the fusion of woman with all nature is attained, that the universality of life is best expressed and most clearly understood.

Paz's poetic technique transforms the philosophical idea into a working system of art, reinforcing the thematic ideas so closely as to become unified with them. His central technique involves the transition between human images and images of nature in which motion plays an important role. The sense of flow and steady transition is aided by rhythmic patterns and periodic repetition. Characteristic of these are frequently recurring lines, series of similar images, and series of lines beginning with the same word and following the same structural pattern with changes only of internal words. Punctuation, or the lack of it, serves in all poems to create a greater sense of rhythm, motion, and unity. Simplicity of vocabulary completes the elements of Paz's poetic technique.

A constant tension is maintained between the real woman and the ideal, between the poet's capabilities and his desires, and between the human figure and the natural form in each of the poems. This tension combines with great sensuality, sensitivity, and sincerity of tone in each development of the theme to produce poems of unique and powerful expression.

MYTH AND CULTURE

7 Recovering the Lost Erotic Priestess of Caribbean Tradition

Matías Montes Huidobro

To begin our study of woman as myth and metaphor in Latin American literature, we must first give some background for the concepts with which we will work.[1] These are the mythic religious notions of woman expressed in the worship of Mary and *hieros gamos* (marriage of woman and divinity). We will then look at the use of these cultural constructs in two works representing Puerto Rican and Cuban theater.

From prehistoric times, there have been mythic expressions of female supremacy. In this respect, J. Edgar Bruns speculates, "Did earliest man think of God as woman, specifically as a great mother? The question is raised because among the more numerous artifacts of pre-historic man is the figure, seated or standing, of an extraordinarily obese woman. The most famous of these is the so-called Venus of Willendorf to which we can add her sisters from Gogarino and, more recently, those discovered at Catal Hüyük."[2] In matriarchal societies woman is believed to rule over both earthly and divine realms. Geoffrey Ashe notes, "Over a large part of the world, before the rise of any verified gods, human beings did indeed worship goddesses. More precisely, they worshipped The Goddess: in Goethe's phrase, the Ewig-Weibliche or Eternal-Womanly. Early Stone Age art gives us no image of male deity. But it does give us female ones—figures with gross breasts and bellies, exaggerated tokens of motherhood."[3] With the rise of patriarchy, man displaces woman from her divine status, and she comes to have a secondary place in the mythic-religious structure. As a consequence, "During the second millennium B.C., male deities took command; partly through the ever-strengthening instituion of kingship, partly through changes in relationships between the sexes, partly through war and conquest."[4] Later, Greek and Judeo-Christian

---

1. This essay was originally written in Spanish and has been translated by Naomi Lindstrom.
2. *God as Woman, Woman as God* (New York: Paulist Press, 1973), p. 7.
3. *The Virgin* (London: Routledge and Kegan Paul, 1976), p. 10.
4. Ibid., p. 15.

civilizations produce powerful cultural myths that place woman at a decided disadvantage. Yet, neither of these cultures succeeds in suppressing one longstanding myth of woman's supremacy: woman as the privileged voice of wisdom. The Zeus-Metis power struggle is an archetypal example from classical antiquity. Here we see the male determination to suppress any female domination. "Athena is actually conceived in the womb of Metis, a goddess who is herself Prudence. Zeus is the father, but when he learns that the wise mother is about to bear a child who might be even more intelligent than she—and certainly more so than he—he devours her."[5] Woman's wisdom is the determining factor in the gestation process. In the Judeo-Christian tradition, the serpent knows that Eve, not Adam, can be tempted with the lure of knowledge and understanding. Let us keep in mind this cultural concept: woman as the possessor of knowledge.

While woman's mythic image deteriorates with the rise of Greek and Hebrew civilizations, when we move from Old to New Testament a positive change occurs. The transition from Eve to the Virgin Mary is a turning point in the cultural myth of woman. The silent wisdom of the Virgin restores to woman some of the prestige she had lost. Though playing a secondary role in the gospel narrative, Mary comes to occupy a large role in the popular culture of Catholic countries. The reason seems to be that "for the Roman Catholic, there is one person in whom this metaphysical mystery of our humanity has become supremely tangible and hence intelligible. That person is a woman named Mary who became the virgin mother of our Lord. The dogmas that cluster about Mary constitute the most significant pronouncements ever made about woman."[6] So, through this almost subversive process, worship of Mary becomes a permitted anomaly against the main patriarchal tradition of Christianity. In John de Satgé's view, "The evangelical has a strong suspicion that the deepest roots of the Marian cult are not to be found in the Christian tradition at all. The religious history of mankind shows a recurring tendency to worship a mother-goddess"; consequently, "the cult of Mary may be an intrusion into Christianity from the dark realms of natural

    5. Bruns, *God as Woman*, p. 24.
    6. Paul K. Jewett, *Man as Male and Female* (Grand Rapids: William B. Eerdmans, 1975), p. 180.

religion."[7] Looking at this recovery of woman's mythic prestige, we must consider also the phenomenon of *hieros gamos*,
that is, the "perfect union" of woman and divinity. Here also,
mythic and metaphoric concepts tend to grant woman prestige.

These cultural patterns travel to America from Spain, but take
on new forms in the New World. Particularly, the mythic structure had to be adjusted so as to cast the best light on the "un-
Christian" sexual relations between Spanish conquerors and
native women. This troubling situation needed to be cushioned
by an accommodating set of myths that would ease the tensions
produced by the clash between the two cultures. We must
remember that racial mixture mingled diverse mythic-religious
notions: Christian, Indian, African. The result was a variety of
pagan-Christian blends influenced by the need to account,
through myth, for the situation in the New World. The Spanish
conqueror develops a dual mythic outlook. He sees himself as
protected by, and worshiping, the Virgin. Yet, in his dealings
with native or African women he discards his Christian respect
for woman's chastity. His behavior is sensual, instinctive, pre-
civilized, pre-Christian.

We will now examine two representative works of Cuban and
Puerto Rican theater with these ideas in mind. The plays concern us because they work out, through myth and metaphor,
conflicts between incompatible notions of woman.

Francisco Arriví is one of the foremost contemporary Puerto
Rican playwrights. His *María Soledad* involves the above-mentioned concerns. It is filled with myths of the vanished Taino
Indians of Puerto Rico and centers on the role of woman in these
myths.

Arriví's play presents a love triangle that, on the surface,
seems blandly contemporary. María Soledad is married to José
Luis, an architect, and courted by Ricardo, a poet. Her marriage
has never been consummated and, compounding the difficulty,
she cannot break out of an incestuous relation with her father,
who made her dance nude in the woods as an adolescent. Some
critics see María Soledad as a damsel in distress whom a
"prince" (Ricardo) must rescue from a "dragon" (José Luis), but
this interpretation does not account for all elements. The true
richness of the play comes from Taino culture erupting in the

7. Quoted in Ashe, *The Virgin*, p. 7.

midst of this apparently cosmopolitan triangle. Interpreted in mythic terms, the work reveals unsuspected depths.

The Cemí, a Taino idol, brings ancient Puerto Rican culture into this cosmopolitan setting. As the curtain rises, we see the double level of the action. The first ambience, a spacious modern living room, is the surface level that distracts attention from the second level, the garden, that reflects the mythic underpinnings of the plot. The living room provides entry back into the Taino past, which constantly lurks beneath the veneer of modernity. The garden is ruled by an idol, the Cemí of the Moon. María Soledad, dressed in a white robe of ritual solemnity, has given herself over to pre-Hispanic Taino worship.

Though Taino culture was disrupted with the Spanish conquest of Puerto Rico, two strong myths persisted. These myths, one male, one female, are important for the analysis of *María Soledad*. The male myth was represented by the Cemí, the stone idol Tainos worshipped. The female myth, which would persist in Puerto Rican culture, was of an Amazon-type dominant woman. For example, one set of Taino myths has to do with the queendom of Loíza, a woman reputed to have ruled the Hayamano region. "Her domain was the fertile land at the mouth of the island's largest river, the Rio Grande de Loíza, where some of the most powerful spirits and gods on the island lived. And still do. Like all the women of Borinquen, the 'lady cacique' of Hayamano had to be respected; she could invoke the spirits."[8] The Amazon figure takes on special significance because of Puerto Rico's history of subjugation. Continually dominated by colonial powers, the Puerto Rican man cannot assume the starring role in the pageant of national life. This humiliating and frustrating phenomenon has been symbolically presented in literary works. In Puerto Rican drama, man is reduced to a passive role in history. Yet woman, in the tradition of the Amazon queen, plays an active role. This circumstance makes woman, not man, the leading figure in the epic of the nation's history. In Arriví's play *Vejigantes*, the solution to the racial problem is brought about by women, Amazons who expose and confront prejudice. In his *Coctel de don Nadie*, a heroine of Amazon strength represents Puerto Rico's hope for the future. The image

8. Stan Steiner, *The Island* (New York: Harper and Row, 1974), p. 24.

of woman is frequently associated with the mythic Amazons of the Taino past.

These circumstances leave the Indian male myth at a disadvantage. With the downfall of Taino culture, literature must be the force that reconstructs its mythic structure and restores the world that existed before the Spanish invasion. This restoration is what Arriví does when he sets forth the concept of a pagan, pre-Christian *hieros gamos*, based on the myth of Cemí, in *María Soledad*. Nowhere to be seen is the cult of Mary the Spaniards brought with them; in *María Soledad* we return to the ancient deities.

The ethnic components in the work create an intellectual gap. While the characters of European descent are lost in the amorous triangle, the Cemí proceeds to form strong pre-Hispanic bonds between himself and María Soledad, who had the idol installed in her home. Though she is adored by the male characters in the work, the young woman worships the Cemí, reversing the pattern; subconsciously giving herself to the Cemí, she feels protected from her own husband. As she becomes a vestal virgin who exists to worship the idol, the passion men feel for her is frustrated by the Cemí.

The Taino idol has been assigned various meanings. Its ethical value has two possible signs. Jacques Bouton sees it as a demon, while François Blanchard states that the Indians considered it a good spirit.[9] The Spanish-Taino duality allows for a two-way interpretation. From the Hispanic point of view, it is a diabolical spirit taking over the house; from a Taino perspective, it symbolizes the mythic recovery of rightful belongings. In this case, it is the woman, María Soledad, that belongs.

If we consider the Cemí as a pre-Spanish male deity, woman's position in the hierarchy does not change entirely. Woman is still below a male deity. There is, in fact, a parallel with Mary, who functions as an intermediate point between God and the world. The difference in the character of the relation is, however, very pronounced. In this case, the vestal virgin's adoration is laden with eroticism. Even with virginity, the notion of purity associated with Mary is lost in the pre-Hispanic metaphor. The

9. See Mercedes López-Baralt, *El mito taino* (Río Piedras, Puerto Rico: Ediciones Huracán, 1976), p. 239.

woman figures as a goddess or semigoddess whose sexual nature is associated with a pre-Christian mythic set. In the cult of Mary, adoration is not consciously erotic and she is seen as an intercessor before a Christian God. In the play we are analyzing, the Mary metaphor goes two ways. María Soledad is adored as a goddess, not to obtain her intercession with God but to move her in the opposite direction. Man seeks to draw María Soledad toward the earthly male sexuality and away from the divine male sexuality. It is the sexual character of the relation that separates it from Christian worship of Mary and makes us realize we are in a different cultural landscape.

José Luis is leery of the Cemí, being separated from it by a cultural and personal barrier. He sees the Cemí and the primitive concept it represents as an anticultural force. This is why we interpret the work as a cultural struggle between the Puerto Rican Indian culture and the material, "civilized" progress of the European culture. Woman is the goal in this tug-of-war, the prize to be won, metaphorically becoming a goddess. José Luis's sexuality is conventionally modern. He has even rid himself, to some extent, of the typically Spanish Marian cult's view of sexuality. On the mythic level of the Cemí, the world of sex, the subconscious and the transcendental fuse together. José Luis has a vague inkling of this process and so proposes to take its place: "He decidido convertirme en cemí."[10] The point is, precisely, to take on the Cemí's aura so as to get hold of the prize, the woman.

In Arriví's play, the theme of incest plays a significant role. María Soledad remains subconsciously bonded to her father, for whom she used to dance nude in the moonlight. There is a link in the play between the spots on the moon and incest, so that one may easily establish a connection between incest and the Cemí-of-the-Moon motif. At the end of the work María Soledad is about to dance nude in the moonlit garden for the Cemí; this reenactment of the key moment of the immediate past will lead the protagonist into a primitive bond where she will be part of pagan, pre-Christian idol worship. But in her Mary-like virginity (we must not forget that her name is María Soledad) it is possible to see the complex reflection of the Mary cult. The

10. Francisco Arriví, *María Soledad*, in *Tres piezas de teatro puertorriqueño* (San Juan: Departmento de Instrucción Pública, 1968), p. 180.

notion that Mary worship is a holdover from ancient idol worship is here easily observable.

We should consider, moreover, that María Soledad is kept apart from her husband for mythic, pagan causes. To be sure, José Luis is an active, well-adjusted, daylight creature, who loves nature in a sense far removed from lunar myths. "We can readily understand how it was that to naive people the sun should be god of the men and the moon of women, because of their characteristics, which seem to correspond to male and female and so justify the choice of these symbols."[11] On both the human and the divine levels, María Soledad cannot feel impelled toward José Luis (the sunlight world), whom she fears, but she feels an identification with the Cemí (the moonlight world).

Like the Marys of Christianity, her life is ruled by the *hieros gamos* concept, but her underlying American Indian nature makes her profane by Catholic standards. "It is to women that the sacred marriage with the Divine Bridegroom is a functional necessity; men do not need to be united with a divine bride to fulfill their functions. But every religion, from the most primitive to the highest, is pervaded with the idea that union with a god, a *hieros gamos*, or 'Holy Matrimony,' is a necessity to every woman."[12] The protagonist has no interest in here-and-now pleasure with men but only in the transcendental sexuality of the idol. María Soledad's nude dance is the pagan ritual that takes her back to the Taino roots of Puerto Rican identity and satisfies the requirements of sacred union.

The myth of woman reflects the cultural conflicts of masculine conquest. Mary-like virginity and "primitive" lasciviousness both exist through rites permitting sexual expression. "During these festivals it is reported that the women displayed an abandon and gross sensuality which did not represent their normal character at all. The participants might be respectable members of the society in everyday life."[13] María Soledad abandons the role of innocent housewife and gives herself to the being she considers her true lover. The male characters fail sexually

11. Esther M. Harding, *Woman's Mysteries* (New York: Harper and Row, 1971), p. 64.
12. Ibid., p. 93.
13. Ibid., p. 92.

because they cannot compete with the god, the Cemí, who can achieve sexual union by means of the moon. María Soledad does not dance nude for Ricardo: the ritual dance is reserved for the Cemí. Man can only be an intermediary. Here is a reversal of Christian tradition, in which the Virgin is the intermediary needed for the birth of the Son. In the Taino meaning of *María Soledad*, man is an intermediary enabling God's sexual union with woman. Woman is her own mistress, firmly defending her body and her rights over it and defying the bourgeois idea of woman as man's property. María Soledad guards her body like a pre-Christian woman devoted to a god. For her, a flesh-and-blood man, existing in time, is not enough. She can only achieve orgasm with God, existing in eternity. In a certain sense, her refusal to become man's property is a metaphor of woman's liberation.

When we look beyond the feminist implications of the text, we see it also makes a statement about the male myth Indian culture has embedded in the Puerto Rican subconscious. The male god Cemí strives to reclaim his rightful place in history. For him, the woman should maintain her virginity in order to give herself in the rite of sacred prostitution. "If the rituals of sacred prostitution are examined in this light it becomes evident that the ancients felt it to be essential that every woman should once in her life give herself, not to one particular man, for love of him, that is for personal reasons, but to the goddess, to her own instinct, to the Eros principle within herself."[14] The idol would no doubt agree with this statement. The woman, giving herself to him, restores to him his rightful heritage—ethnic, historical, and mythic. Woman is also a metaphor of cultural "property rights" because she has the power to give back the usurped legacy of Indian culture and gods.

The play's myth of woman then takes on yet another metaphorical dimension, one harking back to the pagan sacred prostitute. This regression to pre-Christian sexuality occurs when María Soledad disrobes to dance for Ricardo, in front of the Cemí. "Women who resided in the sacred precincts of the Divine Ancestress took their lovers from among the community, making love to those who came to the temple to pay honor to the Goddess. Among these people the act of sex was considered to

14. Ibid., p. 144.

be sacred, so holy and precious that it was enacted within the house of the Creatress of heaven, earth and all life."[15] The characters in the play do not carry the notion of sacred prostitution to its consummation because they are inhibited by contemporary Western culture. Ricardo does not understand that his role is to be the god's intermediary; Luis cannot accept such a ritual, for it would be an affront to his masculine honor; and María Soledad cannot free herself from her mental set. Even without sexual union, the value of the ritual is affirmed. The erotic bond between the woman and the Cemí grows so powerful that María Soledad is transformed into the moon itself. As she becomes a moon goddess, the mystical union with the Cemí leaves her virginity intact. This is, of course, what happens in the Mary story, in which virginity is retained through conception and birth. "It is in this sense that the moon goddess can rightly be called virgin."[16] Both the Cemí and María Soledad are idolatrous representations of the moon, androgynous by nature. "Thus the goddess has the same name as the god, the same attributes and powers, or perhaps she has the feminine version of his more masculine qualities. They form a pair, undifferentiated except in sex."[17] María Soledad becomes the powerful goddess figure of prehistorical times, a metaphor of the moon, and rules over her ancestral queendom as the Venus of pre-Hispanic Puerto Rico.

María Soledad shows the Latin American cultural conflict in one aspect: modern Europeanized existence versus the persistent Indian cultural concepts that may rear their head. However, we must keep in mind that this tug-of-war between cultural sets is really between three competing elements: Indian, European, and African. For this reason, it is useful to look at an Afro-Cuban play, *Réquiem por Yarini* by Carlos Felipe. Again, cultural dissonance is at issue and the mythic projection of woman receives attention.

The Yarini of Felipe's play is based on an actual person. Yarini was a fabled pimp and a prominent figure in the sexual underworld. For Felipe, Yarini reveals unexpected insights into the persistence of Afro culture in Cuba: he is an affirmation of Afro culture against Spanish colonialism. His awareness of the world is collective, in opposition to bourgeois individualism. Felipe

15. Steiner, *The Island*, p. 154.
16. Harding, *Woman's Mysteries*, p. 104.
17. Ibid., p. 104.

points out the antibourgeois and anti-Marxist implications of Afro-Cuban sexual mysticism.

To understand what Yarini shows about the image of woman, let us consider the type of statements this character makes. For Yarini, "The pimp is very close to being a god who feels compassion for men."[18] He sees himself as performing a merciful service by providing men with women who will satisfy their longing for love and beauty. In this, Yarini echoes to some extent the Catholic notion of the marriage sacrament. That is to say, woman is the biological remedy for all the ills of men, the balm that will soothe and comfort them. However, this Christian concept is not very favorable to women. In effect, woman becomes an object and is wholly the possession of male sexuality. But a close analysis of the play discloses that Yarini's image of woman is much more positive. Woman becomes not merely the agent of man's satisfaction, but takes on a more exalted role as a goddess—as in sacred prostitution. The *hieros gamos* concept gives her access to knowledge and the power to determine matters of life and death.

Yarini initially appears as a Don Juan figure. He competes with Lotot, echoing the sexual rivalry between Don Juan and his fellow lady-killer. Their efforts to win over La Santiaguera parallel the bet in *Don Juan* over who will win Inés's favors. The metaphor of woman, however, is different. Inés has an immaculate convent life in imitation of the Virgin Mary, so Don Juan in effect lives out his adventures in an ambience of Mary worship. La Santiaguera has instead a tainted life within a convent whose rules are those of sacred prostitution. The Afro-Cuban world is opposed to the Catholic dogma through the intercession of the Virgin (Inés). Orthodox Catholicism is thus able to reconcile two Spanish archetypes: Don Juan and the Virgin.

Felipe alters this Catholic-Spanish picture just as Catholicism itself was forced to change during the Spanish conquest of Cuba, when modifications accommodated Indian and African religions within Catholicism. These blended religions also had the function of easing the conflicts produced by white supremacy. The Marian cult, strong in Spain, weakened in the

18. Carlos Felipe, *Réquiem por Yarini*, in *Teatro cubano* (Las Villas, Cuba: Universidad de Las Villas, 1961), p. 68. For additional discussion of this work, see my book *Persona, vida y máscara en el teatro cubano* (Miami: Ediciones Universal, 1973), pp. 284–302.

Caribbean under African influence, and other figures appeared next to the objects of orthodox Catholic worship. Especially important for our analysis is Changó, a Yoruba god who is a licentious hermaphrodite, willing to do anything to gain erotic satisfaction.

Réquiem por Yarini reflects this cultural history. The hero is white, but his concept of *hieros gamos* is heavily African influenced. He starts out as apparently a Spanish-style Don Juan, but in his person reveals the changes Afro-Cuban culture wrought in the Spanish concept of Don Juan. He in fact "naturalizes" Don Juan, claiming this originally Spanish figure for Cuba by Africanizing him. The entire work is a proclamation of the Yoruba tribal religion, brought to Cuba by slaves. It is this myth that can save Yarini, who experiences rituals that are far from Christian, such as an Afro-Cuban exorcism. Changó succeeds in imposing his sexuality and his kingdom. As happened with the Cemí, the representative of the enslaved culture conquers the conqueror.

Since *Yarini* has a male hero, one could easily overlook the key importance of the myth of woman in this work. Just as Don Juan becomes Afro, so does the Mary cult. The adoration of virgin's blood becomes a sacred ritual of prostitution. The bordello becomes a temple, a convent of sexuality, where priestesses devote themselves to the phallic cult of Changó, represented by Yarini. On the most visible level, there are two antagonistic forces. On the one side is the well-ordered, "civilized" white community, represented by the forces of the palace, government agents who seek to destroy Yarini. On the other side is the "primitive" religious community, needing no "civilization," Afro, represented by the bordello and Changó's agents, who seek to save Yarini. The action culminates in the hero's death, in his apparent destruction. But this is only a temporary victory for the established order. Through the rites of *hieros gamos* and marriage in death, Yarini is saved for eternal life. In this case, as in that of Don Juan, woman is the agent of divine intervention, represented by La Macorina, a beautiful prostitute who has been dead for some years. She is the one who leads Yarini to the transcendental realm. This afterlife is not a material victory but a spiritual one. The woman wins Yarini for eternal pleasure.

On the earthly-Afro level, the bordello is the temple and La Jabá the prostitute priestess who reigns over the cult of Changó/

Yarini. Beyond this earthly arrangement is a religious structure, with a transcendent order that wants to pull Yarini in, to draw him into the kingdom of death. This order is ruled by the legendary La Macorina, whose voice on earth is La Santiaguera. La Macorina possesses the earthly woman's body to attract and "destroy" the hero. So, Afro-Cuban myth presents three metaphorical signs of woman: (a) La Jabá, the priestess, who reclaims for woman her prestige as a religious actor and a natural intermediary of the divinity, whose role is to serve in temples and guard the secrets of the cult; (b) La Santiaguera, the agent of the orgiastic abandon and sexual freedom women are reputed to have enjoyed in primitive matriarchal societies; and (c) La Macorina, transformed into a goddess with the exuberant body of a primitive Venus. Together they are three aspects of one underlying female reality in a process of transformation. The three women form a sacred sexual cult and live out an erotic ritual centered on a symbol, Yarini, who is the earthly representation of Changó. While Yarini believes that he possesses the women, they actually possess him. La Jabá is the woman in charge of his earthly world, his "temple," and must protect him from evil. Yarini's fate on earth depends on La Jabá. La Santiaguera possesses him sexually. Though this woman is a package of sexual goods in Yarini's and Lotot's rivalry, she moves out of this "merchandise" role. Yarini's attraction to her lures him to his destruction, possessed by desire.

La Macorina, already dead, is the strongest of these manifestations of woman. As queen, she is the one to rule on life and death. She obtains the ultimate satisfaction of *hieros gamos* in the kingdom of the afterlife. Both La Jabá and La Macorina represent knowledge, in this world and the other, which links these characters to the mythic tradition of female wisdom represented by Metis in Greek antiquity and Eve in the Old Testament. La Macorina is also associated with the knowledge that allows woman to dominate sexually. She is the supreme prostitute of the temple, its goddess, who guides Yarini through erotic experiences leading to transcendental sexual knowledge. Like the Egyptian myth of Isis sexually revitalizing Osiris in the afterworld, La Macorina revives, in her realm beyond death, the virility of the man she has conquered. By assigning women these magic strengths, the play restores to women the powerful role they enjoyed in prehistoric myth. Woman reclaims her divine status through such metaphorically charged strong women. In his Afro-Cuban cultural context, Yarini can experience La Macorina's antivirginal taintedness, just as the Spanish Don Juan enjoys the untainted virginity of Inés. In both cases a religious concept is upheld (Afro-Cuban or Christian) and the woman is the means of salvation. Immaculate Inés, an agent of Catholicism and the Spanish social order, reaches out to the sinner to take him, via sanctified union, down the road to eternal joy. Contaminated with eroticism, La Macorina, agent of Afro-Cubanism, a rebellious resurgence of the conquered culture, likewise offers to take the sinner, via the *hieros gamos*, down the path of heavenly joy. The Virgin and the prostitute are as one in carrying out the sacred rites of death.

Both the Puerto Rican and the Cuban plays present myths of women in remarkably favorable terms. The positive, strong image of woman is not readily apparent, for each play features a male deity whom women passionately worship. Nonetheless, analysis shows that it is precisely in their role as worshipers that the women come to assume a much more dominant role than first appears.

In *María Soledad*, the heroine has broken free of the bourgeois Western requirement that she be her husband's possession. She reclaims her body and chooses to dedicate it to the cult of the Cemí, in which she occupies a high priestess role. The flesh-and-blood men in her life become her inferiors. She spurns them for her priestess duties and nearly makes one her attendant in a rite of sacred prostitution. The woman approaches apotheosis while the men become her perplexed and inept suitors, excluded from the special bond between a human woman and a god-lover who elevates her to priestess-goddess status.

In *Yarini*, the initial impression is of a Don Juan figure who exercises control over women. However, the more we know about Yarini's three chief women, the clearer it is that he is far from possessing or manipulating them. Through their cult worship of the pre-Spanish god they see in Yarini, these women assume power over him, guiding him even beyond death and into an afterworld governed by female wisdom. Again the woman's drive to achieve sexual union with a god results in the increased exercise of her magic and mythic powers.

In both plays, the *hieros gamos* concept is highly favorable to woman. The strength attributed to women does not correspond to the Catholic notion of "perfect union," in which woman is not the possessor of such powerful forces and knowledge. Rather, it corresponds to a pre-Hispanic cultural set in which matriarchal elements are likely to be extremely strong. This non-Christian notion of *hieros gamos*, resurfacing in two modern plays, privileges the women it mythifies with wisdom, power to control, and, above all, special access to the gods through sexual union. While these mighty, arcane, and highly eroticized myths of woman were officially displaced by the Catholicism of the conquerors, the two plays we have just examined remind us of their latent persistence in Caribbean culture and their ability to manifest themselves even in the most Europeanized settings.

8 From Dusky Venus to Mater Dolorosa: The Female Protagonist in the Cuban Antislavery Novel

Lorna V. Williams

During the nineteenth century, it was generally assumed throughout the Americas that blacks were creatures of nature rather than of culture. Since blacks were primarily engaged in agricultural tasks, the essence of their being was readily equated with the field of their economic activities. In the case of the black woman, the tendency to perceive her as an elemental creature was even more pronounced because she shared the social environment of the black male and consequently was displaced from the moral domain assigned to the members of her sex. In a slave society like nineteenth-century Cuba, where social contact between blacks and whites was regulated by custom and by law, the black woman came to be regarded as an exotic presence, at once a productive member of the society, yet outside the prevailing norms of accepted feminine behavior.

Writers who attempted to portray the social conditions of the time invariably represent the black woman in paradoxical terms. On the one hand, the black female protagonist, whether slave or free, is usually presented as a figure of incomparable beauty, thereby setting her over and against all other women. However, the literary exaltation of black beauty in a slave society implies a negation of the values of the existing social order. Consequently, there is a retreat from the disruptive implications embedded in the celebration of black female beauty. Even though the female protagonist is said to be remarkably beautiful, she is shown, on the other hand, to be beautiful in a superficial sense, possessing merely beauty of body and, therefore, a fundamental incapacity to evoke genuine admiration.

At the same time, there is a disjuncture between the protagonist's outward appearance and her innermost desires. While her body seems to point only in the direction of sensual pleasure, she experiences her body primarily as the means through which to improve her socially marginal status. For her, satisfying the erotic desires of others is secondary to her own attempt to find fulfillment within the setting of the nuclear family.

121

For women in nineteenth-century Cuba, the ability to achieve domestic bliss depended on the strength of their own family ties. Parents exchanged their daughters for suitable marriage partners.[1] But in the novels to be discussed in this essay, the black women are all members of a disintegrated kinship system. Separated from their parents for one reason or another, the female protagonists are without effective mediators for giving them in marriage. Thus, their basic desire for domesticity stands in marked contrast to their inability to achieve it.

The disparity between the protagonist's aspirations and her lack of the sociocultural means of fulfilling them is also expressed in the love relationship that constitutes the thematic focus of the novels. In all three instances, the black woman is the object of the competing desires of two racially different men. She herself merely seeks to be happily married to the man who is racially similar to her. However, because she is a virtual orphan and therefore outside the system of marital exchange, she is denied the possibility of resolving the opposition between the rivals in a manner that would be satisfactory to her.

The polar categories with which all three novels abound serve to place their treatment of the black woman in the realms of myth. According to Claude Lévi-Strauss, the mythical mode of thought is essentially dualistic. Grounded in a conceptual framework of binary oppositions, myth presents relationships that are at once contradictory and identical. However, in the course of the narrative, a third term is generated in an effort to overcome the contradictions inherent in the mythical view of the world.[2] Given the "constituent ambiguity of mythical speech,"[3] the characters who express its intentions are portrayed as eternal essences even though they are embedded in history. Since myth presents characters in action without offering a causal interpretation of their behavior, it empties human conduct of historical meaning, thereby transforming history into nature.[4] As a result, the temporal perspective in myth is

1. See Verena Martínez-Alier, *Marriage, Class and Colour in Nineteenth-Century Cuba: A Study of Racial Attitudes and Sexual Values in a Slave Society* (London: Cambridge University Press, 1974), pp. 11–21.

2. Claude Lévi-Strauss, "The Structural Study of Myth," *Myth: A Symposium*, ed. Thomas A. Sebeok (1955; rpt., Bloomington: Indiana University Press, 1974), pp. 83–92, 96–103.

3. Roland Barthes, *Mythologies*, trans. Annette Lavers (1963; rpt., New York: Hill and Wang, 1972), p. 124.

4. Ibid., pp. 121–27, 129–31, 142–43.

double. The narrative moves forward in time even as it points toward a timeless dimension. The characters enact events that take place in a particular moment and that are necessarily non-revertible. Yet, in the words of Lévi-Strauss, "the specific pattern described is everlasting."[5] Moreover, according to Scholes and Kellogg, the mediating devices of myth serve to resolve catastrophe.[6] Since myth, in this view, is "the expression in story form of deep-seated human concerns, fears, and aspirations,"[7] the tragic outcome of the narrative would identify it as an attempt to mediate an irresolvable contradiction.

For example, the social world depicted in the Cuban antislavery novel is polarized along the axes of race, sex, and class. Blacks are opposed to whites, men to women, masters to slaves. The constituent elements of each of these polar categories seem fundamentally different from each other: whites are the embodiment of civilization, blacks of barbarism; men act, women and slaves are house-bound and/or plantation-bound. Yet, beneath the apparent differences, the members of each contrary pair are profoundly similar. The master in Anselmo Suárez y Romero's *Francisco* and in Antonio Zambrana's *El negro Francisco (Black Francisco)* who falls in love with his own slave relinquishes his freedom and thereby becomes as metaphorically enslaved to passion as she is enslaved in fact. The male protagonist of *Cecilia Valdés* who admits to an inexplicable preference for black women reveals himself to be as much a creature of instinct as is Cecilia.

Like Cecilia Valdés, Suárez y Romero's Dorotea and Zambrana's Camila are mulatto and therefore occupy a racial position midway between blacks and whites. Dorotea and Camila are both house slaves and as such, they, like Cecilia Valdés, the free black, are socially halfway between masters and field slaves. By virtue of the social gap that separates them from the average black, the three women are located at a cultural midpoint between "uncivilized" Africans and "civilized" *criollos* (American-born whites). Thus, all three women are ideally suited to act as intermediaries between members of the opposing groups.

5. *Myth: A Symposium*, pp. 84–85, 87.
6. *The Nature of Narrative* (New York: Oxford University Press, 1966), pp. 234–35.
7. Ibid., p. 220.

Because they are situated between contrary terms, these women are marked by the duality inherent in their indeterminate position. Considered the social superiors of the dark-skinned Pimienta and the African-born Franciscos, they are the social inferiors of the white master. Their beauty, the very quality that renders them irresistible to both black and white men, becomes, in the course of the narrative, their tragic flaw. In all three instances, the women's interaction with black men is seen as socially regressive in that it leads the men to commit some form of murder. On the other hand, the women's relations with white men are regarded as unnatural because, in each case, that relation results in a form of incest. Thus, the female protagonist of the antislavery novel is presented as an aberration from both nature and society because the narrative erodes the middle ground on which she is initially placed.

In the prologue to *Francisco*, Suárez y Romero refers to the historical circumstances prevailing in Cuba at the time the novel was written (it was begun in 1838 and published in 1880). He mentions, for example, the official practice of censoring antislavery material. Similarly, both Cirilo Villaverde and Antonio Zambrana refer in their texts to contemporary historical events, such as the abolitionist movement and the incipient movement for national independence. Nevertheless, the female protagonist of all three novels exists on the margins of history. For her, the narrative becomes an origin myth in that it recounts how she came to repeat her mother's fate. Inasmuch as she appears to be her mother's equivalent, she is displaced from the linearity of the historical process because her future will be identical with her past. As a result, the empirical world that she seems to inhabit is transformed into the mythical realm of the eternal feminine.

For instance, in the opening paragraphs of Zambrana's *El negro Francisco* (1875), Camila, the female protagonist, is seemingly individualized when the narrator states that she is "una joven mulata (. . .) de sorprendente hermosura" (a young mulatto woman of surprising beauty).[8] However, when we are subsequently given a detailed description of the character, it is

8. Havana: Editorial Letras Cubanas, 1979, p. 24. Further references to this

evident that she has assumed a supra-personal identity:

> Ese tipo: la mulata hija de blanco es, como tipo físico, una maravilla que trae a la memoria las sirenas de la leyenda; la mujer en que se encarna bien posee un don superior al de la hermosura, el de la gracia, es decir, que posee esa elegancia espontánea que hace con el algodón lo que se puede hacer con el terciopelo. . . .
> Camila poseía la mayor pompa y el mayor encanto que son dables en el tipo. (p. 30)

> That type: the mulatto daughter of a white man is, as a physical type, a marvel who reminds you of the legendary sirens; the woman who embodies it well possesses a gift superior to beauty: namely, charm; that is to say, she possesses that spontaneous elegance which does with cotton what can be done with velvet. . . .
> Camila possessed the greatest style and charm possible in the type.

Through the narrator's superlatives and the reference to the mythological sirens, Camila's race ceases to be a simple biological fact and acquires symbolic significance. Once racial origin is imputed to be the privileged source of Camila's allure, her physical appearance is presented as a force for social disorder rather than as a sign of her existence as an individual:

> Había en ella no lo que causa la suave embriaguez de su alma, sino lo que enciende la delirante embriaguez de los sentidos. La morbidez de sus formas, la felina gracia de sus movimientos, su palpitante seno, sus labios hechos para el beso más que para la palabra, su voz en cuyos tonos se adivinaba esa dulce flexibilidad que hace tan ardientes las caricias del lenguaje; su profusa y ondulante caballera, su talle, que tenía el imprevisto repliegue de la serpiente, y sobre todo sus ojos, negros, húmedos y lánguidos ojos, que parecían contener apasionadas y misteriosas promesas: todo hacía de ella la Venus radiante y espléndida de quien se enamora la materia y no la psiquis. (p. 52)

> There was in her not what causes the gentle rapture of the soul, but what excites the delirious rapture of the senses. Her soft shape, the feline grace of her movements, her palpitating breast,

---

work are cited parenthetically in the text by page number. All translations in the text are by the author.

her lips made for kisses rather than speech, her voice, in whose
tones one detected that sweet inflection which makes the
caresses of language so passionate; her thick, wavy hair, her waist
which had the unexpected coils of a serpent, and above all, her
eyes, black, tearful and languid eyes, which seemed to contain
passionate, mysterious promises: everything made her a radiant,
splendid Venus, with whose body one falls in love rather than her
soul.

As a paradigm of seduction, Camila exists primarily as an
object of erotic desire for men. Thus, even though she was
brought up like a daughter by the Orellanas, she arouses sexual
desire in Carlos, her "hermano de juego" (brother in play). Similarly, despite the negation of African heritage that she initially
represents for Francisco, she eventually inspires his undying
love. In this regard, Doña Josefa's attempt to consider Camila as
a "monja enclaustrada" (cloistered nun) (p. 68), an asexual
being who should never marry, appears to be a betrayal of
Camila's essential self. For the narrator's obsessive focus on
Camila's anatomy and his repeated references to her mulatto
origins suggest that for Camila, the fall into nature is inevitable.

Just as Camila's elegant clothing is said to be incapable of
masking the provocativeness of her body, so too the culture to
which she was exposed in the Orellana household proves incapable of erasing the memory of her dead mother's example. And
even though Camila thinks that by identifying with Francisco
she has made a conscious break with her natural heritage, her
relations with Francisco signify a closer step toward that past
inasmuch as Francisco is the embodiment of the racial past.
Moreover, when Camila is obliged to yield to Carlos's advances
in an effort to save Francisco's life, she reenacts the primal scene
of her own beginnings. Her recognition at that moment of her
similarity to her mother signifies the collapse of the temporal
distinction between two generations of women.

As a mulatto living in a slave society, Camila, like her mother,
bears visible testimony of the sexual resolution of the opposition
between blacks and whites—a situation that is perpetuated by
Camila's relationship with Carlos. Yet, the social distance separating master and slave makes it impossible to acknowledge this
means of overcoming the polarity between the racial groups, for
the conjunction of master and slave introduces a discontinuity
in the social order. Since sexual relations between master and

slave subvert the established pattern of social intercourse, continuity in society can only be restored by a drastic reversal of the social irregularity. Carlos's betrayal of his civilized aspect will be counterbalanced by Francisco's betrayal of his physical nature when the slave commits suicide. And as the being who lured both men into acts of social excess, Camila must compensate for her transgression by languishing in madness until her death.

Camila's ultimate fate merely dramatizes her lifelong situation. Her lapse into madness graphically exposes her existence as a creature whose function is to be rather than to act. Having been defined as a member of a biologically determined class, she can exist only within the material contours of her biological category. And her exclusion from the sociohistorical domain is exemplified by the fact that her only significant act results in catastrophe for her and for the natural term of the racial polarities that she mediates. On the other hand, Carlos, the historical pole of the relationship, is not adversely affected by his contact with Camila.

Zambrana's emphasis on Camila's genealogy calls attention to the disproportionate influence of the two ethnic traditions conjoined in Camila's person. While her *criollo* ancestry is the source of her cultural aspect, her African heritage is believed to pollute that aspect so irremediably that it reduces all her learned behavior to the level of the irrational. Paradoxically, in Camila's case, the *criollo* influence that predominates in the sociohistorical realm is incapable of negating the primal antisocial force that the African element evidently represents in the symbolic order. And since sexuality is the domain in which the black threat to the sociocultural order is expressed, Camila's relationships with men are necessarily self-destructive.

By presenting Camila as a symbol of defeat, Zambrana neutralizes the threat represented by black female sexuality, particularly insofar as it appears as a natural force whose primary purpose is to distract the white master from his social responsibility of founding a family. Hence, Camila is only permitted to express her sexuality outside the accepted system of marital exchange, thereby signaling her devaluation as a social being. The intent to displace Camila from the sociohistorical realm culminates in her loss of sanity. But since insanity is a socially defined state, Zambrana's attempt to reduce Camila's existence to its biological aspect leaves her still anchored in the social domain. Even though in his text Zambrana suspends the connection between black female sexuality and its social mediation, thereby causing the seductiveness of the black woman to appear as a physical given, he locates his protagonist between the great house and the asylum, and thereby allows the reader to perceive the sociocultural framing of an existence that the author seeks to portray as natural. Camila's overpowering sensuality, which Zambrana presents as a statement of fact, thus derives from the author's mythical intention to empty his protagonist's biography of its contingency and to equate her entire existence with the unfolding of the single attribute of physical love.

Similarly, in Anselmo Suárez y Romero's *Francisco* (1839), Dorotea, the female protagonist, embodies the black woman whose sexual allure places her outside the boundaries of social legitimacy. But whereas Camila's love for Francisco was unconsummated, rendered impossible through Carlos's mediation, Dorotea's relationship with Francisco produces a daughter. Thus, to a certain extent, Dorotea fulfills the unique social function for which the presence of women in literature has usually been required.

Unlike her white owner, Dorotea is not permitted to regard her child as an extension of her social authority. Since the daughter is the product of a union not sanctioned by her culture, she cannot be regarded as a sign of genealogical continuity because she lacks a nameable father. Without a patriarchal line to define her identity, Dorotea's child can only serve as proof of her mother's irregular sexual conduct, just as Dorotea herself attests to her mother's sexual excesses. Mother and child are therefore different from each other, but also similar to each other since both lack a socially recognized origin.

Dorotea's awareness of her child's identity as a metaphorical orphan leads her to seek to give her daughter a family history by legitimizing her relationship with Francisco. But the fact that her daughter's birth precedes the rite through which familial continuity is ensured means that Dorotea will be unable to erase her daughter's equivocal origin. Marriage in this case is rendered unnecessary because it would not reverse the cycle of sexual irregularity that Dorotea and her daughter represent.

Interestingly enough, the conception of her daughter marks the end of Dorotea's sexual relations with Francisco. Thereafter, she assumes the paradoxical identity of a virgin mother, whose virtue belies the evidence of her sexual experience. On the other hand, her daughter's birth heightens her desirability for Ricardo, her "hermano de leche" (foster brother) inasmuch as her daughter's existence signals her violation of the moral code of orderly succession. To Ricardo, Dorotea is now beyond morality and therefore free from the cultural constraints against consummating his passion:

> —yo debía desde el principio, desde que te azoraste porque te propuse que vivirías conmigo, haberte pegado un puntapié. ¿De cuándo acá tanta virtud, señorita? ¿No se acuerda usted de lo que hizo con Francisco, no se acuerda de la barriga que tuvo en la Habana? ¡Y ahora se escandaliza la muy sinvergüenza! (p. 149)[9]

> "Right from the start, ever since you got upset because I proposed that you live with me, I should have kicked you. Whence all that virtue, young lady? Don't you remember what you did with Francisco? Don't you remember the stomach you had in Havana? And now the very shameless woman is scandalized!"

Thus, motherhood removes Dorotea from the natural sexual process even as it calls attention to her sexual nature.

The incongruence between Dorotea's past sexual activity and her present chastity leaves her morally defenseless against Ricardo. And since her enforced separation from Francisco excludes her from any social claim to having founded a family, she must perform her maternal function without the customary male defender of her family honor. Indeed, it is she who assumes this symbolic role when she intercedes to save Francisco from the overseer's whip. Nevertheless, she is unable to shield her daughter from Ricardo's anger when her daughter receives the blows intended for Dorotea. Like another Virgin Mary, she is reduced to being a helpless onlooker at her child's physical suffering.

The metaphorical link between Dorotea and the Virgin Mary is underscored when Dorotea makes a final effort to strengthen her fragile family structure:

> Veíase ciertamente en un gran conflicto para una muchacha de condición esclava y de sus pocos años: o dejar que Francisco muriese por su causa, o libertarlo de tantos infortunios a costa del

---

9. Citations are from Anselmo Suárez y Romero, *Francisco: El ingenio o Las delicias del campo* (Miami: Mnemosyne Publishing, 1969).

más tremendo sacrificio . . . . Cuando acabó de estas reflexiones, acostó a Lutgarda, que ya se había dormido, y se arrodilló delante de una Virgen de los Dolores implorando su misericordia. Esas oraciones, la esperanza de que el Cielo se lastima de nosotros cuando padecemos en este valle de miserias, y el comparar sus pesadumbres con las que tendría la Madre del Señor, viendo crucificado por los infieles al hijo de sus entrañas, la fueron consolando poco a poco. (p. 167)

Certainly, for a very young slave girl, she found herself in a big predicament: either to let Francisco die because of her, or to free him from his many misfortunes through the greatest sacrifice. . . . When she finished these reflections, she put to bed Lutgarda who had already fallen asleep, and she knelt before Our Lady of Sorrows, imploring her mercy. Those prayers, the hope that Heaven takes pity on us when we suffer in this vale of misery, and comparing her grief with that of the Mother of our Lord, as she watched her son being crucified by the heathen,—all this consoled her little by little.

In equating Dorotea's situation with that of the Virgin, the paradigmatic Christian portrait of suffering, Suárez y Romero points to the futility of Dorotea's gesture. At the same time, the author introduces a significant variation on the Christian myth[10] in that Dorotea, the grieving mother, will not mourn the loss of a child. Instead, she will mourn the loss of her child's father, whose absence will become definitive when he commits suicide. Presumably, as the novel's retrospective focus suggests, the daughter who survives will, in turn, reproduce her mother's experience.

The cyclical pattern of female destiny that forms Zambrana's *El negro Francisco (Black Francisco)* and Suárez y Romero's *Francisco* is also evident in Cirilo Villaverde's *Cecilia Valdés o La loma del Angel* (1839). Like Zambrana's Camila and Suárez y Romero's Dorotea, Villaverde's protagonist is a dusky Venus endowed with the fatal sexuality possessed by her mother. Nevertheless, Cecilia's equivocal origin poses a greater threat to the sociocultural order than that of Camila or Dorotea. Whereas Camila and Dorotea were slaves like their mothers before them, and as

10. Here I use the word *myth* in the original Greek sense of "a traditional tale." Regarding this definition, see G. S. Kirk, *Myth: Its Meaning and Functions in Ancient and Other Cultures* (Cambridge: Cambridge University Press, 1970), p. 8.

such had a clearly defined position within the social hierarchy, Cecilia, like her own mother, is born free in a slave society and therefore represents instability within the social order. Hence, Cecilia seems white, even though she is not; she thinks she is a Valdés, but she is not.

Cecilia's ignorance of her own origin causes the Oedipus theme, latent in the two previously discussed works, to become explicit in Villaverde's novel. In a manner reminiscent of Sophocles' hero, Villaverde's protagonist fails to recognize a relative, and therefore she violates sacred familial bonds by engaging in sexual relations with a blood relative and bringing about his violent death. Moreover, Cecilia meets her tragic end precisely because of the steps she takes to avoid the fate that was determined for her.

The implacable sequence of events is set in motion when Cecilia's father rejects her at birth by denying her his name so as not to jeopardize his position within his legally constituted family and in the larger society. The child is therefore removed to an orphanage where the conferral of the name Valdés effects the necessary legal break between father and daughter. The child is also separated from her mother, who by then has gone crazy with the thought that the virtually white child despised having a colored mother. The child's detachment from her mother becomes definitive through the conspiracy of silence surrounding her mother's existence. As a result, Cecilia grows up not knowing her true parents.

Despite her physical separation from both parents, Cecilia is still recognized as her mother's daughter. Several women in the neighborhood perceive Cecilia's striking resemblance to her mother, and the wet nurse employed by her father to transfer her to and from the orphanage knows that Cecilia is his daughter. Nevertheless, Cecilia herself is blind to the evidence of her identity. When she accidentally wanders into her father's neighborhood and her ancestry is questioned by her half-sisters and her father's wife, she denies having either a living mother or father. Her statement, "Yo conozco a ese hombre que está ahí acostado" (I know that man lying down over there),[11] is singularly ironic, because while she recognizes Don Cándido Gam-

---

11. Havana: Consejo Nacional de Cultura, 1964, p. 37. Further references to this work are cited parenthetically in the text by page number.

boa visually, she seems unaware that he is her father. Nor does she perceive her resemblance to one of her half-sisters, which others will point out. Her grandmother's subsequent allusions to her identity are interpreted by Cecilia as a rhetorical gesture rather than as the truth about her origins:

> —Vamos, dime, hija mía, ¿qué harías tú si tu protector, tu amigo constante, tu único apoyo en el mundo, como si dijéramos, tu mismo padre, que es verdaderamente un padre para nosotras pobres, desvalidas mujeres, sin otro amparo bajo el cielo, ¿qué harías tú si te aconsejaba, vamos, si te prohibía el que hicieras una cosa? Di, ¿tú lo harías? ¿Tú le desobedecerías? (p. 208)

> "Now, tell me, my child, what would you do if your protector, your constant friend, your only support in the world, let's say, your own father, who is really a father to us, poor, helpless women, without any other support under the sun, what would you do if he advised you, or rather, if he forbade you to do something? Tell me, would you do it? Would you disobey him?"

The logic with which Cecilia refutes her grandmother's argument is basically sound, but she neglects to follow her deductions to their logical conclusion and therefore misconstrues the testimony of her own eyes and ears:

> —Pues bien, el tal no se puede tener en rigor por viejo. Le sobra el dinero y ha sido toda su vida, según dice mamita, un correntón y enamorado como hay pocos. Hasta ayer, como quien dice, según me ha contado mamita, a pesar de ser casado y con hijos, mantenía mujeres, con preferencia las de color. Ha perdido más muchachas que pelos tiene en su cabeza; y mamita parece empeñada en hacerme creer que su generosidad conmigo es inocente y desinteresada. Quien no lo conozca que lo compre. (p. 211)

> "Well, the gentleman in question can't really be considered old. He has a lot of money and according to Mammy, all his life he has been a playboy and lover like none. Up to yesterday, as it were, from what Mammy has told me, even though he was married and had children, he kept women, preferably colored women. He has ruined more young girls than the hairs on his head; and Mammy seems intent on making me believe that his generosity to me is innocent and disinterested. You can buy that only if you don't know him."

Thus, once again, an opposition exists between knowledge and truth because Cecilia's presumed knowledge of Don Cándido's character does not enable her to decipher the true meaning of his actions toward her. The concordant set of reasons that should reveal her actual relationship to him are perceived by Cecilia as merely signs of the inconceivable.

As the two passages quoted above indicate, the absent father, whom Cecilia considers dead, is the primary source of parental authority in her family. He not only takes care of Cecilia's economic needs, but he also makes the major decisions about her welfare and even attempts to discipline her behavior. Consequently, he arouses hostility, fear, and resentment. On the other hand, Don Cándido stands as a model of the ideal love object. While Cecilia refuses to identify with him in reality, she assumes that identification at the level of unconscious desire, as is evident in the following statement: "mucho que sí me gustan más los blancos que los pardos. Se me caería la cara de vergüenza si me casara y tuviera un hijo *saltoutrás*" ("It's true that I prefer white men a lot more than mulattoes. I would die of shame if I got married and had a throwback child") (p. 358). Since mulattoes are the group to which both her natural mother and her surrogate mother belong, Cecilia's stated preference for white men represents a rejection of her mother and an embrace of her father.

Cecilia's disavowal of her father means that Don Cándido himself cannot become the object of her conscious desire. Nevertheless, the repressed attachment to her father manifests itself in another form when Cecilia transfers her affections to Leonardo, Don Cándido's son. The warnings expressed by both Don Cándido and Cecilia's grandmother against this alliance are misconstrued and unheeded because their message is contrary to Cecilia's desire. As a result, Cecilia becomes Leonardo's mistress and bears him a daughter.

When Cecilia's jealousy causes Leonardo's death on his wedding day, the very situation occurs that both Don Cándido and Cecilia's grandmother had sought to prevent during her childhood. By withholding his name from her and thus symbolically expelling her from his family, Don Cándido had hoped to divert misfortune from his home. Similarly, by separating Cecilia from her natural mother, her grandmother had expected to deflect disaster from her household. Despite their precautions, Cecilia's persistence in satisfying her desires in a socially unacceptable manner brings about the catastrophe that both father and surrogate mother had attempted to ward off.

That Leonardo is killed unintentionally—Cecilia had intended his bride to be murdered instead—does not diminish Cecilia's transgression because she has already committed incest. The commitment of unnatural acts like incest and fratricide demand the ritual expulsion of the wrongdoer in order to protect the community from the danger of pollution. Thus, after Leonardo's death, Cecilia is not permitted to continue living as before. At the instigation of Leonardo's mother, she is made to expiate her twin crimes against society by being confined to the same mental institution in which her mother languishes to death.

In retracing the steps of her own beginnings, a return underscored by the final embrace of mother and daughter in the hospital, Cecilia finds herself in the very situation that she had attempted to avoid. Rather than becoming the wife of a white man, and therefore inscribing herself in the sociohistorical order, Cecilia must resign herself to having been the temporary mistress of one and giving birth to his daughter, just like her mother, her grandmother, and her great-grandmother. What had appeared to be an opportunity to attain what neither her natural mother nor her surrogate mother had achieved—a good marriage—proves instead to be the fatal step toward Cecilia's inevitable fulfillment of an inherited biological destiny.

Cecilia's situation, like Camila's and Dorotea's, is defined primarily by her bodily experience. In this respect, the existence of all three women is identical to that of their female ancestors. Each woman appears as an embodiment of the past, and therefore the nature of her activities is anterior to her performance of them. The leap out of history that this implies for the protagonist is marked by the ending of the novels, where all protagonists end their days in madness, social isolation, or death.

Nevertheless, this timeless structure of female experience is grounded on a contradiction, for the protagonists exist in a historically specific moment in nineteenth-century Cuba. In the slave society in which they live, masters have the power of life and death over their slaves. Consequently, when Suárez y Romero and Zambrana present Dorotea and Camila as having sexual power over their respective masters, what is brought into focus is the disparity between the masters' socioeconomic power and their sexual powerlessness. The link between sexuality and power is made transparent when both Carlos and Ricardo perceive Francisco, their slave, as the obstacle to the fulfillment of their desires. In an economy in which slaves are regarded as valuable pieces of machinery, both masters jeopardize their economic self-interest by incapacitating their male slave for labor on the plantation, with a view to being rewarded sexually by their female slave. By subordinating the pursuit of material wealth to their desire for sexual pleasure, Carlos and Ricardo reveal that they equate true mastery with the sexual possession of their female slave. Similarly, in *Cecilia Valdés*, there is an incongruence between Leonardo's objective situation as the only son and heir in one of the island's wealthiest and most powerful families and his acknowledged weakness for the sexual charms of Cecilia Valdés. The tension becomes apparent when Leonardo defers the consolidation of his social power to the pursuit of sexual satisfaction with Cecilia, his social inferior.

In all three novels, the underlying conflict between sexuality and power is resolved by the authors' presentation of the mulatto heroine as an aesthetically pleasing object of desire. But this resolution itself is based on a contradiction, for the idea of the mulatto woman as the paradigmatic object of desire implies a profound rejection of the black woman, a rejection articulated by one of the male characters in *Cecilia Valdés*. That each protagonist is the daughter of a white father entails the devaluation of her darker mother. Indeed, all three novelists indicate that the protagonist derives her positive attributes either from her father or from her lengthy association with *criollos*. The authors' intent to resolve the contradiction embedded in their novels recalls Lévi-Strauss's statement that "the purpose of myth is to provide a logical model capable of overcoming a contradiction."[12] But while the literary exaltation of the tragic mulatto mediates the conflict between socioeconomic power and sexual potency, it fails to resolve the initial problem of how the white founding father overcame his repugnance of the black woman in order to create the primal mulatto.

12. *Myth: A Symposium*, p. 105.

MYTH AS LANGUAGE

9 Woman as Metaphorical System: An Analysis of Gabriela Mistral's Poem "Fruta"

Carmelo Virgillo

Fruta

En el pasto blanco de sol,
suelto la fruta derramada.

De los Brasiles viene el oro,
en prietos mimbres donde canta
de los Brasiles, niño mío,
mandan la siesta arracimada.
Extiendo el rollo de la gloria;
rueda el color con la fragancia.

Gateando sigues las frutas,
como niñas que se desbandan,
y son los nísperos fundidos
y las duras piñas tatuadas . . .

Y todo huele a los Brasiles
pecho del mundo que lo amamanta,
que, a no tener el agua atlántica,
rebosaría de su falda . . .

Tócalas, bésalas, voltéalas
y les aprendes todas sus caras.
Soñarás, hijo, que tu madre
tiene facciones abrasadas,
que es la noche canasto negro
y que es frutal la Vía Láctea . . .

from Cuenta-mundo[1]

Fruit
Onto the sun-white grass
I free the spilled fruit.

That gold comes out of Brazilian lands
enclosed in dark wicker baskets where it sings

---

1. Gabriela Mistral, *Poesías completas*, 3d ed. (Madrid: Aguilar, 1966). Henceforth, all references to Mistral's poetry will apply to this volume. The English translation of "Fruta" is mine.

from out of Brazilian lands, my child,
they send the siesta in bunches.
I stretch out the roll of glory;
color rolls out with fragrance.

You go after the fruits on all fours,
like little girls they skitter off,
and they are melting-soft loquats
and hard tattooed pineapples . . .

And everything scents of Brazilian lands,
Bosom of the world that nurses it all,
that, if not for Atlantic waters,
would overflow its skirt . . .

Touch them, kiss them, turn them over and over
and you will learn all their faces.
You will dream, child, that your mother
has seared features,
that night is a black hamper
and that the Milky Way is a fruit tree . . .

Gabriela Mistral has all too often been taken to task for allegedly offering in her work too literal or mimetic a representation of woman. If this were true, one could understandably quarrel with the type of statement she would then be making about womanhood. Her insistent theme of maternity as female fulfillment would therefore take on unpleasant overtones befitting the Freudian dictum "biology as destiny."[2] However, in this paper I argue that Mistral's treatment of the maternal function should be separated from any possible implication about how real-world women are to realize their potential. After all, we shall be looking here at autonomous poetic texts and, moreover, at texts of a highly metaphorical nature—not at all at a set of directives concerning how women ought to feel or behave.

I propose to look instead at the larger poetic system wherein woman and maternity are simply elements, albeit prominent ones. This system in its scope goes far beyond the question of women's social role. In effect, it is so globally inclusive that, as we shall see, it seeks to take in the entire cosmos. At issue, then, is an immense spiritual quest whose goal is the generation of meaning and whose proof lies in the symbolic code or system

2. For a thought-provoking discussion of this topic, see Robert Seidenberg, "Is Anatomy Destiny?," in *Marriage in Life and Literature* (New York: Philosophical Library, 1970), pp. 119–56.

developed by the poet. Within such a code, woman and procreation are present as meaning-bearing signs in a larger, all-encompassing poetic language.

While the above-mentioned issues can be traced throughout Mistral's lyric production, the short collection of poems *Cuentamundo* must be considered exemplary of the type of mythic coding that interests us here. As the title indicates, the idea of working out a language capable of "speaking" or figuring the world is strongly present. Furthermore, woman and female powers of procreation play a prominent role as terms through which this symbolic and metaphorical "speaking" is to become possible.

Though the collection deserves to be studied as a whole, since it constitutes a mythic reconstruction of the cosmos that is uniquely feminine in the lexical framework in which Roland Barthes places myth,[3] in this paper I shall limit my observations to only one poem, "Fruta." In it Mistral, transcending the familiar sexual connotations of fruit and asserting her favorite themes and sub-themes (namely solitude, maternity, and mysticism, with their variants, grief, love, nature, and death), explores the internal reality of an entity emblematic of woman's ambivalence. She invests fruit with new dimensions, making it a symbol of the lonely messianic role of the female, implying that grief and self-immolation are necessary for the creation and survival of mankind.[4] In addition, we propose to examine how the text discloses a probing into the primordial enigma surrounding procreativity and equates the latter with artistic creativity.

3. Lisa Appignanesi indicates that the term *femininity* is one generally misunderstood because it is vague. "As such it constitutes what Roland Barthes calls a 'myth': a statement which bears no *direct* relationship to the object it describes (woman) and evokes a range of suggestions which is culturally determined" (*Femininity and the Creative Imagination* [London: Vision, 1973], p. 2). The implication is that *feminine* is an adjective denoting not sociological characteristics, but rather constituent factors such as creativity, sensibility, suggestiveness, intuitiveness, etc.—traits that may be found in man as well as woman. Consequently, the artist can be said to possess all of those characteristics, regardless of sex. In this respect, *Cuenta-mundo* is more than just a woman's view of the world; it is instead a hymn to the spiritual nature of Creation and to all that is good, beautiful, and everlasting on earth.

4. Gabriela Mistral's view coincides, albeit fortuitously, with Erich Neumann's pronouncement that "woman experiences herself first and foremost as the source of life. Fashioned in the likeness of the Great Goddess, she is bound up with the all-generating life principle, which is creative nature and a culture-creating principle in one. . . . Abduction, rape, marriage or death, and separation are the great motifs underlying the Eleusinian (matriarchal) mysteries" (*The Great Mother*, 3d ed. [New York: Pantheon, 1963], p. 306).

To begin with, let me refer briefly to the four-line ennea-syllabic composition "La cuenta-mundo," which sets forth an overall scheme while it introduces the conceptual and most of the formal characteristics of "Fruta" and other poems:

> Niño pequeño, aparecido
> que no viniste y que llegaste,
> te contaré lo que tenemos
> y tomarás de nuestra parte.[5]

> Little ghost child,
> who never came and yet arrived,
> I'll tell you about our world
> and you will share it with us.

One notices at once how the text evokes a set of associations with the educative aspect of the maternal function, the transmission of knowledge from mother to child. The mother is, in this context, familiar with the world's workings and ready to pass this information on to her offspring. Also evident are other possible meanings of motherhood. The physical production of the child is here alluded to in a lament over barrenness ("Niño pequeño, aparecido, que no viniste"). This lament is then countered by an affirmation of the notion that, even in the absence of physical procreation, a child may be created through other means ("y que llegaste").

Given the prominence of this theme of mothering-without-mothering in Mistral's poems, it is safe to assume that the allusion is to the creative work viewed as a correlative of and substitute for physical motherhood. In this respect, the paradox expressed in the antithesis "que no viniste . . . y que llegaste" leaves one no alternative but to consider mother, child, and world as mere abstractions. Interpreted symbolically, they then transcend rigid temporal and spacial limitations to represent instead immanent elements of eternal truth. As a result of this transformation, Mistral loses in the text the earthly traits of the sterile woman and reacquires, in this new realm of artistic rebirth, the inalienable rights of her sex. This introductory quatrain and the poems that follow constitute a subtle invitation

5. *Poesías completas*, p. 287.

to return via the imagery of her verse to the poet's own child-hood—a mythic world of innocence, illusion, and dream where objective, adult logic disappears and the subjective concept of primal universal order rules.[6] It posits the world we find in "Fruta."

Almost casually, a female persona using the lyrical "I" announces she is casting onto a sunny meadow the fruit pre-sumably brought along:

> En el pasto blanco de sol,
> suelto la fruta derramada.[7]

> Onto the sun-white grass
> I free the spilled fruit.

Following the overall scheme that predominates in *Cuenta-mundo*, "fruta" becomes a word-symbol for the decomposition of the external world and the creation of a new *poetic* one wherein the more profound connotations of fruit can be exam-ined. In this symbolic framework, *fruit*, understood as *offspring*, discloses woman's maternal mission: *freeing* the life she brought or *spilled* into the world. Underlying this message are further inferences prompted by the rhetorical context in which the verbs *soltar* (to free) and *derramar* (to spill) appear. The first sug-gestion is that the cleavage implicit in childbirth at some unspec-ified time in the past (past participle *derramada*) is predestined because the act of spilling is involuntary. The second is that a mother gives birth cognizant that the fruits of her love, once liberated from her dark womb into the light, are to be con-

6. Thus, Mistral's transmutation supports the theories of such researchers as Otto Rank and Carl G. Jung, who "believe that artists try to recapture the spirit of childhood, when freedom and innocence accompanied security and nourish-ing love given by parents—a golden age. The attempt to recapture paradise lost is repeated in mythic patterns and images of the quest" (Grace Stewart, *A New Mythos: The Novel of the Artist as Heroine 1877–1977* [St. Albans, Vt.: Eden Press, 1979], p. 8). Mistral's eminent capacity for mythmaking is brought to the fore by Juan Villegas (in "La aventura mítica en 'La flor del aire' de Gabriela Mistral," *Revista Iberoamericana*, no. 95 (1976), pp. 217–32), who maintains that Mistral consistently structures her works according to certain myths and mythic images consonant with both her universal concerns and personal experience.

7. *Poesías completas*, p. 296.

sciously freed like newborn animals scattered in a warm pasture.[8]

The second stanza contains the second and third movements:

> De los Brasiles viene el oro,
> en prietos mimbres donde canta
> de los Brasiles, niño mío,
> mandan la siesta arracimada.[9]

> That gold comes out of Brazilian lands
> enclosed in dark wicker baskets where it sings
> from out of Brazilian lands, my child,
> they send the siesta in bunches.

The most discernible variant in this second movement is the introduction of the third-person narrative voice and the addition of yet another poetic persona expressed by the directive vocative "niño mío." Both replace the first-person voice of the initial stanza, thus amplifying the poetic dimension. The impression immediately derived from these four lines is that of a cradle song, as the metric rhythm reproduces a swinging and rocking movement that matches the fruit's swaying journey from Brazil in dark wicker. Ultimately, the singing and rhythm insinuate the image, sound, and movement of a mother lulling her child to sleep.

---

8. The message conveyed by the imagery of this couplet corresponds admirably to the Spanish *dar a la luz*: to give birth. It is worth noting how a similar imagery representing infants as young animals put out to pasture emerges from *Lecturas para mujeres*: "Vosotras, madres, decís: ¡Los hombres lo han querido! ¡Los hombres se han vuelto fieras! ¿Y quiénes son los hombres? Miradlos, pues: son cosa diminuta que engorda y sonríe a la sombra de vuestro seno, como se agranda y dora el grano de uva a la sombra del parral.

"De vosotras salieron; vosotras los cargásteis mientras no pudieron caminar; vosotras los trajisteis de la mano. Ahora os sentís extrañas a ellos; os asustáis de sus crímenes y exlamáis: ¡Los hombres! ¡Los hombres!—como gritarían las madres del rebaño devorado en la noche: ¡Los lobos! ¡Los lobos!"

("You, mothers, say: Men do this! Men have wanted it this way! Men have turned into wild beasts! And who are these men? Well, just look at them: they are diminutive things that fatten and smile in the shade of your bosoms, like grapes growing and brightening in the shade of the vine arbor.

"They came out of you: you carried them while they were unable to walk; you led them by the hand. Now you feel as strangers before them; their crimes frighten you and you exclaim: 'Men! Men!'—as mother-sheep would cry: 'Wolves! Wolves!,' when their flock is devoured in the night") (*Lecturas para mujeres*, 3d ed. [San Salvador: Ministerio de Educación, Departmento Editorial, 1961], pp. 111–12).

9. *Poesías completas*, p. 296.

The interior structure of this second movement derives from symbolism and imagery. The noun "Brasiles," or Brazilian lands, is of capital importance, for it gives rise to an intricate series of associations further revealing and reinforcing the central theme—woman's ambivalent, mysterious nature, which presupposes her ties with earthly and divine power. The figure of Brazil is commonly linked with the legendary, fathomless riches of those dark and secret recesses that have captivated humanity's imagination for centuries. Aside from this image, Brazil conveys an even deeper symbolism. It recalls the figure of the bare-breasted Amazon, the mythic hermaphrodite whose traits epitomize the strength this vast and complex land draws from the interplay of its many components. The text, by making Brazil—the source of the fruit—a symbol of pluralistic totality, endows womanhood with the traits of the Amazonic virago. Brazil as origin suggests further implications for the Amazonic myth: it becomes an extraordinary place whose integrity rests on the harmonious coexistence of opposites and implies the mythological paradise free of discord, discrimination, unrest, suffering, or conflict. The hermaphrodite, uniting dominant traits of male and female, symbolizes an ideal condition, largely unknown in our world.[10] Thus the text is transcending earthly reality and describing instead a mythic-mystic journey in a timeless, paceless context, with Brazil functioning as mother and paradise and perhaps even God.[11] Such interpretation is substantiated by the verb form "mandan" (they send) and by the plurality of the noun "Brasiles." Together, verb and noun suggest the anonymous and magnanimous will that chooses woman's deceptively fragile womb, the "prietos mimbres" (dark wicker baskets), for the purpose of delivering to earth forms of life conceived in it own precious image. The noun "oro," or gold, is thus used to mean life, reflecting its radiant, loving source. In the same framework, the metaphor "siesta arracimada" (siesta in bunches), understood as a reference to the prenatal condition of living beings in which it is still possible to exist in a perfect state of peace and unity, would call to mind the image of the ideal world whence all life originates and flows naturally from one generation to another.

10. Juan Cirlot, *A Dictionary of Symbols* (London: Routledge and Kegan Paul, 1971), pp. 40–41.
11. Ibid.

In the third movement, represented by the last two lines of the second stanza—"Extiendo el rollo de la gloria; / rueda el color con la fragancia" ("I stretch out the roll of glory; / color rolls out with fragrance")[12]—the text reinstates the lyrical "I," which now figures again as the dominant poetic voice. The maternal persona behind it seems to be retracing her steps to elaborate on what she had stated in the first stanza. She no longer addresses herself to her would-be child but to the reader to remind one how the fruits fall out as a result of her unfolding or opening out their container—traditionally a paper cone.

From a strictly logical standpoint, the conceptual and formal characteristics of the third movement would indicate that this couplet could have followed or been incorporated into the first stanza. In effect, the third movement continues and reinforces the imagery of the first one, for it infers the preestablished natural dictates of childbirth. Moreover, with the introduction of the image produced by the metaphor "rollo de la gloria," depicting the mother's womb-cornucopia, the complex levels of symbolism and imagery stratify. At this point, "siesta arracimada" of the second movement, previously understood as an allusion to the child being lulled to sleep, now suggests that this infant is a "frutita," a small fruit himself hanging in a bunch (hence the Spanish "arracimada"—a play on the words "racimo" and "rama") from his mother's breasts ("prietos mimbres"), seen as the branches of the dark tree of her body. With this new symbolic dimension, it is understood that as the mother is singing her child to sleep she pulls out her breast ("Extiendo el rollo") against which the sleeping child lies while nursing.

The third movement, with the reappearance of the first-person singular voice and the reiteration of the third, also completes a cycle wherein one witnesses the image of fruit becoming more and more abstract. What was "fruta" in the first stanza turns successively into "oro" and "siesta arracimada," ultimately achieving full transparency in the metaphor "rueda el color con la fragancia." This systematic disintegration of fruit as a one-dimensional entity into particles evoking optical, tactile, gustatory, and olfactory sensations can be attributed to the poet's effort to recreate the synesthetic totality of fruit with her breast and with her child. Subsequently, if one carries a step

12. *Poesías completas*, p. 296.

further the symbolism of fruit's container within its rhetorical framework—"rollo de la gloria"—a number of other images surface. "Rollo," first seen as the mother's womb-cornucopia and then as her breast, now denotes the female genealogical sphere as well as astrological completeness and even divine perfection.[13]

Structurally, the imagery integrates the superficially fragmentary nature of the first three movements. The strophic order represents the reconstruction of the feminine mission in antiempirical, transcendental terms, rejecting any human systematization of the cosmic process. The text's view may be summarized as consisting of (1) *creation* ("en el pasto blanco de sol, / suelto la fruta derramada"); (2) *conception* ("De los Brasiles viene el oro"); (3) *gestation* and *sustenance* ("en prietos mimbres . . . mandan la siesta arracimada"). This new poetic logic not only explains the tying of the strophic knot ("suelto la fruta . . . Extiendo el rollo de la gloria") but also constitutes the end of a cycle and the return to the initial process of continuous creation.

The fourth movement reestablishes the multiple symbolic perspectives. On the first level of illusion the child is the object of the mother's scrutiny as he pursues on all fours the elusive fruits that she identifies for him: soft loquats and hard, tattooed pineapples. On the second symbolic level, the child is seen groping for his mother's hard breasts with their soft nipples.

> Gateando sigues las frutas
> como niñas que se desbandan,
> y son los nísperos fundidos
> y las duras piñas tatuadas . . .

> You go after the fruits on all fours
> like little girls they skitter off,
> and they are melting-soft loquats
> and hard tattooed pineapples . . .

The text, by making explicit the relationship between "frutas" and "niñas," both feminine nouns, attaches feminine characteristics to fruit. The lack of grammatical elision deliberately makes the child and fruits dependent on the same verb form, "sigues" of the main clause. By this means it is possible for the

---

13. "Signs and Symbols," in *The Random House Dictionary of the English Language*, college ed., (New York: Random House, 1968), p. 1535. Also, see Neumann, *The Great Mother,* p. 141.

text to link the act of following and that of the fruits' dispersing, fruit and offspring, and finally, the poet's imaginary child and all living beings that abandon their matrix after creation. In the realm of this new logic, the lexical forms of the stanza can only be interpreted in highly polysymbolic terms. "Sigues" corresponds to the infant's effort to grope for the breasts as they separate from his mouth and from each other while the mother moves her torso. As a dual image, it also corresponds to the fruit following the same predestined path of all little girls whose mission demands that they cut their maternal bond—an idea made explicit by the Spanish "desbandarse."

Furthermore, one notices portrayed symbolically in the exotic, soft, molten loquat and hard, tattooed pineapple a tolerance for extremes that, by allowing softness and sweetness to coexist with durable and indelible strength, emphasizes the feminine, hermaphroditic nature of fruit. The suspension marks ending the stanza suggest that behind the aforementioned polarity of external and internal characteristics of fruit lie the opposite forces of feminine reality, the continuum of life, and, in an even broader sense, the concept of the self-renewing creative process.

The fourth stanza, representing movement five, melds the entire relationship between the fruit, breast, and child triplicity:

> Y todo huele a los Brasiles
> pecho del mundo que lo amamanta,
> que, a no tener el agua atlántica,
> rebosaría de su falda . . .

> And everything scents of Brazilian lands
> bosom of the world that nurses it all,
> that, if not for Atlantic waters,
> would overflow its skirt . . .

A new level of imagery is now attained with Brazil portrayed as a huge, enormous woman or even as a single breast. Yet, this quatrain could have more logically followed the second movement, forming the following chain: "De los Brasiles viene el oro," "de los Brasiles . . . / mandan la siesta arracimada," where "oro" and "siesta" can now be viewed as milk. The strophic dislocation therefore reflects the composition's own subjective cosmic vision, and one looks then for a different poetic logic resting on a symbolic plane: in the interior imagery of the first movement. Therein the earlier image of Brazil as a hermaphroditic Amazon is brought back to complement and highlight the image of feminine completeness of movement four.

The new plane of imagery representing woman as bosom *of the world* now establishes the female figure as a complex entity, and this is achieved by the integration of cosmic elements. Here, feminine ambivalence, expressed in the interaction of offspring and mother, mother and earth, earth and water, water and human flesh, dissolves the apparent ambiguity engendered by the relative pronoun "que" at the beginning of the third line. Brazil is now equated with both fruit and breast, all three over-running land boundaries to flow throughout the world, for the implication here is that Brazil's milk *is* her fruit.

In the two movements of the last stanza, the mother-fruit motif advances, along with the major and minor themes. The imperative is used to assert motherly and spiritual authority in an explicit way:

> Tócalas, bésalas, voltéalas
> y les aprendes todas sus caras.
> Soñarás, hijo, que tu madre
> tiene facciones abrasadas,
> que es le noche canasto negro
> y que es frutal la Vía Láctea . . .

> Touch them, kiss them, turn them over and over
> and you will learn all their faces.
> You will dream, child, that your mother has seared features,
> that night is a black hamper
> and that the Milky Way is a fruit tree.

The external structure of the stanza indicates that this is the only sextain representing a whole poetic unit. The first two lines are topical and form movement six, uniting with the last four, which in turn produce the composition's seventh and final movement. Between these last two movements is a continuity that brings to the foreground the integrity of the poem's message before con-cluding it. Thus, fruit, breast, milk, woman, mother and child, humanity and creation, earth and universe are irrevocably fused. Even the rhythm integrates diverse elements as it echoes the cadence of the earlier cradle song before sounding a slower, reflexive, concluding tempo, indicating that the child has fallen asleep.

In the first couplet, the imperative and the reiteration of the same grammatical ending reproduce the rhythm of the fruits or breasts turned over and over. Concomitantly, there emerges the maternal invitation to have her body explored, suggested by the addition of the metaphor "y les aprendes todas sus caras" in the second line. After all, fruit is meant to be touched, kissed, sucked, like a mother's breast. The visual, tactile, and gustatory sensations in the phrase "Tócalas, bésalas, voltéalas," coupled with the implications of the following parallel clause "y les aprendes todas sus caras," lead not only to the physical but also to the spiritual discovery of woman. At this symbolic level, one visualizes fruit and breasts submitting voluntarily to a pre-destined task intended to surprise and gratify both the mother's offspring and the world that partakes of Brazil's abundance. All discover with each touch, each kiss, each turn a new pleasure that will nourish and fortify.

In the closing movement, the poetic persona seems to be whispering to her child, whom she has finally lulled to sleep in the silence of the night. Here the verb form "soñarás," on which the parallel clauses "tu madre tiene facciones abrasadas," "es la noche canasto negro," and "es frutal la Vía Láctea" all depend, serves as a key word. First of all, the allusion to the oneiric experience of the child establishes a bond between the consciousness of the mother and the subconscious mind of the child. Furthermore, the future tense almost confirms that, in this state representing the meeting of two perceptions of human reality, the offspring will discover in dream what the mother as woman already senses. This intuitive capacity, so integral a part of the feminine character and so essential to creativity, is revealed by the structural function of the verb "soñar" in its symbolic form. It fuses the two movements by disclosing their intrinsic characteristics. Thus the *mother* created by the poet's imagination identifies spiritually with the other half of the artistic creation: the fruit child.

Having linked Brazil and fruit, mother and offspring, woman and creation, we now also understand woman's presence, essence, and ascendency. The key words "facciones abrasadas," "noche," "frutal," and "Vía Láctea" are employed to integrate externally and internally the structural aspects of the entire poem. The common link between these word-symbols is their relationship to the four basic cosmic elements: air, fire, earth, and water. They are also the cardinal points of woman that are used in the text to accentuate female completeness.[14] Thus woman becomes synonymous with mother nature and associated with complexity, contradiction, and mystery. Through the same symbols, the ritual (the innate and natural sacrifice of woman—the freeing of a nurtured child), which had remained implicit up to this point, surfaces in the last three lines, where it is ultimately substantiated by the reference to the mythic-mystic ascendency of the female figure. If one recalls the ocean voyage of fruit from a remote, bountiful, sunny Brazil and remembers the separation of fruit from its source to make the long trip in tight, dark, wicker hampers—a mission intended to please and nourish the world—it should not be difficult to grasp the symbolic level of the closing movement.

As before, the symbology of this final movement is pluralistic. The "facciones abrasadas" could intimate the mother-poet's point of origin: the sun, which symbolizes light, life, Heaven, and God, and the divine inspiration that guides the artist. On the other hand, the adjective "abrasadas" could also correspond to *abraded, seared*, or *burned*, referring to Brazil's parched soil and the mother's dried breast after she has weaned her child. Moreover, the choice of this particular adjective denotes pain and anguish as well as abuse. Night, mankind's silent reminder of the dark and mysterious infinity that surrounds us all, fulfills here a dual function: it is correlative to both "prietos mimbres" and "rollo de la gloria." Both are containers, the former to transport the child to a future he cannot, at this point, visualize—perhaps even his death—and the latter the child's physical and spiritual container, suggestive of the dark, peaceful womb. The last two symbols, "frutal" and "Vía Láctea," complete the poem's entire cycle. Both function as coordinates in the dualistic structure of the composition since they imply source of life and nourishment. They also bring together the two planes on which the composition is constructed: "frutal" as the telluric level, "Vía Láctea" as the nebulous, distant realm of the imagination— a child's vision of Heaven or paradise. The ensuing imagery portrays the fruit tree and the Milky Way suckling and then releas-

14. Cirlot, *A Dictionary of Symbols*, p. 4, appropriately claims that according to the most elemental cosmogonies, nature is depicted as a hermaphrodite: "Of the four Elements, air and fire are regarded as active and male: water and earth passive and female."

ing their offspring—fruit and heavenly bodies—to float all alone in darkness and silence on their eternal mission: the former in their wicker hampers across the great ocean,[15] the latter abandoning their luminous source so that they might brighten the universe. From their distinct yet similar acts of cleavage, new fruit trees and new constellations will be formed whose children will then carry on the creative, lonely, sacrificial, self-fulfilling, and metaphorically maternal assignment.

15. By giving the fruits' container a definitive shape, "prietos mimbres," the poet finalizes her conviction that woman is essentially a mother, whose symbol is the womb. As such she is preordained to shelter her children and then release them from her bond.

10 Arlt's Exposition
of the Myth of Woman

Naomi Lindstrom

In *Le Deuxième Sexe* (1949), Simone de Beauvoir denounces soci-
etally fostered strategies to avoid granting women fully human
status.[1] In Beauvoir's analysis, one of the most pervasive tactics is
a process she calls "the myth of woman." By myth, she means the
widespread reliance on prestructured patterns that organize—
and thus falsify—one's perception of woman:

> The myth is one of those snares of false objectivity into which the
> man who depends on ready-made valuations rushes headlong.
> Here again we have to do with the substitution of a set idol for
> actual experience and the free judgment it requires. For an
> authentic relation with an autonomous existent, the myth of
> Woman substitutes the fixed contemplation of a mirage.[2]

Beauvoir's formulation would appear to have considerable
psychological reality for readers. Analysis akin to that of Beauvoir has subsequently appeared in writings by both feminists
and those interested in the workings of myth. In the first group,
one may count Betty Friedan, Kate Millett, Germaine Greer, and
Adrienne Rich; in the second, Roland Barthes and Edgar
Morin.[3] Further confirmation for Beauvoir's contentions lies in
the fact that Margaret Mead's classic sex-role analysis, *Male and
Female*, published the same year as *Le Deuxième Sexe*, contains
strikingly analogous assertions.[4]

1. *The Second Sex*, trans. H. M. Parshley (New York: Vintage, 1974); see
especially "The Myth of Woman in Five Authors," pp. 224–85, and "Myth and
Reality," pp. 285–97.
2. Ibid., p. 294.
3. Betty Friedan, *The Feminine Mystique* (New York: W. W. Norton and Co.,
1963); Kate Millett, *Sexual Politics* (Garden City, N.J.: Doubleday, 1970); Germaine Greer, *The Female Eunuch* (London: MacGibbon and Kee, 1970); Adrienne
Rich, *Of Woman Born: Motherhood as Experience and Institution* (New York: W. W.
Norton and Co., 1976); Roland Barthes, *Système de la mode* (Paris: Julliard, 1960);
and Edgar Morin, *Les Stars* (Paris: Seuil, 1965). Some of these writers use concepts closely akin to those that underlie Beauvoir's analysis without reference to
her writings. Others proclaim a specific indebtedness. For example, the Morin
volume of essays contains an overt tribute to the tenth anniversary of the publication of *Le Deuxième Sexe*.
4. *Male and Female: A Study of the Sexes in a Changing World* (New York: Morrow,
1949).

This paper looks at how one author, the Argentine Roberto Arlt (1900-1942), makes society's mythification of woman one element of his fictional representation. It should be emphasized that I am not accusing Arlt of falsely mythifying woman. On the contrary, Arlt invokes the mythification process precisely in order to expose and to reveal its mechanisms and thus deconstruct it.[5] This exposition is effected through the creation of a female character, Hipólita, who appears in Arlt's novel *Los siete locos* (1929) and its sequel, *Los lanzallamas* (1931). Hipólita is notable for, among other things, her power to provoke men to feats of extravagant mythmaking.

Reading the novels, one receives remarkably little reliable information about the "real" Hipólita, although this fact has not stopped critics from characterizing her in definitive terms.[6] As any reader must immediately note, the novels lack a reliable central narrator. To read, one must continually heed the distortions and falsifications of the unstable Arltian characters.[7] Thus, Hipólita herself is not in the foreground, either as individual or as representative of her sex. What claims attention is the mythic mechanisms by which men seek to make sense of her. Hipólita's femininity is only significant in that it elicits this paradigmatically—and appallingly—human behavior. Arlt is by no means

5. Critics disagree as to whether Roberto Arlt shares his characters' more confused and sentimental notions or stands apart to comment ironically. See Eduardo González Lanuza's summary of the debate in his *Roberto Arlt* (Buenos Aires: Centro Editor de América Latina, 1971), pp. 36–37. González Lanuza chooses to view Arlt as a perpetual adolescent who simply imbues his characters with his own fanciful elaboration of realty. Among those who see Arlt as a sophisticated and analytic "deconstructor" are Naomi Lindstrom, *Literary Expressionism in Argentina* (Tempe, Ariz.: Center for Latin American Studies, Arizona State University, 1977); Noé Jitrik, "Entre el dinero y el ser," lectura de *El juguete rabioso* de Roberto Arlt, *Dispositio*, 1, 2 (1976), 100–103; and David William Foster, "Roberto Arlt or the Neurotic Imperative," in his *Currents in the Contemporary Argentine Novel: Arlt, Mallea, Sábato, and Cortazar* (Columbia: University of Missouri Press, 1975), pp. 20–45.

6. For instance, Stasys Gostautas, "La evasión de la ciudad en las novelas de Roberto Arlt," *Revista Iberoamericana* 80 (1972):460, gives the "carácter de Hipólita" as "frío y calculador." However, other critics have stressed that Hipólita is *not* characterized in any definitive manner; see González Lunuza, *Roberto Arlt*, p. 83.

7. At the same time, the way in which Arltian characters distort their experience of events represents patterns of conceptualization common among real people. This representativity is one of the motivating premises of Oscar Masotta's *Sexo y traición en Roberto Arlt* (Buenos Aires: Jorge Alvarez, 1965). See in particular pp. 11–19.

writing feminist literature, but his utilization of Hipólita confirms Beauvoir's statements about woman's treatment.

One sees Hipólita mythified by two different men. The process begins with her husband, the deranged Ergueta. Ergueta succeeds in communicating his mythmaking ardor to Erdosain, the unhappy antihero of the two novels. Between the two men's efforts, Hipólita is re-elaborated into three separate versions of womanhood.

Ergueta's account of Hipólita is the most suspect, for the man is unmistakably insane. When Ergueta first appears, he has met Erdosain in a café in order to give an account of his recent actions. As Erdosain already knows, Ergueta has met a prostitute in his low-life wanderings and subsequently married her. To transform this sordid anecdote, Ergueta relies on his private apocalyptic mythology. In his scheme, the seedier milieux of Buenos Aires have become an eschatological backdrop against which he and Hipólita play out a drama of sin and redemption. Through a system of paradoxical relations, Ergueta is both a redemptive prophet and a sharpster. Hipólita is both a virginal creature, a *donna angelica,* and a street-wise whore.

The first part of this conversation goes badly. Ergueta's discourse is clearly a mythic one, but Erdosain persists in attempting to engage him in rational discourse. Erdosain points out that Hipólita cannot be the Lame Whore of the Apocalypse since she is an able-bodied young woman. This literal-mindedness has no effect on Ergueta, who continues to fit experience to myth: "pero ella es la descarriada, y yo el fraudulento, el 'hijo de la perdición'" (but she is the woman gone astray, and I am the deceiver, the "son of perdition").[8] Particularly baffling to Erdosain is Ergueta's inclusion of very worldly realities in his apocalyptic elaboration. For example, Ergueta is proud of his astuteness in marrying under Uruguayan law, thus rendering divorce possible.

At midpoint in the conversation, Ergueta produces a photograph of Hipólita. This image corresponds to Ergueta's exalta-

8. Roberto Arlt, *Los siete locos* (Buenos Aires: Losada, 1968), p. 169. Further citations from this work are cited in the text, designated by *SL* and the page number corresponding to this edition. Citations from *Los lanzallamas* (Buenos Aires: Fabril, 1968) are also cited in the text, designated by *L* and the page number corresponding to this text.

tion of Hipólita as a divine creature. Overwhelmed by this pseudo-objective documentation, Erdosain abandons his rationalistic approach to the woman. Now he begins to work out his own myth of Hipólita as a pure being. In effect, he accepts Ergueta's account with only one alteration: Ergueta now appears as Hipólita's beastly oppressor. The narrator exposes Erdosain's mental processes: "Pensó en la deliciosa criatura y se la imaginó soportando a este bruto bajo un cielo oscurecido por grandes nubes de polvo e incendiado por un sol amarillo y espantoso. Ella se marchitaría como un helecho transplantado a un pedregal" (He thought of the delicious creature and imagined her suffering under that great brute beneath a sky dark with dustclouds and set ablaze by a dreadful yellow sun. She would wilt like a fern planted into lava rock) (*SL*, p. 172).

This goddesslike image of Hipólita, the "deliciosa criatura" (delicious creature) of "gran sensibilidad" (deep sensitivity) (*SL*, p. 163), is short-lived. It is shattered when the "real" Hipólita shows up on Erdosain's doorstep, seeking aid. The man immediately notes features incompatible with Hipólita's supposed ethereality: her freckles, her red hair, her sharp features, her seeming unconcern over her husband's descent into madness. Consequently, Erdosain spends the first part of their encounter questioning the woman about key elements in her *donna angelica* myth. In Ergueta's elaboration, one proof of Hipólita's spiritual purity is her history of self-abnegating and charitable acts. Now Hipólita denies this history: "pero, ¿así que a usted le dijo que yo había regalado mi collar a una sirvienta? . . . ¡Qué hombre!" (but, so he told you I gave my necklace to a servant? That man!) (*SL*, p. 156).

In response to the new situation, Erdosain remolds his perception of Hipólita. He now perceives her following a pattern Millett discusses as the "vagina dentata."[9] Whereas before Hipólita's gaze seemed otherworldly and spiritual, it now appears as a "malévola mirada verdosa" (malevolent green gaze) attacking Erdosain with "haces de mirada" (a host of bolts streaming from her eyes) (*SL*, p. 158). Hipólita's thin facial features before signaled refinement and delicacy; in the new version, they are harsh and sharp. After reorganizing his

9. *Sexual Politics*, p. 150. Millett's analysis attributes this type of mythification to authors of fiction and poetry, rather than to characters within the work.

perceptions of the woman, Erdosain concludes that she must be "fría . . . una mujer perversa" (cold . . . a perverse woman) (*SL*, p. 158). In a complete inversion, Hipólita has moved from being the pure and vulnerable girl to the callous predator.

This highly unfavorable mythic treatment is not Erdosain's final version of Hipólita. Another alteration begins to take place when the man notices the woman's fatigue. This small sign is an indication for Erdosain to incorporate Hipólita into another of his mental categories, the world's "insulted and injured." He begins to imagine a pathetic scenario for her: "[Hipólita] lo miraba con fijeza, pero la dureza de líneas que estaba rígida bajo la epidermis de su semblante como una armadura de voluntad se descompuso de fatiga. Con la cabeza inclinada a un costado, a Erdosain le recordó a su esposa . . . quizá fuera a parar en un hotel de muros sucios, y entonces, apiadado, dijo:—Discúlpeme" ([Hipólita] stared at him steadily, but the hardness of the lines held taut under the skin of her face like an armor of will broken down under the strain. With her head tilted to one side, she reminded Erdosain of his wife . . . maybe she'd end up in a hotel with dirty walls, and then, seized with pity, he said, "I'm sorry") (*SL*, p. 159).

When Erdosain has fully integrated Hipólita into his mythic race of suffering souls, he engages her in a rather bathetic ceremony in which they confess their respective histories of personal humiliations and degradations. Erdosain is moved to tears by this ritual and declares the couple profoundly united as two of life's losers. Willing to accord Hipólita favorable treatment, he once more perceives her gaze as attractive, emanating "un calor súbito" (a sudden warmth) (*SL*, p. 185).[10] Exhausted by his efforts to remold the woman's image, he drifts into a state of half-sleep.

As Erdosain falls silent, the reader becomes privy to the woman's thoughts on the recent events. These reflections show exactly how unproductive and false Erdosain's mythmaking has

10. *Magic* is the term used by David Viñas to describe the gaze of the novel's "mad" characters. "El escritor vacilante: Arlt, Boedo y Discépolo," in his *Literatura argentina y realidad política, de Sarmiento a Cortázar*, rev. ed. (Buenos Aires: Siglo Veinte, 1971), pp. 67–73, offers the hypothesis that the characters seduce and hypnotize followers with their eyes, seeming to offer fulfillment of fantasies. The element of fantasy is stressed by Adolfo Prieto, "Las fantasía y lo fantástico en Roberto Arlt," in his *Estudios de literatura argentina* (Buenos Aires: Galerna, 1969), pp. 83–103.

been. The man has assumed that the woman would be pleased to figure as one of the world's noble underdogs. In fact, Hipólita rejects this image of herself and the maudlin scheme that supports it. She sees Erdosain as "un débil y un sentimental" (weak and sentimental) (*SL*, p. 194). Moreover, she knows that he cannot establish an adequate relation with her, but will always remain dependent and irresponsible, substituting sentimentality for much-needed "empuje" (drive) (*SL*, p. 195).

Erdosain's relations with Hipólita largely repeat Ergueta's failure. Both men exhibit a lack of interest in knowing the woman as an existent human being, capable of reacting, choosing, and changing. Rather, they seek to impose upon her a fixed pattern that will satisfy their private world schemes. Hipólita offers herself as the *materia prima* of men's private myths because she finds financial benefit in this practice. However, the procedure is unsatisfactory to all concerned. Hipólita can please Ergueta by playing along with his apocalyptic myth, yet his obsessions destroy him and he ends up reviling her. Erdosain makes a fool of himself in front of her and nearly kills her later. Hipólita, meanwhile, feels a growing revulsion for men: "Todos son así. . . . Los débiles, inteligentes e inútiles; los otros, brutos y aburridos" (That's how they all are. . . . The weak ones, intelligent and useless; the rest, a lot of boring animals) (*SL*, p. 195).

Given Hipólita's history of failures, one takes special note when a new man succeeds in his relations with her. This individual is the Astrologer, an enigmatic revolutionary. His ability to reach the alienated young woman helps reveal Ergueta's and Erdosain's inadequacy.

Immediately upon meeting Hipólita, the Astrologer submits her to a bizarre process of testing and evaluation. Among other things, he refuses to admit her to his house, conducting their initial interview on the lawn. There, he bombards her with a curious and trying set of utterances. Miscellaneous hostile remarks, impertinent questions, and reflections on the human condition force Hipólita to react to the man.

While Hipólita's initial response is one of disorientation, she soon enters into the Astrologer's type of irrational discourse. She begins to reveal some of her most disturbing experiences "sin poder explicarse el porqué" (for reasons she couldn't figure out) (*L*, p. 21). This spontaneity is a departure from Hipólita's previous habit of calculating her remarks to fit the man's fantasies.

Eventually, the Astrologer is satisfied with Hipólita's potentialities as revealed by her behavior under his peculiar interrogation. Subsequently, she becomes a member of his inner circle and the person he most confides in. When disastrous events overtake the Astrologer's band of revolutionaries, Hipólita is the one he chooses to take with him into underground exile.

The relation between the Astrologer and Hipólita is no idealization of the man-woman bond, for many reasons. Both partners remain engaged in trickery, criminal activities, and manipulation of others, yet the Astrologer does keep in mind that woman is a being who can make decisions and alter herself willfully. One might describe his intervention by saying that he lends support to Hipólita's labors to work out her own myth, a system that can give direction to her vital energies and provide existential satisfactions. In this sense, the Astrologer meets Beauvoir's requirement that, just as "man is defined as a being who is not fixed, who makes himself what he is," woman must receive the same treatment.[11] He forces Hipólita to confront her past actions and to start seeing herself as a unique being, not just the malleable stuff of men's mythmaking. At the least, one can say that he allows her to glimpse what she is capable of becoming: "a human being in quest of values in a world of values."[12]

As Hipólita ceases to be the object of mythmaking and learns to collaborate in the creation of an archetype, what must change in her behavior and in that of the men around her? Beauvoir, again, can suggest an answer. *The Second Sex* contains a strong implicit statement that discourse, verbal behavior, is the realm in which woman wins or loses her "authenticity." Although Beauvoir does not claim to be working in the area of discourse analysis, she frequently carries out just such investigation. She scrutinizes a large corpus of female utterances and writings, including remarks made in casual conversation as well as on more formal occasions, private diaries and letters, confessions, and testimonial statements. She also examines men's habits in speaking with or writing to women as well as the fictional repre-

11. *The Second Sex*, p. 38.
12. Ibid., p. 58.

sentations of female or female-male discourse situations. Her purpose in bringing together and analyzing this mass of examples is twofold: (a) to see how women gain, or lose, the ability to formalize their life experience in words, even if those words are only addressed to a diary or an intimate confidant; and (b) to examine women's ability to "make their voices heard," to participate efficaciously in verbal exchanges.

When the reader first learns about Hipólita, the woman has been entirely "robbed" of her own discourse. This figurative theft occurs as her mad husband, Ergueta, insists on forcing her to fit a preexisting text, the Book of Revelation. If Hipólita is to be "her own woman," then the discourse that defines her must be the speech she herself produces; but that discourse has been entirely displaced by the words of St. John and Ergueta.

Gostautas has pointed out the most important device operant in this displacement. To use Gostautas's example, Ergueta narrates to Erdosain a beatific vision supposedly related to him by Hipólita. What is immediately striking is the lack of correspondence between the woman's story and everything else one learns about her. The visionary tale has manifestly grown out of Ergueta's beliefs and experiences, not his wife's.[13]

The incongruity becomes even more apparent when Ergueta cites his wife "verbatim." These reported utterances stand out for their highly figurative, emotive language—for example, "Entraré en tu casa desnuda" (I will enter your house naked) (*SL*, p. 167). Such expression is identical to Ergueta's more lyrical flights of speech, based on a scriptural paradigm, but bears no resemblance to the remarks made by Hipólita.

Perhaps most curiously of all, the madman reports verbal actions Hipólita has allegedly used to disrupt conventional situations. For example, he claims that she declared herself a prostitute in front of her ultrarespectable in-laws and that she rejected worldly wealth in front of her demimondaine associates. The use of inappropriate speech acts to disturb and disorient is very much a characteristic of Ergueta, but one does not see Hipólita perform such disorderly actions.

A systematic pattern governs Ergueta's crazed insistence on "misquoting" his wife. The madman has devised an entire set of verbal practices that he considers suited to the Whore of the

13. Gostautas, "Las evasión," p. 460.

Apocalypse, a corrupt-virginal creature living in the last days of sinful man. Whatever the real, noneschatological Hipólita may have said is entirely accidental and can safely be discarded as insignificant. This substitution of invented discourse for a woman's real remarks is a crude myth-creating device, but an extremely powerful one. Confronted with the evidence of its falsity, Erdosain can only wonder at the hold it exercised upon him: "Yo le creía en estas circunstancias" (I believed him when I was there) (*SL*, p. 167). Ergueta's very persuasiveness suggests that he is only carrying to a deranged extreme a pattern already present in male-female verbal interactions.

Erdosain is considerably saner than his Bible-reading friend. Therefore, his practices more closely approximate those of "normal" speakers. Such a move toward relative sanity is noticeable in his early exchanges with Hipólita. He confronts the woman with the image of her discourse that Ergueta supplied; she rejects this image as alien and unrecognizable, unrelated to anything she ever said or might say. The two agree that Ergueta's distortion of his wife's speech is simply a sign of his madness. Neither seems to note the organized, purposeful character of this eccentric behavior.

Erdosain may dismiss Ergueta's outlandish procedures as lying and madness, but he, too, is eager to supply Hipólita with a discourse suited to his mythic image. Their first encounter goes badly because the woman unwittingly violates the man's notions of how she should speak. Erdosain finds profoundly disturbing those aspects of Hipólita's language he deems "impestivo y prostibulario" (rough bordello talk) or "canalla" (gutter language) (*SL*, p. 158). He can only accept her as the long-suffering, great-spirited female, the *donna angelica* who loves and shelters men even at the cost of great personal suffering. He cannot allow such a creature to coarsely address him as "m'hijito" (kid) or to employ such a vulgar proverb as "Paciencia, mala suerte" (That's the way the cookie crumbles) (*SL*, p. 158).

During this exchange, Erdosain gives Hipólita clues to indicate how she should express herself. He complains that her words sound too cold and unfeeling: "me habla de todo este drama con una tranquilidad que asombra" (you're telling me this whole drama so coolly it's unnerving) (*SL*, p. 158). When she still fails to speak as the emotive, sweet woman he has in mind, he prompts her with less and less subtlety: "dígame . . .

¿sufrió mucho al lado de él?" (tell me . . . did you suffer much with him?) (*SL*, p. 160). Hipólita's unresponsiveness to this prompting disgusts Erdosain so deeply he is driven from her presence.

However, the next interaction between Erdosain and Hipólita proceeds much more smoothly because the man has replaced the real Hipólita with an imaginary simulacrum of her, an "interlocutora hipotética" (imaginary conversation partner) (*SL*, p. 165). Unlike the original, the fantasized Hipólita satisfies Erdosain. Now he enjoys Ergueta's privilege: he can control both what he says and what his female companion "says." This conversation in fantasy restores the completeness of Hipólita's "sweet creature" myth, which was severely damaged by the woman's autonomous verbal behavior.

Erdosain eventually attempts to reestablish contact with the real Hipólita. During this interchange, Hipólita is much more able to supply the man with the type of speech he demands of her. After her initial clumsiness, she appears to have mastered the key elements of this expression: she must speak a great deal about suffering, both hers and his; she must express abundant, even maudlin, compassion for the wretched; she must continually sweeten and soften her discourse.

Now Hipólita, who formerly insisted upon a stoical attitude, encourages the man to pour out his tribulations to her: "¿Por qué está triste?" (Why are you sad?) (*SL*, p. 184). Formerly, she had distressed Erdosain by the tart, cynical tenor of her remarks. Now she tells him that he must never commit suicide because "Eso está en manos de Dios" (That's in God's hands) (*SL*, p. 185). Erdosain responds with warm enthusiasm to this sentimentalized mode, encouraging Hipólita to tell him the story of her misfortunes. Here, he pushes her toward bathetic expression through small clues and promptings. When her story strikes him as too detached and neutral, he reminds her, "Debe ser triste" (It must have been sad); Hipólita, willing to follow these signals, responds, "Sí, es muy triste ver felices a los otros y ver que los otros no comprenden que una será desdichada para toda la vida" (Yes, it's very sad to see other people happy and see how other people don't understand that you're going to be unhappy your whole life long) (*SL*, p. 186). In this way, she produces an account of her life virtually to order. The reader will find this impromptu autobiography mawkish and improbable-sounding, but for its intended consumer it is a source of enormous listening pleasure. "Cuente, la deliciosa criatura" (Tell me, delicious creature) (*SL*, p. 187), he says, rewarding her with immoderate praise for her absurd and disjointed narrative efforts.

Arlt's text indicates the inauthenticity of such speech through both Hipólita's disgust as soon as she is able to disengage herself from the encounter, and the fact that Erdosain elicits from Hipólita a verbal response largely identical to the one he earlier had obtained from his wife, Elsa. Since the two women are otherwise quite unlike, this last circumstance is especially striking.

To look at this parallelism, one may turn briefly away from the consideration of Hipólita and toward an examination of Erdosain's most important exchange with Elsa. Here, Erdosain has cause to be offended, for his wife is leaving him in the midst of his misfortunes; moreover, she is accompanied by a man who appears to be her lover. Elsa manages to distract her husband from these unhappy facts by allowing him to engage her in a melodramatic conversation about suffering. First, she impresses upon him the personal sacrifices she has made as his wife. Apart from her obvious argument that the man has been "a poor provider," Elsa is using a calculated strategy. She knows that Erdosain is unable to resist his own myth of the wretched, self-abnegating female.

The sentimental element in their talk grows stronger until Erdosain and Elsa finally move into a totally bathetic exchange. A sample of this dialogue shows the extreme point of Erdosain's "heart-wrenching" male-female discourse:

> —Mirá . . . esperame. Si la vida es como siempre me dijiste, yo vuelvo, ¿sabés?, y entonces, si vos querés, nos matamos juntos . . . ¿Estás contento?
> Una ola de sangre subió hasta las sienes del hombre.
> —Alma, que buena sos, alma . . . dame esta mano—y mientras ella, aún sobrecogida, sonreía con timidez, Erdosain se la besó—. ¿No te enojás, alma?
> Ella enderezó la cabeza grave de dicha.
> —Mirá Reme . . . yo voy a venir, ¿sabés?, y si es cierto lo que decís de la vida . . . sí, yo vengo . . . voy a venir.
> —¿Vas a venir?
> —Con todo lo que tenga.
> —¿Aunque seas rica?

—Aunque tenga todos los millones de la tierra, vengo. ¡Te lo juro!

—¡Alma, pobre alma! ¡Qué alma la tuya! Sin embargo, vos no me conociste . . . no importa . . . ¡ah, nuestra vida! (*SL*, p. 56)

"Look, wait for me. If life is the way you always told me, I'll come back, see?, and then, if you want, we'll kill ourselves together . . . Are you happy?"

A wave of blood suffused his whole face in warmth.

"Dearest, how good you are, you sweet soul . . . Give me your hand," and she, though startled, smiled shyly. Erdosain kissed it. "You're not mad at me, darling?"

She raised her head, somber with happiness.

"Look Remo . . . I'm going to come, see?, and if it's true what you say about life . . . yes, I'll come . . . I'm coming back."

"You'll come?"

"With everything I've got."

"Even if you're rich?"

"Even if I have all the millions in the world, I'll come. I swear!"

"Poor, dear, sweet soul! What a soul you have! But still, you never knew me . . . it doesn't matter . . . ah, our lives!"

This ridiculous verbal performance, which continues far beyond the transcribed fragment, shows Elsa soothing her husband with an abundant supply of the talk he craves. It is certainly not the speech of a "human being in quest of values," as Beauvoir would say, but of a woman seeking to conform to a myth of woman.

The end of these oppressive patterns comes when Hipólita meets the Astrologer. This significant encounter occurs as the first episode of *Los lanzallamas*, the second book of the Erdosain story. This segment is entitled "El hombre neutro" (The Neuter Man); the obvious reference is to the Astrologer's castrated condition, revealed in the course of the exchange. However, one must note that the Astrologer is also neuter and neutral in much of his verbal behavior toward Hipólita. With his extraordinary insight into human nature, he correctly guesses the essential fact of the Erdosain-Hipólita encounter: an impulsive man has imprudently poured out too much of his story to a designing woman. The present intention of Hipólita is, clearly, to practice her Delilah-like wiles on the Astrologer. The latter, however, is already on his guard; he refuses to react to Hipólita and subjects her behavior and remarks to careful scrutiny. In a very short

time he has accurately diagnosed her new strategy: "El Astrólogo sin mostrarse sorprendido la miró tranquilamente. Solilo-
quió: 'Quiere hacerse la cínica y la desenvuelta para dominar'"
(The Astrologer, showing no surprise, looked at her coolly. He
mused to himself: "She wants to come across as the tough dame
to get the upper hand") (*L*, p. 16).

The first counterstrategy of the Astrologer is simply to break
with the major conventions governing conversation. For some
time, he refuses to show any reaction to Hipólita or to respond
to her "tough" remarks. The woman becomes increasingly
flustered, speaking more and more pointless words in a futile
attempt to display self-possession. When the man does speak, a
further rupture with norms occurs. Though her identity is per-
fectly evident to him, he subjects her to redundant inquiries
about it. All this anomalous behavior finally succeeds in causing
the woman to abandon her conversational role of "tough
cookie":

> —¿Así que usted es amiga de Erdosain?
> —Va la tercera vez que me lo pregunta. Sí, soy amiga de Erdo-
> sain . . . pero, ¡Dios mío!, qué hombre desatento es usted. Hace
> tres horas que estoy parada hablando y todavía no me ha dicho:
> "Pase, ésta es su casa . . ." (*L*, p. 16)

> "So you're Erdosain's friend?"
> "This is the third time already you've asked me. Yes, I'm Erdo-
> sain's friend . . . but, my God, what a rude man you are! Here
> I've been standing for three hours talking and you still haven't
> said to me, 'Come in, make yourself at home'."

Hipólita's disconcerted state allows the Astrologer to speak to
her more freely. He further breaks down her defenses by telling
her he considers her "una charlatana" (a bluffer) (*L*, p. 17) and
by making sport of her plan to blackmail him.

The conversation now enters a second phase in which the
Astrologer actually seeks to communicate with Hipólita. Here,
too, he is exceptionally cautious not to allow her to slip back into
her old discourse habits. The woman is accustomed to listen to
men's talk for signs of personal involvement, which she can
then use in devising a response. She habitually responds as a
woman to a man. The Astrologer frustrates this practice by
keeping her discourse severely impersonal and abstract, almost
like a lecture addressed to an anonymous public. The woman

has no idea how to deal with such dehumanized expression of ideas and information: "Hipólita asintió, presa de malestar. Todo aquello era innegable, pero ¿con qué objeto le comunicaba tales verdades?" (Hipólita agreed, full of misgivings. All that was undeniably true, but what was he doing telling her all this true stuff?) (*L*, p. 20).

The barrage of cold, general talk is a test to which the Astrologer is subjecting Hipólita. Now she must respond without recourse to her "female wiles," with no fixed mythic pattern to guide her. The Astrologer places the burden of the conversation on her by demanding abruptly that she show she has been following the ideas he has been setting forth.

Given the novelty of this task, Hipólita performs well. Her impromptu speech brings together abstract meditations, reminiscences, and reflections on her experiences. The narrator reports not only Hipólita's words but also the reactions of the Astrologer. In every case, the man is pleased with the freshness and vividness of the woman's expression: "El Astrólogo asienta con la cabeza, sonriendo de la precisión con que la muchacha roja evoca la llanura habitada por hombres codiciosos" (The Astrologer nods his head yes, smiling at the accuracy with which the red-headed girl evokes the plains inhabited by greedy men) (*L*, p. 22). While his response to her attempts to "decipher" and exploit him was an impassive coldness, he greets her efforts toward independent expression with enthusiastic smiles and verbal encouragement.

The myth of woman has been an implicit issue throughout the dialogue: first, because of the Astrologer's refusal to let Hipólita speak as a myth; and second, because of Hipólita's remarks concerning the role of woman in society. Only toward the end of the interchange does the issue of the mythification of woman in society become an explicit topic.

At this juncture, the Astrologer must meet the challenge of describing woman's mythical-magic potential without reverting to the old, confining patterns. He does so by couching his thoughts in an "open" language, a mystical-sounding, highly ambiguous language that invites multiple interpretations and amplifications. For example, when Hipólita asks him to justify his belief in woman by giving a reason, he replies, "Porque ella es principio y fin de la verdad" (Because she is the beginning and the end of truth) (*L*, p. 32).

This "open" discourse is, in a certain sense, an answer to Beauvoir's complaint. Beauvoir denounces the discussion of woman when it relies on the concept of myth and on a mythic mode of expression. Her point is that myth has traditionally been used to constrain woman to a limited number of fixed roles and images. The authors she examines speak of woman in such a way as to cut off some of her possibilities—most notably, the possibility of full autonomy. The Astrologer's mystical speech emphasizes the diversity of individual women, their need to choose their own existential paths. He is certain that such authenticity can occur within a mythic conception of woman-hood.

Hipólita, who serves as questioner and examiner, offers an argument impressively similar to Beauvoir's. She points out how little benefit women have enjoyed from the cosmic life-force that mythifiers attribute to them: "hasta ahora no han hecho más que tener hijos" (up till now all they've done is have children). The Astrologer insists that his dynamic, utopian vision of woman contains a fundamental difference: "Deje que [las mujeres] empiecen a despertar. A ser individualidades" (Let [women] begin to awaken. To be individual beings) (L, p. 32).

During this exchange, Hipólita displays an unaccustomed and surprisingly vivid speech. Yet, she is still under the guidance of a male sponsor, even if that male sponsor insists on her individuality. It still remains for Hipólita to speak on her own. This is the particular importance of the woman's lengthy interior monologue and soliloquy, transcribed in the chapter "Hipólita sola" (Hipólita Alone) (L, pp. 107–11). The narration here relies on varying techniques for rendering the changes in the woman's consciousness resulting from her conversation with the Astrologer. Direct and indirect interior monologues give the reader access to a process of self-definition in its earliest stages. Hipólita, though chaotic in her organization, comes closer and closer to affirming her right to self-determination. When her thoughts on this subject are most fully formalized, she literally gives voice to them in an assertive statement of her need for individualistic fulfillment and choice.

The fact that Hipólita has no audience for her personal declaration of independence does not indicate the defeat of communication. Rather, it shows that she can now speak without relying on the cues provided her by a male interlocutor to whose

needs she must cater. The lengthy interior monologue and soliloquy constitute Hipólita's last significant appearance in the
work—significantly so, for her story here reaches a point of
closure. By assuming "her own voice," by effectively articulating her need for choice, the former prostitute also pronounces
an end to her old, myth-governed discourse and a beginning to
the elaboration of a new mythic self.

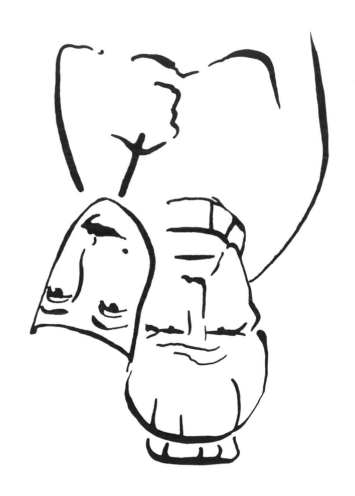

FOLK-POPULAR CULTURE

11 Women, Men, and Ambivalence within the Brazilian *Literatura de Cordel*

Candace Slater

Today, in open-air markets throughout northeastern Brazil, as well as in fairs in Rio de Janeiro and São Paulo, vendors continue to offer the stories in verse known as *folhetos* or *literatura de cordel*.[1] The genre, which first came to Brazil from Portugal some five centuries ago, offers rare, and for that reason all the more significant, insights into the thoughts and feelings of the Brazilian masses.[2]

The role of woman within the *literatura de cordel* may not initially strike one as a particularly fertile area of inquiry. Because *cordel* stories, like their European counterparts, are so highly stereotyped, one might expect to find little that could be considered interesting, let alone surprising. The usual cast of lovely maidens, wicked stepmothers, and compassionate angels can be found in *folhetos* from many times and many places.

And yet, while there is no doubt that *cordel* authors, who are always male, draw upon a limited number of highly ritualized

1. I am grateful to the Tinker Foundation for supporting my research in Brazil and in Palo Alto, California, during 1977–1979. The term *folheto* (colloquial, *folhete*), meaning "pamphlet," was used for these stories in verse until about ten years ago when researchers, newly interested in them, introduced the Portuguese term *literatura de cordel* (the *cordel* refers to the cord along which these booklets were suspended for display in marketplaces). Book-length studies and collections of a general nature on the *cordel* tradition include Sebastião Nunes Batista, *Antologia da literatura de cordel* (Natal: Fundação José Augusto, 1977) and Luís da Câmara Cascudo, *Vaqueiros e cantadores* (Porto Alegre: Editorial Globo, 1939). See also Mark J. Curran, *Literatura de cordel* (Recife: Universidade Federal de Pernambuco, 1973); Manuel Florentino Duarte et al., *Literatura de cordel: Antologia*, 2 vols. (São Paulo: Global Editora, 1976); *Literatura popular em verso: Antologia*, vols. 1–4, *Catálogo, Estudos* (Rio de Janeiro: MEC/Fundação Casa de Rui Barbosa, 1962–1977); and Liêdo Maranhão de Souza, *Classificação popular da literatura de cordel* (Petrópolis: Vozes, 1976). For an English-language overview of the *cordel* tradition see Candace Slater, *Stories on a String: The Brazilian Literatura de Cordel* (Berkeley: University of California Press, 1982).

2. For a detailed study of the ties between the Portuguese and Brazilian chapbook tradition see Luís da Câmara Cascudo, *Cinco livros do povo* (Rio de Janeiro: José Olympio, 1953). For a comparative summary see Candace Slater, "Why One Evil King Could Not Be Brazilian: A Comparison of Portuguese and Brazilian *Literatura de Cordel*," *Luso-Brazilian Review* (in press).

characters, these characters may interact unpredictably. Analysis of sex roles within the *cordel* is therefore useful not only for what it may or may not suggest about male/female relationships in everyday life,[3] but also for the contradictions it inevitably unearths. This paper looks briefly at female roles within the *cordel* tradition, then moves on to examine the male/female balance in one *folheto* about an outlaw called the Valiant Vilela.[4]

Before turning to this *folheto*, however, it is worth reviewing some of the most common stereotypes of women within the Brazilian *literatura de cordel*. The first three types outlined below are actually positive mirror images of the second three, which serve as negative examples of feminine behavior. Thus 1 and 4, 2 and 5, and 3 and 6 are closely related.

To be sure, not every *folheto* heroine fits one of the half-dozen roles exactly. Especially in news stories called *folhetos de época* or *folhetos de acontecimentos*, the protagonist—who may be a president's wife, the center of a sordid drug scandal, or a local journalist—may be more of an individual, less of a specific type.[5] Then too, there are a few common figures such as Maria Bonita, the outlaw Lampião's companion, who seem to belong to their own special category.[6] Nevertheless, the great majority of female characters represent variations on one of the following models:

(1) The poor but virtuous maiden. After successfully responding to a series of trials, thereby proving the excellence of her character, the beautiful young heroine is rewarded with a handsome, wealthy, and equally exemplary husband. Thus in

3. For a discussion of male and female roles in a specifically Latin American context see Evelyn P. Stevens, "Marianismo: The Other Face of Machismo in Latin America," in *Female and Male in Latin America,* ed. Ann Pescatello (Pittsburgh: University of Pittsburgh Press, 1973), pp. 89–101.

4. The Vilela story (*O Valente Vilela,* Recife: N.p., n.d.) is attributed to João Martins de Ataíde, an important Recife-based *cordel* author and publisher who died in 1959. For another version of the Vilela story see Jorge Amado, "Biblioteca do Povo e Coleção Moderna," in *Novos estudos afro-brasileiros,* ed. Gilberto Freyre et al., 2 vols. (Rio de Janeiro: Civilização Brasileira, 1937), 2:262–324.

5. Eva Perón, Angela Diniz, a young woman murdered as the result of her involvement with a Rio de Janeiro drug ring, and a Recife-based reporter, Cristina Tavares, have all been subjects of circumstantial *folhetos.*

6. Maria Bonita should, in keeping with traditional *cordel* values, be treated as a representative of evil since she left her husband to follow Lampião. Nevertheless, *cordel* accounts of her are generally either positive or at least neutral in tone. See, for example, *A Verdadeira História de Lampião e Maria Bonita,* by Manuel Pereira Sobrinho, reproduced in *Liberatura Popular em Verso: Antologia,* 1:369–88.

The Story of Rose White, or the Fisherman's Daughter, the lovely but destitute young heroine ends her days playing hymns on the piano as the wife of a blue-blooded millionaire.[7]

There are also, one should note, many rich and virtuous maidens, usually the daughters of kings or wealthy ranchers. Unlike their impoverished sisters, these women generally play a secondary role in *cordel* stories, functioning primarily as prizes for a poor but virtuous hero. Sometimes a protagonist of this sort will defy a tyrannical father by running off to marry a penniless but pure-hearted man. These young women, who are exemplified by the lovely Creusa in *The Mysterious Peacock,* soon regain their docile bearing and, like their less wealthy counterparts, become model wives.[8]

(2) The willing martyr. The protagonist in this case is often a married woman of superior status. Accused of imaginary wrongs by a malicious individual, she is temporarily stripped of her rank and possessions until such time as her faith in God results in the restoration of her position. The centuries-old story of the Empress Porcina is a classic example of Virtue Maligned. One particularly successful northeastern variant would be Caetano Cosme da Silva's *The Madwoman in the Garden,* in which the falsely accused protagonist wanders about crazed with sorrow for some fourteen years. When her innocence finally becomes apparent to her husband, he calls home his grieving wife and all ends happily ever after.[9]

(3) The faithful aide. Mothers, faithful wives, older sisters, fairy godmothers, and maiden aunts often play a beneficent, tutelary role in *cordel* stories. Often these persons counsel the hero or heroine and lend the steadfast support that allows him or her to triumph. In the tale of *Juvenal and the Dragon,* for

7. Luis da Costa Pinheiro, *História de Rosa Branca ou a Filha do Pescador* (Juazeiro do Norte: Tipografia São Francisco, 1976). *Folhetos* often go through multiple printings. The date given here simply refers to that edition of the text used by the author of this paper. Although considerable bibliographical research is presently underway (see, for example, Átila de Almeida and José Alves Sobrinho, *Dicionário bio-bibliográfico de repentistas e poetas de bancada,* 2 vols. (João Pessoa/ Campina Grande Editorial Universitária/Centro de Ciências e Tecnologia, 1978), most *folhetos* remain difficult to date.

8. João Melquiades Ferreira da Silva, *Romance do Pavão Misterioso* (Juazeiro do Norte: Tipografia São Francisco, 1974).

9. Caetano Cosme da Silva, *O Assassino da Honra ou a Louca do Jardim* (Juazeiro do Norte: Tipografia São Francisco, 1974).

instance, the hero owes his success largely to the intervention of three old women who give him food, shelter, and three talismanlike dogs.[10] In another sort of story, *The Man Who Sold the Cow,* a loyal wife insures both her own and her husband's good fortune by approving of his apparently foolish decisions.[11]

(4) The deluded prostitute. Brazilian pamphlet literature is full of deluded women who abandon happy homes and loving husbands for an ill-fated life of luxury. After describing with no little relish the high life they choose, the poet does an inevitable about-face, going on to portray the fallen woman's end in lurid detail. Thus in one of at least a half-dozen versions of the Mary Magdalene story, none of which has much to do with the biblical account, the poet concludes with a scene in which the errant woman's husband tosses a coin to the now thoroughly wretched creature whom he fails to recognize.[12]

(5) The sharp-tongued wife or mother-in-law. A favorite personage in satiric *folhetos,* the shrewish woman usually gets her comeuppance. In the interim, however, she engages in a series of comic exploits designed to serve as examples for men as well as women. In *The Young Man Who Got Beaten Up by Young Women,* for instance, the protagonist, Oscar, is a henpecked laughingstock until he perceives the error of his ways.[13] In *The Alligator Woman,* a virago continues to terrorize the husband who fails to resist her ludicrous orders.[14]

(6) The deceitful stepmother. Although *folheto* villains are more apt to be men than women, there are a fair number of female Iagos within the pages of the *literatura de cordel.* These women generally attempt to turn husbands or sons against an innocent son or daughter through a series of unjust insinuations. Thus in *The Story of the Greek Slave,* the treacherous Rosina tries to eliminate her stepdaughter by making a series of deceptive observations before the girl's father, the king. When the young princess emerges triumphant, she magnanimously par-

10. João Martins de Ataíde, *Juvenal e o Dragão* (Juazeiro do Norte: Tipografia São Francisco, 1978).

11. Francisco Sales Areda, *O Homem da Vaca e o Poder da Fortuna* (n.p., n.d.).

12. João Martins de Ataíde, *A Triste Vida da Meretriz* (Recife: n.d.).

13. Caetano Cosme da Silva, *O Rapaz que Apanhou das Moças por não Saber Namorar* (n.p., n.d.).

14. Francisco de Souza Campos, *A Mulher Jacaré* (Olinda: Casa de Crinça, 1977).

dons her stepmother, who, seeing the error of her ways, goes on to live "for her husband, her castle, and nothing else."[15]

As the preceding summary should make clear, the *cordel* author has a very definite view of how women—and people in general—ought to act. Because *folheto* personages are meant to serve as embodiments of virtue *(firmeza)* and vice *(falsidade)*, rather than as full-fledged individuals, it is not difficult to pick out the values that these stories seek to reinforce.[16]

Male and female characters may embody many of the same traits. Both heroes and heroines, for instance, are likely to be not only sincere, loyal, and God-fearing, but also well-educated, given that the ability to read is a mark of coveted upper-class status. In a Brazilian retelling of the European story of the Princess Genevieve, for instance, the poet proudly notes that his protagonist excels not only in embroidery, cooking, and sewing, but also in reading, writing, arithmetic, and foreign languages ("She spoke Portuguese, / Italian, Latin, / Greek, German, and French / very well").[17]

There are, nevertheless, other traits that vary depending on the actor's sex. As the following partial list should make clear, women are supposed to be less aggressive, more reticent than their male counterparts. They are also more apt to be condemned for sexual misconduct.

Given the kind of stereotyping found in Brazilian literature, as in so many other popular literatures, one can expect a certain uniformity throughout *cordel* stories. Nevertheless, these tales are not wholly predictable, for the apparently cardboard figures often reveal flickers of emotion. *Cordel* protagonists may say one thing and do another. Thus, although there are definite standards that *folheto* heroes and heroines are expected to meet, their behavior is not always consistent with these standards or with aspects of their own character. It is possible to find docile princesses suddenly throwing a cantankerous father into a

15. João Martins de Ataíde, *Romance do Escravo Grego* (Juazeiro do Norte: Tipografia São Francisco, 1977), p. 48.

16. For a discussion of *cordel* values see Alice Mitika Koshiyama, *Análise de Conteúdo da Literatura de Cordel: Presença de Valores Religiosos* (São Paulo: Universidade de São Paulo, Escola de Comunicações e Artes, 1972).

17. Leandro Gomes de Barros (?), *Martírios de Genoveva* (Juazeiro do Norte: Tipografia São Francisco, 1976), p. 2.

Cordel Virtues (Firmeza)

Male and Female	Male	Female
sincere	strong	sweet-tempered
loyal	brave	modest
hard-working	without compassion	pure-hearted
resigned	for enemies	gentle
courteous	intelligent	pleasant
honest	demanding of respect	cautious
trusting in God	protector of	serene
charitable to all	the innocent	smiling
generous in regard	frank	chaste
to the poor	persevering	
educated	quick to act	
attractive (fair,		
tall, well-fed)		

Cordel Vices (Falsidade)

Male and Female	Male	Female
vain	cowardly	shrewish
deceitful	seducer of women	given to gossip
stingy	weak	unyielding
bad-tempered	heartless	(disobedient)
blasphemous	cynical	disrespectful
given to excess	violent	foolish
(drink, etc.)		promiscuous
greedy		
harsh		
quick to forget		
promises		
overly ambitious		

cauldron of boiling oil or a supposedly pure-hearted maiden rushing to lay hands on a deceased villain's money.[18]

Furthermore, the ambiguity characterizing a number of *cordel* stories is not limited to individual personages. On occasion, the poet will not only reveal mixed emotions toward one or another actor but may actually undercut the moral his story ostensibly illustrates.

The case of the Valiant Vilela is an example of a story that lends

18. The *folhetos* in question are Severino Borges Silva, *A Princesa Maricruz e o Cavaleiro do Ar* (Recife: João José da Silva, n.d.), and José Bernardo da Silva, *Mariana e o Capitão do Navio* (Juazeiro do Norte: Tipografia São Francisco, 1976).

itself to multiple interpretations. Apparently clear-cut, it actually reveals two quite different story lines. Most *cordel* readers see the Vilela tale as a funny story, a purposely exaggerated confrontation between one outlaw and an ill-matched State.[19] And yet, although it is Vilela who occupies center stage in this *folheto*, the story's meaning ultimately depends on one's interpretation of the relationship between the backlands rebel and his wife. At first glance the wife would appear to be a variation on the faithful-aide stereotype described earlier in this paper. It is not certain, however, that the role she plays is wholly positive.

In order to understand the Vilela story, a summary of its plot may be useful. The sixteen-page text, which is composed of some fifty six-line stanzas, may be reduced to these key incidents:

(1) From an early age, Vilela reveals his tyrannous nature by killing people for the most trifling motives (an argument over a pipe, dissatisfaction with the felling of a tree). His victims include his brother-in-law and two young men whom he does not even know.

(2) Reacting to these murders, the local police commissioner unsuccessfully attempts to bring Vilela to justice.

(3) Alerted to the situation, the state police commissioner sends two separate forces after Vilela. When these groups are defeated, a second lieutenant named Negreiro (which means either "slave driver" or "black") volunteers to go after the outlaw with a specially selected force of 180 black men.[20]

(4) Negreiro arrives in Vilela's district, surrounds his home, and begins a prolonged exchange of words with the outlaw.

(5) When Vilela finally responds to his adversary's taunts by emerging from his house, the lieutenant finds himself alone; all 180 soldiers have deserted.

(6) The two men engage in a physical combat from which Vil-

---

19. For a study of the figure of the outlaw in Brazilian pamphlet literature see Ronald Daus, *Der epische Zyklus der Cangaceiros in der Volkspoesie Nordostbrasiliens* (Berlin: Coloquim Verlag, 1960).

20. Racial slurs are common in the *literatura de cordel*, due in part to the poor man's need to feel that someone is worse off than himself. A number of the best *cordel* poets have, however, been mulatto or black. See Jeová Franklin, "O preconceito racial na literatura de cordel," *Vozes* 64 (1970):35–39, and Clóvis Moura, *O preconceito de côr na literatura de cordel* (São Paulo: Editora Resenha Universitária, 1976).

ela ultimately emerges triumphant. He is about to kill the vanquished lieutenant when the outlaw's wife appears and pleads for the man's life.

(7) Vilela initially rejects, then accepts his wife's call for mercy.

(8) Free to return home, the lieutenant hangs himself instead because of his shame at his men's desertion.

(9) Vilela, "very repentant," leaves home without a word to his wife or children. Forgotten by the world at large, he takes refuge in the woods as a hermit for forty years before dying as a backwoods saint.

It is important to note from the very beginning that a large part of the Vilela story is a verbal duel *(desafio, peleja)*. As such, it looks to the oral tradition of improvised ritual insults common in the northeastern backlands.[21] The body of the *folheto* is not devoted to a description of Vilela's heinous deeds, which are rapidly summarized in the first six stanzas, but to a long, thoroughly delightful debate between the outlaw and the lieutenant, occupying fully half of the booklet. In these circumstances, Vilela's initial misdeeds function largely as an excuse for the confrontation in which the two men act like singers attempting to outdo their opponents in the wit and force of their challenges.

It is true that the conflict, which remains one of words in the *peleja*, eventually turns into a physical confrontation here. Nevertheless, the eight pages of paired stanzas in which the two opponents exchange evenly-matched insults are clearly an offshoot of the verbal dueling tradition with which the typical *cordel* buyer is thoroughly familiar. In fact, a number of the taunts made by Vilela and the lieutenant can actually be found in other oral and written duels.

And yet, although the Vilela story owes a great deal to the northeastern verbal dueling tradition, it is more than a *peleja*.

21. Classic works on Brazilian poet-singers, called *repentistas* or *cantadores*, include Gustavo Barroso, *Ao som da viola* (Rio de Janeiro: Livraria Leite Ribeiro, 1923); Francisco das Chagas Batista, *Cantadores e poetas populares* (Paraíba: F. C. Batista Irmão, 1929); José Rodrigues Carvalho, *Cancioneiro do norte* (Rio de Janeiro: MEC, 1967); Francisco Coutinho Filho, *Repentistas e glosadores* (São Paulo: A. Sartoris and Bertoli, 1937) and *Violas e repentes*, 2d rev. ed. (São Paulo: Editora Leitura/INL, 1972); and Leonardo Mota, *Contadores*, 2d ed., *Violeiros do norte*, 2d ed., and *Sertão alegre*, 2d ed. (Fortaleza: Imprensa Universitária do Ceará, 1961, 1962, 1963). An English translation of one poetic contest written in *cordel* form is available as *The Warriors: Peleja between Joaquim Jaqueira and Manoel Barra Mansa*, trans. Ernest J. Barge and Jan Feidel (New York: Grossman, 1972).

Unlike the overwhelming majority of oral and written contests, which skip from one topic to another without any transition, the *folheto* in question has, as we have seen, a definite story line. The spirited confrontation between the outlaw and the lieutenant is embedded in a narrative frame and is therefore just one part of a larger whole. It is thus necessary to ask what this larger whole may mean. As every *cordel* story must reinforce the values to which its audience professes to adhere, the Vilela story must comment on some level about the way that people ought to act. In the most obvious reading of the *folheto*, Vilela emerges as the archetypal strong man who goes about enforcing his will on others. In this case, he shows his strength by killing anyone (that is, any male contemporary) who displeases him. Because he is stronger than anyone else, he continues to do as he pleases until vanquishing the unlucky lieutenant. At this point, just as he is about to dispatch the man with his usual savage zeal, his wife intervenes on the would-be victim's behalf.

The outlaw initially rejects his wife's pleas for the lieutenant, whom, after all, he has defeated through superior force. "All you do is make trouble," he insists. "If the lieutenant had succeeded in killing me / you would be singing a different tune! / But now that it is my turn to kill him, you butt in where you have no business." He goes on to denounce the fickle nature of women ("I don't know what it is . . . / that makes them so deceitful"), berating her for having abandoned her responsibilities: "Without doubt you have left the house untended / and the baby all alone."

Nevertheless, it is the wife who has the last word in this case. She finally manages to move Vilela by pointing out that the lieutenant is a husband and father: "If you kill him / who is going to bring up his children?" As a final argument, she notes that the outlaw is in much the same boat as the lieutenant: "After all, we too are married and could find ourselves in the same situation some day."

Vilela's decision to free the man whom he was about to kill is, at best, grudging ("Let him tell all the world / that my wife served as his lawyer," he grumbles). This concession is, however, dwarfed by a much larger change of heart. Suddenly "most repentant," the outlaw leaves his home and family for "a hermit's existence in the woods," becoming a saint after forty years of ostensible atonement.[22]

In this reading of the *folheto,* it is the wife who gains her husband's salvation by softening his heart. Looking back over the key events, one can pose the following interpretation: (1) violence visited upon men of near-equal status; (2) intervention of woman; (3) recognition of error by man; (4) acceptance of social role (implied renunciation of violent behavior); (5) repentance for evil deeds; and (6) salvation.

Seen from this viewpoint, the Vilela story becomes a saga of the triumph of Christian charity over the concept that might makes right. The female principle appears here as the one force capable of humanizing a violent, exclusively male universe. The recognition of social responsibilities and of brotherhood through shared concerns ("we could well find ourselves in the same situation") makes a continuation of one-to-one combat among males impossible.

And yet, something does not quite fit this ready framework. Looking back over the last few pages of the story, one cannot fail to perceive a bothersome inconsistency.

Vilela's wife is clearly a prime exponent of the New Testament concept of forgiveness, which has never been overly popular among nominally Catholic backlanders. "Husband, don't kill the man, / because he did not offend you," she argues. "Why is it that you want to take the life / of a person who never did you any harm?" Going a step further, she offers to exchange her own life for the lieutenant's. "If you really must murder someone," she tells her husband, "then let it be me instead of him."

There is no doubt about the compassionate nature of these statements. In terms of the story, however, they are not strictly correct. Vilela's wife insists that the lieutenant never did anything to hurt her husband when, in reality, the man swore on more than one occasion to take the outlaw dead or alive ("This

22. This pattern of atonement is common in the *literatura de cordel.* See for instance the story of Dimas the good thief *(História de Dimas, O Bom Ladrão)* by Francisco das Chagas Batista (Juazeiro do Norte: Tipografia São Francisco, 1977). Usually, however, it occupies a substantial part of the narrative and is not simply tacked on as it is here.

time you are going to leave here / tied up in a rope headed for prison / or wrapped in a hammock bound for the cemetery"). She claims that her husband has no motive for revenge, but what better motive could there be than the instinct for survival? ("If you are not going to open up, say so," the lieutenant tells Vilela, "and I will knock it down / so that blood flows in rivers / on the threshold.") Finally, she says that the lieutenant "did not know what he was doing," an assertion clearly not backed by the facts. The officer's defeat is not a result of any uncertainty on his part about his aims, but bad luck, and by implication within the world of the *peleja*, inferior skill.

It is possible to argue that the lieutenant had no personal feud with Vilela and was simply doing his duty. As the wife notes, Jesus, "who was so badly wronged," did not retaliate against his persecutors. Therefore Vilela, who has been treated comparatively well, should pardon a man who has had the courage to live up to his word.

It is also true, however, that Vilela gave the lieutenant a number of at least nominal chances to call off a suicidal mission. "Go see your wife and child," Vilela tells him from the start, advising him to make a run for the trees when the officer finds himself alone. Although the outlaw broaches these opportunities to call off the fight in a taunting manner on which a proud man would be loathe to act, they are nevertheless offers. His assertion that the lieutenant "insisted on bothering me" is therefore not without a certain logic.

Looking back over the *folheto* from a second perspective, one might argue that it is actually Vilela, not his wife, who is right. In terms of the patriarchal honor code, she has left her designated sphere—the home—to meddle in a domain in which she has, as Vilela says, "absolutely no place." Certainly, the role of intercessor is frequently attributed to the Virgin Mary within the world of the *cordel*. One can find stories in which she pleads for Getúlio Vargas, former president of Brazil, others in which she takes the side of a penniless rogue. Nevertheless, Mary is not Christ's wife but his mother, and female parents command a respect seldom shown to wives in northeast Brazilian literature and life.

The fact that the outlaw finally succumbs to his wife's pleas

does not necessarily mean that either he or the lieutenant genu-
inely endorses the merciful stance she espouses. Although the
officer, for his part, has beseeched God to allow him to return to
his family ("Have mercy on me, / a husband and father!"), he
does not rush home in thanksgiving to his loved ones but
promptly hangs himself from the nearest tree. Shamed by his
debt to a woman and determined to fulfill his initial promise to
his commander ("If I cannot bring back Vilela dead or alive / I
will not bother returning"), he goes on, as the author notes in his
concluding stanza, to prove his valor by refusing to return home
defeated.

Vilela, for his part, is similarly unhappy. Slinking out the back
door, he isolates himself from the world over which he once
exerted all but absolute power. In the concluding stanzas,
whose brevity borders on abruptness, the poet tells us nothing
more than that "he died and became a saint."

The dissatisfaction, if not outright resentment, hinted at in
the concluding stanzas suggests a second, quite different, reading of the Vilela story in which the key elements are as follows:
(1) violent game limited to men of equal status (contest in which
the rules—superior skill in one-to-one combat—are unknown);
(2) intervention of a woman (imposition of new rules—combat
involves moral considerations because persons other than opponents are involved); (3) resultant disintegration of game; and
(4) destruction of both opponents.

In this interpretation, the principle of might makes right
rather than Christian charity is ultimately supported. Women
are seen as weak, even treacherous individuals who, if not kept
in their place, guarantee destruction. Although the poet uses
humor liberally, he is serious in his underlying message that
social ties are dangerous because they cancel out a man's ability
to act freely and for himself. No longer able to act at will in the
world he once dominated, Vilela has no other choice but to
retreat to the woods, the one place where he may make his own
decisions and continue an autonomous existence.

The author's presentation of the Vilela story as a humorous
combat rather than a serious encounter between the forces of
good and evil makes it unnecessary for the *cordel* buyer to go
searching for a moral. Nevertheless, while most readers regard

the *folheto* as little more than "a funny story," they are quite willing to talk about their reactions to the outlaw and his wife.[23] It is interesting to note the comments of *folheto* buyers about the wife of the outlaw in particular and female *cordel* characters in general. Although it would be a mistake to assume that male buyers respond the same way to women in literature as they would to real members of the opposite sex, it nevertheless seems fitting to close with a brief look at some of their reactions. If one talks at any length with *folheto* buyers about the Valiant Vilela, it becomes clear that the story means something to them. It is remarkable, for instance, to note that many buyers interviewed in Recife's central marketplace believe that Vilela was a real person. Although the remainder doubt his existence, many of these persons hedge their denial ("I don't think that Vilela existed, but there were so many outlaws in the old days that it is hard to say for sure," says one).[24] The persons who claim that there was a Vilela often provide specific details. "He was from around Teixeira in the state of Paraíba," states one buyer, "because my father saw him once and told me."[25] One old man

23. The following comments were recorded in the São José Marketplace in Recife during June 1978. I do not, unfortunately, have data about the informants other than their age, sex, occupation, and birthplace if other than Recife, because of the difficulties in obtaining quantifiable data from northeastern *cordel* buyers. In Rio de Janeiro, I was able to interview 200 *cordel* buyers in the São Cristóvão Fair and the Largo do Machado, using a more or less standard list of questions and a tape recorder. (See Slater, "Joe Bumpkin in the Wilds of Rio de Janeiro," *Journal of Latin American Lore*, 6, 1 (1980), pp. 5–53. The questionnaire approach was, however, impossible in northeastern marketplaces, partly because changes in the traditional market structure have made the once crucial weekly fair less important, with the result that customers are less apt to congregate at one time and one place. Even more important, however, I found that people were either intimidated, or else fascinated, by the tape recorder to the point that they forgot all else. Furthermore, whereas the somewhat more sophisticated Rio buyer assumed that I must be "another one of those reporters," and accordingly responded with patient courtesy, northeasterners were simply not interested in answering a list of questions. Although I talked at length to several hundred individuals in northeastern marketplaces, I found that I had to rely on extended conversations, which I later summarized on paper. This approach, while not ideal, yielded great quantities of invaluable information. In Recife I was actually able to assist in the sale of *cordel* stories, thanks to the good will of poet José de Souza Campos.
24. The speaker here is a 61-year-old unemployed man born outside Caruaru, Pernambuco. He has been in Recife for the past 31 years.
25. Janitor, age 37; born Campina Grande, Paraíba; 4 years in Recife.

from Bom Jardim goes so far as to describe seeing the outlaw when he himself was a child.[26]

Given the degree of psychic if not material reality that the Vilela story has for many persons, reactions to the question of whether the outlaw's wife should have intervened in the quarrel between the two men are particularly interesting. Not surprisingly, responses to her behavior vary.

Young men along with women of all ages are, for instance, more apt than older men to think that the wife did the right thing. Similarly, persons born in the city appear quicker than those born in the countryside to take her part. Defense of the wife's intervention often entails a more general condemnation of Vilela's heinous deeds. "If it weren't for his wife, Vilela would still be killing people in cold blood," a young woman notes.[27] "If Vilela had gone on the way he was going we would all be a couple of feet under the ground by now!," jokes a slightly older man.[28]

A minority claim to have no opinion. "I don't say that she should and I don't say that she shouldn't have interrupted because after all, it's not my story and it's not for me to say what happened," one buyer asserts.[29] The majority of respondents think, however, that the wife was not correct in intervening. Significantly, their feelings in most cases are based less on whether they think it was right for Vilela to kill the lieutenant than on objections to her intervention in and of itself. "Of course she was right," one old man says,

> but that doesn't mean that she had to go and argue with her husband in front of another man. There's a time and a place for everything and that other man, the lieutenant, went and killed himself anyway, didn't he? So what good did her making a nuisance of herself do?[30]

Responses to the particular case of the Valiant Vilela fit a more general pattern of mixed reactions on the part of *cordel* authors and buyers toward female characters in the *literatura de cordel.* When asked if he found it just that the Madwoman in the Gar-

26. Doorman, age 67; born Bom Jardim, Pernambuco; 8 years in Recife.
27. Housewife, age 19; born Surubim, Pernambuco; 6 years in Recife.
28. Ice cream vendor, age 23; born Recife.
29. Janitor, age 63; born João Pessoa; 18 years in Recife.
30. Farmer, age 70; born São Lourenço da Mata, Pernambuco.

den should be forced to wander about for fourteen years before her innocence could be proven, the author's response is "yes and no." "Look," Caetano Cosme da Silva says:

> Her husband could have killed her. Instead, he let her live, all he did was to make her leave the house. If you ask me, I think that she was lucky because he took her back in the end and everything turned out all right.[31]

And yet, even the case of the unfortunate Madwoman is not as cut and dried as may appear at first glance. Asked why the Madwoman's daughter should conclude the story with a promise never to marry, the same author shrugs and says with a grin, "Who knows, maybe she was afraid that the same thing would happen to her!"

Although it is not this paper's intent to illustrate any direct relationship between *cordel* stereotypes and everyday interaction between men and women, it is possible that seemingly contradictory attitudes toward woman in Brazilian pamphlet literature may reflect similar, though not identical, attitudes toward them in life. The fact that *cordel* stories are not always as simple or straightforward as they may appear at first glance owes at least something to tensions between ideal, literary expectations and more everyday feelings and experiences.

The ambiguity, however, is not necessarily a negative factor. The story of the Valiant Vilela—and wife—has been popular for decades thanks not only to its vibrant dialogue and humor but in part to its success in allowing people to interpret the facts at will. By offering the reader a large dose of violence without threatening those values of charity and order to which that reader feels he must adhere, the story is successful on two fronts. Undercutting the correctness of the wife's position by making her a meddlesome, somewhat comic variant of the typical *cordel* helpmate, the poet allows Vilela to be ultimately wrong without making his wife really right.

In conclusion, it is worth reemphasizing the value of sex-role analysis within the *literatura de cordel*. Although *cordel* stories routinely employ those stereotypes of women initially outlined in this paper, the interrelationships between *folheto* personages are often significantly ambiguous. The *cordel*'s complexity and

---

31. Caetano Cosme da Silva, interview in Campina Grande, Paraíba, 4 March 1978.

capacity for contradiction are particularly obvious in stories such as *The Valiant Vilela.*

Moreover, buyers' reactions to female protagonists in this and other *folhetos* underline the need for further studies of male and female roles in folk and popular literature. *Cordel* personages clearly cannot be equated with flesh-and-blood individuals. Nevertheless, the degree of response that these stereotypes awaken suggests that we are dealing with powerful emotions. Continued analysis of texts and further investigation of their human context will no doubt help us in better evaluating the relationship between social realities and literary representations.

Selected Bibliography

This brief listing is intended to provide a representative sampling of critical writings concerning the mythic and metaphorical representation of women in literature and, in some cases, in forms of popular writing. Coverage focuses principally on works in the Latin American area, but a more schematic preliminary listing sets forth some of the more important titles reflecting international developments in this area of study.

A note is in order explaining the criteria we used to determine the relevancy of critical writings to our central topic. Many works of myth-centered criticism make some reference to woman, the feminine principle, or the *anima*. Indeed, it is a tenet of Jungian-archetypal thought that the female side of the universe and human nature ought to be kept continually in consideration. However, simple occasional reference to woman and womanly forces does not classify an analysis as fundamentally concerned with the issue of the representation of woman. We have chosen to list only those works in which there is a substantial amount of discussion devoted to this topic and in which the problem of representing feminine entities is an explicitly formulated question. In addition, works containing theoretical background to some of the issues discussed in the essays appear in our listing.

Another area of inquiry close to our own, and to which readers may well care to direct attention, is the reexamination of women's roles as special mediators between large cosmic forces and everyday events. Examples of this topic are the new examinations of women as traditional healers and magical intercessors, as witches and sorceresses and as diviners of the future. This particular area of study is primarily the terrain of cultural anthropology, although it should be noted that its concerns go beyond the bounds of traditionally delineated anthropological studies.

The limits in our bibliography preclude the listing of works of creative writing. This is not to say, by any means, that creative writers are not also instrumental in diffusing new ideas about woman's mythic and metaphorical images.

It should be emphasized that this is, indeed, a selection out of the many materials related to the topic. Beyond the above-delineated restrictions of subject matter, we have also established limitations based on considerations of general accessibility. Therefore, materials appearing in little-circulated form have generally not been included. In the area of periodical publications, we have only listed the standardly organized and distributed journals—the so-called "mainstream" of academic publishing. This is not, however, to imply that only these professional outlets carry interesting or worthwhile material on our chosen topic.

As a last remark, we would like to clarify that in view of the nature of this collection, which represents a reexamination of the topic of myth in general and feminine myth in particular, we have listed only those works that reflect modern investigation of theoretical-critical issues.

Agosin, Marjorie. *Las desterradas del paraíso, protagonistas en la narrativa de María Luisa Bombal*. New York: Senda Nueva, 1982.

Andermatt, Verena. "Hélène Cixous and the Uncovery of a Feminine Language." *Women and Literature*, 7, 1 (1979), 38–48.

Appignanesi, Lisa. *Femininity and the Creative Imagination*. London: Vision, 1973.

Araújo, Helena. "Narrativa femenina latinoamericana." *Hispamérica*, no. 23 (1982), 23–24.

Arciniegas, Germán. *América mágica, II, las horas y las mujeres*. Buenos Aires: Sudamericana, 1961.

Arrom, José Juan. "Cambiantes imágenes de la mujer en el teatro de la narrativa virreinal." *Latin American Theater Review*, 12, 1 (1978), 5–15.

Auerbach, Nina. *Woman and the Demon: The Life of Victorian Myth*. Cambridge: Harvard University Press, 1983.

Avendaño, Fausto. *Jung, la figura del ánima y la narrativa latinoamericana*. Ph.D. diss., University of Arizona, 1973.

Barradas, Efraín. "El machismo existencial de René Marqués." *Sin nombre*, 8, 3 (1977), 69–81.

Barthes, Roland. *Mythologies*. Paris: Seuil, 1963.

———. *Système de la mode*. Paris: Seuil, 1967.

Beauvoir, Simone de. *The Second Sex*. Trans. H. M. Parshley. New York: Knopf, 1953.

Belford, Ann Ulanov. *The Feminine in Jungian Psychology and in Christian Theology*. Evanston, Ill.: Northwestern University Press, 1971.

Bellough, Vern L. *The Subordinate Sex*. Urbana: University of Illinois Press, 1973.

Bischoff, Efraín U. "La mujer en el Martín Fierro." *Letras de Buenos Aires*, 2, 6 (1982), 35–53.

Boschetto, Sandra María. "El canto de las sirenas: aproximaciones al mundo femenino en algunos relatos de Juan Carlos Onetti." *Explicación de textos literarios*, 7, 2 (1983–1984), 3–18.

———. "La inversión de la figura femenina en 'El güero,' de José Donoso." *Crítica hispánica*, 6, 1 (1984), 1–10.

Bruns, Edgar J. *God as Woman, Woman as God*. New York: Paulist Press, 1973.

Campbell, Joseph. *The Mythic Image*. Princeton: Princeton University Press, 1974.

Chapman, Arnold G. "The Barefoot Galateas of Bret Harte and Rómulo Gallegos." *Symposium*, 18 (1964), 332–41.

Cixous, Hélène. "The Laugh of the Medusa." Trans. Keith Cohen and Paula Cohen. *Signs*, 1 (1976), 875–93.

―――. "Entretiens avec Françoise van Rossum-Guyon." *Revue des Sciences Humaines*, no. 168 (1974), 479–93.

Colomina, Marta. *La Celestina mecánica*. Caracas: Monte Avila, 1976.

Cornillon, Susan Koppelman. *Images of Women in Fiction: Feminist Perspectives*. Bowling Green, Ohio: Bowling Green University Popular Press, 1972.

Corteau, Joanna. "The Image of Woman in the Novels of Gracialiano Ramos." *Revista/Review interamericana*, no. 4 (1974), 161–71.

Culler, Jonathan. *The Pursuit of Signs: Semiotics, Literature, Deconstruction*. Ithaca: Cornell University Press, 1981.

Devereux, Georges. *Femme et mythe*. Paris: Flammarion, 1983.

Dolziel, Margaret, ed. *Myth and the Modern Imagination*. Dunedin: University of Otago Press, 1967.

Dorfman, Ariel. *Imaginación y violencia en América*. Santiago, Chile: Editorial Universitaria, 1970.

―――. *The Empire's Old Clothes: What the Lone Ranger, Babar and Other Innocent Heroes Do to Our Minds*. With translations by Clark Hausen. New York: Pantheon, 1982.

Douglas, Ann. *The Feminization of American Culture*. New York: Knopf, 1977.

Douglas, Wallace. "The Meaning of 'Myth' in Modern Criticism." *Modern Philology*, 50 (1953), 232–42.

Durán, Fray Diego. *Book of the Gods and Rites and the Ancient Calendar*. Trans. Fernando Horcacitas and Doris Hayden. Norman: University of Oklahoma Press, 1971.

Durán, Gloria. *La magia y las brujas en la obra de Carlos Fuentes*. Mexico City: Universidad Nacional Autónoma de México, 1976.

―――. *The Archetypes of Carlos Fuentes: From Witch to Androgyne*. Hamden, Conn.: Anchor, 1980.

Edwards, Lee. *Psyche as Hero: Female Heroism and Fictional Form*. Middletown, Conn.: Wesleyan University Press, 1984.

Eichner, Hans. "The Eternal Feminine: An Aspect of Goethe's Ethics." *Transactions of the Royal Society of Canada*, 4, 9 (1971), 235–44.

Eliade, Mircea. *Cosmos and History: The Myth of Eternal Return*. New York: Harper and Row, 1959.

―――. *Myth and Reality*. Trans. Willard R. Trask. New York: Harper and Row, 1963.

El-Saffar, Ruth. "Tres imágenes claves de lo femenino en *Persiles*." *Revista Canadiense de estudios hispánicos*, 3, 3 (1979), 219–36.

Englekirk, John. "Doña Bárbara, Legend of the *Llano*." *Hispania*, 31 (1948), 259–70.

Erhart, Virginia. "Corín Tellado: la Cenicienta en la sociedad de consumo." *Crisis* [Buenos Aires], no. 3 (1974), 71–80.

Feral, Josette. "Antigone or the Irony of the Tribe." *Diacritics*, no. 8 (1978), 2–14.

Ferrante, Joan M. *Woman as Image in Medieval Literature*. New York: Columbia University Press, 1975.

Fiedler, Leslie. *Love and Death in the American Novel*. New York: Criterion, 1960.

Fiorenza, Elizabeth Schussler. *In Memory of Her: A Feminist Theological Reconstruction of Christian Origins*. New York: Crossroads, 1983.

Fishburn, Katherine. *Women in Popular Culture: A Reference Guide*. Westport, Conn.: Greenwood Press, 1982.

Fisherova Book, Vera. "Las heroínas en la novelística argentina." *Revista hispánica moderna*, nos. 3–4 (1944), 111–24.

Fitz, Earl E. "Freedom and Self-Realization: Feminist Characterization in the Fiction of Clarice Lispector." *Modern Language Studies*, 10, 3 (1980), 51–61.

Fontanella, Lee. "Mystical Diction and Imagery in Gómez de Avellaneda and Carolina Coronado." *Latin American Literary Review*, 9, 19 (1982), 47–55.

Foster, David W. "The Demythification of Buenos Aires in Selected Argentine Novels." *Chasqui*, 10, 1 (1980), 11–14.

Friedan, Betty. *The Feminine Mystique*. New York: Norton, 1963.

Frye, Northrop. "The Archetypes of Literature." *Kenyon Review*, 13 (1951), 92–100.

———. *Anatomy of Criticism: Four Essays*. Princeton: Princeton University Press, 1957.

———. "Myth as Information." In *Northrop Frye on Culture and Literature: A Collection of Review Essays*. Chicago: University of Chicago Press, 1978; rpt. Phoenix Ed., 1980.

Gillman, Linda. "The Looking-Glass Through Alice." In Janet Todd, ed. *Gender and Literary Voice*. New York: Holmes and Meier, 1980, pp. 12–23.

Ginsberg, Judith. "From Anger to Action: The Avenging Female in Two *Lucías*." *Revista de estudios hispánicos*, 14, 1 (1980), 51–64.

Goertz, Clifford, ed. *Myth, Symbol, and Culture*. New York: Norton, 1974.

González, Patricia, ed. *La sartén por el mango: actas del Congreso de Escritoras Latinoamericanas*. San Juan, Puerto Rico: Huracán, 1983.

188 Bibliography

González Lanuza, Eduardo. "Poesía y sexo: a propósito de *Tala.*" *Sur,* no. 8 (1938).

Gramcko, Ida. "La mujer en la obra de Gallegos." *Revista Shell,* no. 37 (1960), 37–40.

Graves, Robert. *The White Goddess: A Historical Grammar of Poetic Myth.* New York: Farrar, Straus and Giroux, 1966.

Guerra-Cunningham, Lucía. "Algunas reflexiones teóricas sobre la novela femenina." *Hispamérica,* no. 28 (1981), 29–39.

————. *La narrativa de María Luisa Bombal: una visión de la existencia femenina.* Madrid: Playor, 1981.

Gyurko, Lanin A. "The Pseudo-Liberated Woman in Fuentes' *Zona sagrada.*" *Journal of Spanish Studies: Twentieth Century,* 3, 1 (1975), 17–43.

————. "The Vindication of La Malinche in Fuentes' 'Todos los gatos son pardos.'" *Ibero Amerikanisches Archiv,* 3, 1 (1977).

————. "The Image of Woman in Two Novels of Carlos Fuentes." *Washington State University Research Studies,* no. 43. Pullman: Washington State University, 1975.

Hall, Linda. "The Cipactly Monster: Woman as Destroyer in Carlos Fuentes." *Southwest Review,* 60, 3 (1975), 246–55.

Hall, Nor. *Mothers and Daughters: Reflections on the Archetypal Feminine.* Minneapolis: Rasoff Books, 1976.

Hancock, Joel. "Elena Poniatowska's *Hasta no verte, Jesús mío*: The Remaking of the Image of Woman." *Hispania,* 66, 3 (1983), 353–59.

Harding, Esther H. *Woman's Mysteries.* New York: Harper and Row, 1971.

Hardwick, Elizabeth. *Seduction and Betrayal: Women and Literature.* New York: Random House, 1947.

Hays, Hoffman Reynolds. *The Dangerous Sex.* New York: Putnam, 1964.

Heilbrun, Carolyn G. *Toward a Recognition of Androgyny.* New York: Knopf, 1973.

Heller, Erich. *The Artist's Journey into the Interior and Other Essays.* New York: Random House, 1965.

Hellerman, Kasey M. "The Coatlicue-Malinche Conflict: A Mother and Son Identity Crisis in the Writings of Carlos Fuentes." *Hispania,* 57, 4 (1974), 867–75.

Hoberman, Luisa. "Hispanic American Women as Portrayed in the Historical Literature: Type or Archetypes?" *Revista/Review interamericana,* no. 4 (1974), 131–35.

Horn, Maurice. *Women in the Comics.* New York: Chelsea House, 1981.

Irigaray, Luce. *Speculum de l'autre femme.* Paris: Minuit, 1974.

————. *Ce Sexe qui n'en est pas un.* Paris: Minuit, 1977.

Jacquette, Jane S. "Literary Archetypes and Female Role Alternatives: The Women and the Novel in Latin America." In Ann Pescatello, ed.

Female and Male in Latin America. Pittsburgh: University of Pittsburgh Press, 1973.

James, E. O. *The Cult of the Mother Goddess*. New York: Barnes and Noble, 1959.

Janeway, Elizabeth. *Man's World, Woman's Place: A Study in Social Mythology*. New York: Dell, 1972.

Jewett, Paul K. *Man as Male and Female*. Grand Rapids: William B. Eerdmans, 1975.

Johnson, Julie Greer. *Woman in Colonial Spanish-American Literature: Literary Images*. Westport, Conn.: Greenwood, 1983.

Jung, Carl G. "The Archetypes of the Collective Unconscious." In vol. 9, pt. 1 of *The Collected Works of C. G. Jung*. Ed. Herbert Read, Michael Fordham, and Gerhard Adler. New York: Pantheon, 1953, pp. 153–60.

Kaminsky, Amy. "The Real Circle of Iron: Mothers and Children, Children and Mothers, in Four Argentine Novels." *Latin American Literary Review*, 4, 9 (1976), 77–86.

Kapschutschenko, Ludvila. "Evita y el feminismo: mito y realidad." *Letras femeninas*, 9, 1 (1983), 43–52.

Kerenyi, Elensis C. *The Archetypal Image of Mother and Daughter*. Trans. Ralph Manheim. New York: Pantheon, 1967.

Kirk, Geoffrey Stephen. *Myth: Its Meaning and Functions in Ancient and Other Cultures*. New York: Cambridge University Press/Berkeley: University of California Press, 1970.

Kirsner, Robert. "De doña Bárbara a Luisiana: feminismo refinado." *Caribe*, 1, 2 (1976), 57–64.

Kleinbaum, Abby Wettan. *The War Against the Amazons*. New York: New Press/McGraw-Hill, 1983.

Kristeva, Julia. "Femininité et écriture." *Revue des Sciences Humaines*, no. 168 (1977), 479–93.

———. "Questions à Julia Kristeva." *Revue des Sciences Humaines*, no. 168 (1977), 495–501.

———. *Polygone*. Paris: Seuil, 1977.

Lafforgue, Jorge, ed. *Nueva novela latinoamericana*. Buenos Aires: Paidós, 1969.

Larue, Gerald A. *Ancient Myth and Modern Man*. Englewood Cliffs, N.J.: Prentice-Hall, 1975.

Lauter, Estelle. *Women as Mythmakers: Poetry and Visual Art by Twentieth-Century Women*. Bloomington: Indiana University Press, 1984.

Lauter, Estelle, and Carol Schreier, eds. *Feminist Archetypal Theory: Interdisciplinary Re-visions of Jungian Thought*. Knoxville: University of Tennessee Press, 1985.

Leavitt, Sturgis. "Sex vs. Symbolism in *Doña Bárbara*." *Revista de Estudios Hispánicos*, 1 (1967), 117–20.

Lederer, Wolfgang. *Fear of Women.* New York: Harcourt Brace Jovanovich, 1968.

Lee, Stan. *Superhero Women.* New York: Simon and Schuster, 1977.

Lévi-Strauss, Claude. *La pensée sauvage.* Paris: Plon, 1962.

———. "Le Temps du mythe." *Annales,* 26 (1971), 533–40.

———. "The Structural Study of Myth." In *Myth: A Symposium.* Ed. Thomas A. Sebeok. Philadelphia: American Folklore Society, 1955, pp. 50–66.

Lima, Robert. "Cumbres poéticas de erotismo femenino en Hispanoamérica." *Revista de estudios hispánicos,* 18, 1 (1984), 41–59.

Lindstrom, Naomi. "Clarice Lispector: Articulating Woman's Experience." *Chasqui,* 8, 1 (1978), pp. 41–52.

———. "A Discourse Analysis of 'Preciosidade' by Clarice Lispector." *Luso-Brazilian Review,* 19, 2 (1982), 187–94.

———. "Norah Lange: presencia desmonumentalizadora y femenina en la vanguardia argentina." *Crítica hispánica,* 5, 2 (1983), 131–48.

López, Yvette. " 'La muñeca menor': ceremonias y transformaciones en un cuento de Rosario Ferré." *Explicación de textos literarios,* 11, 1 (1982–1983), 49–58.

Madsen, William. *The Virgin's Children.* Westport, Conn.: Greenwood, 1969.

Marcus, Roxanne B. "An Application of Jungian Theory to the Interpretation of doña Inés in Valera's *Juanita la larga.*" *Revista Canadiense de estudios hispánicos,* 3, 3 (1979), 259–74.

Martí, Nelly. *El gato eficaz* de Luisa Valenzuela: la productividad del texto." *Revista Canadiense de estudios hispánicos,* 41 (1979), 73–80.

Martin, Eleanor J. "Carlota O'Neill's *Cuarta dimensión* [*Fourth Dimension*]: The Role of the Female and the Imagination in Everyday Existence." *Latin American Literary Review,* 8, 15 (1979), 1–11.

Marx, Elaine. "Women and Literature in France." *Signs,* 3, 4 (1978), 832–42.

Mead, Margaret. *Male and Female: A Study of the Sexes in a Changing World.* New York: Morrow, 1949.

Meireles, Cecília. "Expressão femenina da poesia na América." In *Três conferências sobre cultura hispano-americana.* Rio de Janeiro: MEC, 1959.

Meyers Spack, Patricia. *The Female Imagination.* New York: Random House, 1971.

Miller, Beth K. *Mujeres en la literatura.* Mexico City: Fleischer, 1978.

———, ed. *Women in Hispanic Literature: Icons and Fallen Idols.* Berkeley: University of California Press, 1983.

Miller, Nancy K. "Emphasis Added: Plots and Plausibilities in Women's Fiction." *PMLA,* 96 (1981), 36–48.

Mora, Gabriela. "La otra cara de Ifigenia: una reevaluación del personaje de Teresa de la Parra." *Sin nombre,* 7, 3 (1976), 130–44.

────. "*Los perros y la mundanza* de Elena Garro: designio social y virtualidad feminista." *Latin American Theater Review,* 8, 2 (1975), 5–14.

Mortley, Raoul. *Womanhood: The Feminine in Ancient Hellenism, Gnosticism, Christianity and Islam.* Atlantic Highlands, N.J.: Humanities Press, 1983.

Neumann, Erich. *The Great Mother: An Analysis of the Archetype.* Trans. Ralph Manheim. Princeton: Princeton University Press, 1955; rpt. 1974.

Nigro, Kirsten F. "Rosario Castellanos' Debunking of the Eternal Feminine." *Journal of Spanish Studies: Twentieth Century,* 8, 1–2 (1980), 89–102.

Nin, Anaïs. *A Woman Speaks: The Lectures, Seminars and Interviews of Anaïs Nin.* Ed. J. Hinz. Chicago: Swallow Press, 1975.

Ocampo, Victoria. "La mujer y su expresión." In *Testimonios. Segunda Serie.* Buenos Aires: Sur, 1941, pp. 286–99.

────. *De Francesca a Beatrice.* 3ª ed. With an epilogue by José Ortega y Gasset. Buenos Aires: Sur, 1963.

O'Connor, Patricia. "Eros and Thanatos in Francisco García Pavón's *El último sábado.*" *Journal of Spanish Studies: Twentieth Century,* 4, 1 (1976).

Olsen, Carl, ed. *The Book of the Goddess: Past and Present.* New York: Crossroad, 1983.

Ordóñez, Elizabeth. "The Decoding and Encoding of Sex Roles in Carmen Martín Gaite's Retahilas." *Kentucky Romance Quarterly,* 27, 2 (1980), 237–44.

────. "The Female Quest Pattern in Concha Alos' *Os habla Electra.*" *Revista de estudios hispánicos,* 14, 1 (1980), 51–64.

────. "Woman and Her Text in the Works of María de Zayas and Ana Caro." *Revista de estudios hispánicos,* 19, 1 (1985), 3–15.

Orenstein, Gloria F. *The Symbol of the Goddess in Contemporary Women's Literature.* Los Angeles: University of Southern California Press, 1983.

Patai, Daphne. *Myth and Ideology in Contemporary Brazilian Fiction.* Cranbury, N.J.: Fairleigh Dickinson University Press, 1983.

────. *The Orwell Mystique: A Study in Male Ideology.* Amherst: University of Massachusetts Press, 1984.

Paz, Octavio. *Sor Juana Inés de la Cruz o las trampas de la fe.* Rev. ed. Mexico City: FCE, 1983.

Pearson, Carol, and Katherine Pope, eds. *"Who Am I This Time?": Female Portraits in British and American Literature.* New York: McGraw-Hill, 1976.

Pérez, Luis A. "*La marquesa de Yolombó* y el mito en la literatura hispanoamericana." *Hispania,* 65, 3 (1982), 377–82.

Pérez Martin, Norma, ed. *Mitos populares y personajes literarios.* Buenos Aires: Casteñeda/Centro de Estudios Latinoamericanos, 1978.

Perrot, Jean. *Mythe et littérature*. Paris: Presse Universitaire de France, 1976.

Pescatello, Ann. *Female and Male in Latin America*. Pittsburgh: University of Pittsburgh Press, 1973.

Piercy, Marge. *The Moon Is Always Female*. New York: Knopf, 1981.

Pitkin, Hanna Fenichel. *Fortune Is a Woman*. Berkeley: University of California Press, 1984.

Pontiero, Giovanni. "Testament of Experience: Some Reflections on Clarice Lispector's Last Narrative *A hora da estrela*." *Ibero Amerikanisches Archiv*, 10, 1 (1984), 13–22.

Pratt, Annis. "Aunt Jennifer's Tigers: Notes Toward a Preliminary History of Women's Archetypes." *Feminist Studies*, 4, 1 (1978), 188.

Rich, Adrienne. *On Lies, Secrets and Silence*. New York: Norton, 1979.

Righter, William. *Myth and Literature*. London and Boston: Routledge and Kegan Paul, 1975.

Rodríguez, Alfred, and John Timm. "El significado de lo femenino en *La familia de Pascual Duarte*." *Revista de estudios hispánicos*, 2 (1977), 251–64.

Rogers, Katharine M. *The Troublesome Helpmate: A History of Misogyny*. Seattle: University of Washington Press, 1966.

Sachs, Viola. *The Myth of America: Essays in the Structures of Literary Imagination*. The Hague: Mouton, 1973.

Schanzer, George O. "Rubén Darío and Ms. Christa." *Journal of Spanish Studies: Twentieth Century*, 3, 2 (1975), 145–52.

Schau, Stacy. "Conformity and Resistance to Enclosure: Female Voice in Rosario Castellanos' *Oficio de tinieblas* [*The Dark Service*]." *Latin American Literary Review*, 7, 24 (1984), 435–57.

Schecter, Harold, and Joanna Gormely Semeiks. *Patterns in Popular Culture*. New York: Harper and Row, 1980.

Scholes, Robert, and Robert Kellogg. *The Nature of Narrative*. New York: Oxford University Press, 1966.

Sebeok, Thomas Albert, ed. *Myth: A Symposium*. Bloomington: Indiana University Press, 1965.

Seidenberg, Robert. "Is Anatomy Destiny?" In *Marriage in Life and Literature*. New York: Philosophical Library, 1970, pp. 119–56.

Shepherd, Simon. *Amazons and Warrior Women: Varieties of Feminism in Seventeenth-Century Drama*. New York: St. Martin's, 1982.

Siemens, William L. "The Devouring Female in Four Latin American Novels." *Essays in Literature*, 1, 1 (1974), 118–29.

Slochower, Harry. *Mythopoesis: Mythic Patterns in the Literary Classics*. Detroit: Wayne State University Press, 1970.

Stevens, Evelyn. "Marianismo: The Other Face of Machismo in Latin America." In *Male and Female in Latin America*. Ed. Ann Pescatello. Pittsburgh: University of Pittsburgh Press, 1973.

Streicher, Helen White. "The Girls in the Cartoons." *Journal of Communications*, 24, 2 (1974), 125–29.

Sullivan, Constance A. "Re-reading the Hispanic Literary Canon: The Question of Gender." *Ideologies and Literatures*, 16 (1983), 93–101.

Taylor, J. M. *Eva Perón: The Myths of a Woman*. Chicago: University of Chicago Press, 1971.

Todorov, Tzvetan. *The Poetics of Prose*. Trans. Richard Howard. Ithaca, N.Y.: Cornell University Press, 1977.

Trudgill, Eric. *Madonnas and Magdalens*. New York: Holmes and Meier, 1976.

Urbistondo, Vicente. "El machismo en la narrativa hispanoamericana." *Texto crítico*, 4, 9 (1978), 165–83.

Van Rossum-Guyon, Françoise. "Questions à Julia Kristeva. À partir de *Polylogue*." *Revue des Sciences Humaines*, no. 168 (1977), 495–501.

Vásquez Arce, Carmen. "Sexo y mulatería: dos sones de una misma guaracha." *Sin nombre*, 12, 4 (1982), 51–63.

Virgillo, Carmelo. "A imagem da mulher no poema 'Frutescência' de Henriqueta Lisboa." *Revista da Académia Brasileira de Letras*, no. 148 (1984), 15–40.

Wheelright, Philip. "The Semantic Appeal to Myth." In *Myth: A Symposium*. Ed. Thomas Albert Sebeok. Philadelphia: American Folklore Society, 1955, pp. 59–103.

White, John J. *Mythology in the Modern Novel*. Princeton: Princeton University Press, 1971.

Williams, Lorna V. "*The Shrouded Woman*: Marriage and Its Constraints in the Fiction of María Luisa Bombal." *Latin American Literary Review*, 10, 20 (1982), 21–30.

Wilson, S. R. "Art by Gender: The Latin American Woman Writer." *Revista Canadiense de estudios hispánicos*, 6, 1 (1981), 135–37.

Wolf, Eric R. "The Virgin of Guadalupe: A Mexican National Symbol." *Journal of American Folklore*, 71, 279 (1963), 34–39.

The Contributors

Richard J. Callan is Professor of Latin American Literature at the University of New Hampshire. He also teaches non-Spanish courses in the Humanities Program. He is author of *Miguel Angel Asturias* (1970), *"América, fábula de fábulas" y otros ensayos de Miguel Angel Asturias* (1972), and *Viajes, ensayos y fantasías de Miguel Angel Asturias* (1981). Professor Callan is noted for his numerous articles applying Carl Jung's archetypal/mythological theories.

Sandra Messinger Cypess is Associate Professor of Spanish and Comparative Literature, as well as Director of the Latin American and Caribbean Area Studies Program at SUNY-Binghamton. Among her essays on the contribution of women writers to Latin American theater are "The Plays of Griselda Gámbaro," in *Dramatists in Revolt*, edited by Leon F. Lyday and George W. Woodyard (1976), and "La difícil esperanza hecha realidad: La dramaturgia de la mujer en Puerto Rico" for a forthcoming anthology.

Peter G. Earle is Professor of Spanish and Latin American Literature at the University of Pennsylvania, where he also serves on the editorial board of the *Hispanic Review*. In addition to his work on Miguel de Unamuno, Professor Earle has distinguished himself in the field of the Latin American essay, where he is best known for *Voces hispanoamericanas* (1966), *Prophet in the Wilderness: The Works of Ezequiel Martínez Estrada* (1971), and, with Robert E. Mead, *Historia del ensayo hispanoamericano* (1973).

Fred P. Ellison is Professor of Portuguese at the University of Texas at Austin, specializing in nineteenth- and twentieth-century Portuguese and Brazilian literatures. He has translated Brazilian works, especially the poetry of João Cabral de Melo Neto and Affonso Romano de Sant'Anna. In addition to research on the Mexican Alfonso Reyes in Brazil, Professor Ellison has published myth criticism of novels by Ferreira de Castro and José Américo de Almeida. In recognition of his many contributions to Luso-Brazilian studies in America, including his classic *Brazil's New Novel* (1954, rev. 1979), he has been named Corresponding Member of the Academia Brasileira de Letras.

David W. Foster is Professor of Spanish at Arizona State University. He is the author, co-author, or editor of over 30 books and 150 articles on Latin American literature. Among his recent works are *Alternative Voices in the Contemporary Latin American Narrative* (1985), *Studies in the Contemporary Spanish-American Short Story* (1979), *Mexican Literature: A Bibli-*

ography of Secondary Sources (1981), and *Jorge Luis Borges: An Annotated Primary and Secondary Bibliography* (1984).

Naomi Lindstrom is Associate Professor of Spanish and Portuguese at the University of Texas at Austin. She chairs the Politics of Culture Program of the Institute of Latin American Studies. Her research specialization is Argentine literature of the 1920s and 1930s. She is the author of *Literary Expressionism in Argentina: The Presentation of Incoherence* (1978) and *Macedonio Fernández* (1981) and translator of Roberto Arlt's 1929 novel *The Seven Madmen* (1984).

Matias Montes-Huidobro is Professor of Spanish at the University of Hawaii at Manoa. He has authored many critical essays and books on Spanish and Spanish American literature. Among these are *XIX: superficie y fondo del estilo* (1971), *Persona: vida y máscara en el teatro cubano* (1984), and the forthcoming *Persona: vida y máscara en el teatro puertorriqueño*. A novelist, playwright, and poet in his own right, Professor Montes-Huidobro has produced the novel *Desterrados al fuego* (1975) and two plays, *La sal de los muertos* (1971) and *The Guillotine* (1973).

Ann Marie Remley Rambo teaches Spanish language and literature, Mediterranean studies, and English as a second language at DePauw University. She is involved in the writing and speech competence programs there. She has published some poems individually and has a special interest in semantics, semiotics, and symbolism.

Candace Slater is Associate Professor of Spanish and Portuguese at the University of California-Berkeley. She is an accomplished scholar in the field of Brazilian popular poetry and has to her credit *Stories on a String: The Brazilian "Literatura de Cordel"* (1982) and *Trail of Miracles: Stories of a Pilgrimage in Northeast Brazil* (1985), as well as a number of critical essays. She is a former Guggenheim, Tinker, and NEH fellowship recipient.

Carmelo Virgillo is Professor of Romance Languages at Arizona State University, specializing in eighteenth-, nineteenth-, and twentieth-century literature. The author and co-author of *Correspondência de Machado de Assis com Magalhães de Azeredo* (1969), *Aproximaciones al estudio de la literatura hispánica* (1983), and articles on Spanish, Spanish American, and Brazilian literature, he teaches Italian, Spanish, and Portuguese. He has also directed the ASU Summer Program in Florence.

Lorna V. Williams is Associate Professor of Spanish at the University of Missouri-St. Louis. A specialist in Latin American literature, Professor Williams has published a number of critical studies on the African element in the Caribbean. Her most significant work in this area is *Self and Society in the Poetry of Nicolás Guillén* (1982). She has been increasingly interested in the feminine presence in the literature of the Spanish-speaking New World, wherein she probes the multitude of myths surrounding the black woman.

Index